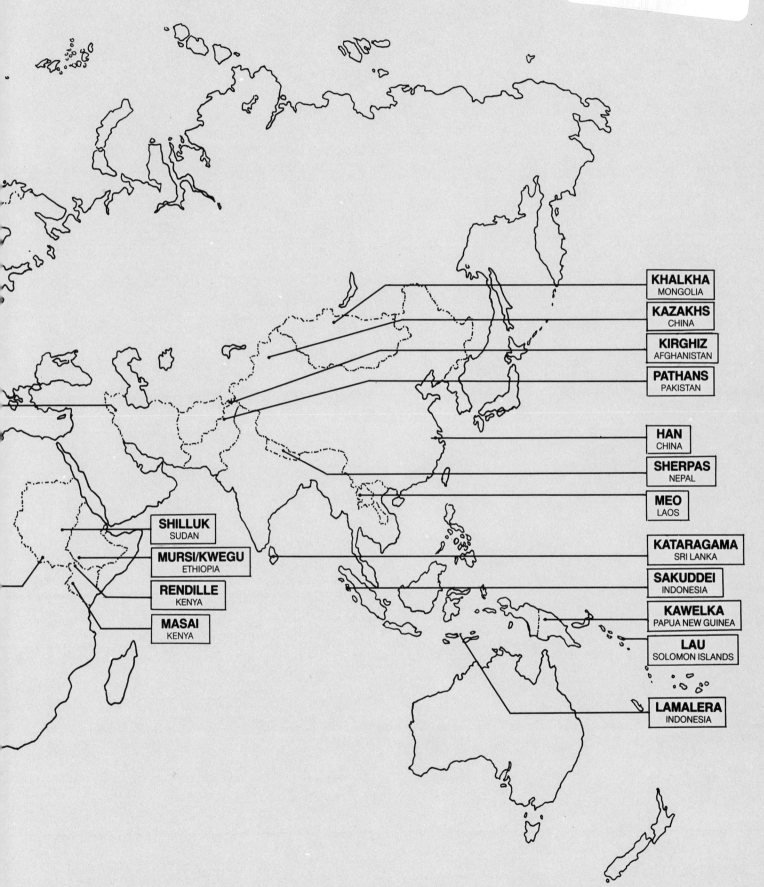

KHALKHA
MONGOLIA

KAZAKHS
CHINA

KIRGHIZ
AFGHANISTAN

PATHANS
PAKISTAN

HAN
CHINA

SHERPAS
NEPAL

MEO
LAOS

KATARAGAMA
SRI LANKA

SAKUDDEI
INDONESIA

KAWELKA
PAPUA NEW GUINEA

LAU
SOLOMON ISLANDS

LAMALERA
INDONESIA

SHILLUK
SUDAN

MURSI/KWEGU
ETHIOPIA

RENDILLE
KENYA

MASAI
KENYA

DISAPPEARING WORLD

DISAPPEARING WORLD

Television and Anthropology

ANDRE SINGER
—WITH—
LESLIE WOODHEAD

BOXTREE

in association with

GRANADA TELEVISION LIMITED

DEDICATION

In memory of Pattie Winter
and
for all the peoples of *Disappearing World*

First published in Great Britain in 1988 by
Boxtree Limited

Text © copyright 1988 André Singer and
Leslie Woodhead
ISBN 185283   211   8

Designed by Groom and Pickerill
Typeset by York House Typographic Limited
Printed and bound by New Interlitho spa, Milan

for
Boxtree Limited
36 Tavistock Street
London WC2E 7PB

Published in association with Granada
Television Limited.

CONTENTS

Acknowledgements   6

PREFACE *by Sir Denis Forman*   7

FOREWORD *by Brian Moser*   9

INTRODUCTION *by André Singer*   15

ON LOCATION *Filming Disappearing World by Leslie Woodhead*   47

1 **THE WINDS OF CHANGE**
TUAREG, ESKIMOS BASQUES   62

2 **CLASH OF CULTURES**
CUIVA, KAYAPO, SAKUDDEI, MAKU AND BARASANA, MEO   82

3 **A MATTER OF CHOICE**
LAU, SHERPAS, MURSI MIGRANTS   107

4 **BEHIND THE CURTAIN**
MONGOLS, KAZAKHS, HAN   124

5 **ORDER, ORDER, ORDER**
MURSI, PUSHTUNS, SHILLUK, KIRGHIZ   139

6 **GAINING CONTROL**
KAWELKA, DERVISHES, KWEGU, MASAI   160

7 **CHRISTIANS AND PAGANS**
AZANDE, UMBANDA, EMBERA   183

8 **CELEBRATION**
CARNAVAL, KATARAGAMA, QUECHUA   199

9 **MEN AND WOMEN**
ASANTE, MOROCCANS, MASAI, MEHINAKU   217

The *Disappearing World* Film Archive   242

Anthropologists contributing to *Disappearing World*   244

Bibliography   247

Index   253

Acknowledgements

That brilliant observer of American society Tom Lehrer, in his song 'Lobachevsky', urged that plagiarism was to be positively encouraged provided it was called 'research'. This book is the product of considerable research. Directors, producers and researchers will recognise material taken from their *Disappearing World* scripts; anthropologists will notice references to and quotations from their published ethnographies and articles. Without their contributions the book would hardly have been possible. The photographs too have come from a variety of sources. In the early 1970s Granada arranged to try to keep all the photographs taken by individual members of the film teams on location in one central archive. Today the *Disappearing World* archive at the Hutchison Picture Library is one of the best collections of anthropological photographs in the world. Our thanks go to the many photographers whose images illuminate this book. Their work is individually credited below.

Above all at Granada, credit for this book must go to Andrew Robinson. It was he who saw the potential of an earlier proposal by André Singer and, with relentless enthusiasm, became the driving force behind the book. Planning the text, reading it, bullying it into final shape and proofing it once written, all became his remit, and they were performed with zealous dedication.

At Boxtree, Sarah Mahaffy could not have been more supportive. Other individuals who have contributed to the book include Ilona Benjamin, Michael Lee, Patricia McKiernan, Steven Seidenberg and David Wason. Our thanks also go to John Leech for the map, John Gilbert for his editing, and Groom & Pickerill for their design.

Finally, it cannot be repeated too many times that the book owes its existence to the peoples from all over the world who were hosts to the film teams who intruded on their lives. We like to believe that most of them will be pleased by it and proud of it, and we will attempt to ensure that as many of them as possible get to see it.

ANDRÉ SINGER and
LESLIE WOODHEAD

The publishers would like to acknowledge the following photographers whose photographs appear in this book:-

David Ash: p 215
Mike Baudo: p 2
Tim Beddow: p 209
Peter Connors: pp 10, 83, 89, 90, 92
Chris Curling: pp 17, 26, 31, 176, 178, 179, 179, 180, 221, 222, 223, 225, 226, 231, 232, 234
Sarah Errington: pp 132, 190
Andy Harries: p 175
Paul Henley: p 57
Richard House: p 200
Melissa Llewelyn Davies: pp 180, 182, 227, 228, 229, 230
Cavan MacCarthy: pp 190, 202
Michael MacIntyre: pp 191, 192, 201
Brian Moser: pp 12, 19, 20, 21, 22, 32, 33, 44, 51, 56, 58, 72, 73, 82, 84, 85, 86, 87, 97, 98, 99, 100, 101, 102, 103, 104, 105, 106, 125, 126, 128, 129, 170, 189, 193, 194, 195, 196, 197, 198, 214
Charlie Nairn: pp 16, 24, 28, 30, 43, 47, 63, 64, 65, 66, 67, 68, 69, 70, 160, 161, 162, 163, 164, 205, 206
A. Obeyesekere: pp 205, 206, 207, 208
Carlos Pasini: pp 210, 211, 212, 213, 234, 235, 236, 237, 238, 239, 240
Nick Plowright: p 78
John Ryle: pp 35, 188, 191, 199, 200, 201, 203, 204
Mike Sallnow: pp 210, 211, 213, 214, 215, 216
John Shepherd: pp 11, 27, 36, 93, 94, 95, 96
André Singer: pp 29, 34, 102, 130, 131, 133, 134, 141, 144, 145, 147, 148, 149, 150, 151, 152, 153, 154, 155, 156, 157, 158, 159, 165, 166, 167, 168, 169, 170, 171, 181, 183, 184, 185, 186, 187
Ivan Strasburg: pp 16, 31, 71, 72, 73, 74
Donald Tayler: p 9
Anna Tully: pp 218, 219, 220
David Wason: pp 41, 52, 112
Leslie Woodhead: pp 11, 13, 14, 18, 23, 25, 36, 37, 38, 39, 40, 42, 45, 46, 48, 49, 50, 53, 54, 55, 56, 59, 60, 61, 75, 76, 77, 78, 79, 80, 81, 90, 91, 107, 108, 109, 110, 111, 113, 114, 115, 116, 117, 118, 119, 120, 121, 122, 123, 135, 136, 137, 138, 140, 141, 142, 143, 172, 173, 174, 176, 177, 241

PREFACE

It is now nearly twenty years since Granada embarked upon the *Disappearing World* series. Ever since I had seen *Grass,* (made in Iran in 1925 by Milton Schoedsack and Merian C. Cooper) I had been seized of the idea that in film we had a means of documenting and capturing a picture of the tribal societies that were bound soon to disappear. Flaherty was working too but his films – *Moana, Nanook of the North* and *Man of Aran* – tended to incline towards the personal.

Later came Jean Rouch, whose work for the Musée de l'Homme covered spectacularly the tribes of West Africa; and so by 1970 I was ready to support wholeheartedly an enterprise that reflected a genuine interest in anthropology, coupled with the professional abilities to make films. It was one of the greatest pleasures of my time in Granada Television to see Brian Moser and other colleagues bring this vision to life and to put on record their studies of tribal societies, now more than forty in number. I am deeply grateful to the anthropologists, to the film crews and to everyone who collaborated to make *Disappearing World* such an enormous success.

DENIS FORMAN

'Tell the Americans about us. Tell them we are not wild Indians who club people. Tell them we are beautiful.'

SHUMOI, a Mehinaku, speaking to the anthropologist THOMAS GREGOR.

'The final goal of which an anthropologist should never lose sight is to grasp the native's point of view, his relationship to life, and to realise his vision of the world.'

BRONISLAW MALINOWSKI

FOREWORD

deas for television series emanate from strange places. *Disappearing World* probably began in a dugout canoe in 1960 as three of us paddled our way down the uncharted head-waters of the north-west Amazon; but it was ten years before the first film was transmitted. Since then, many individuals have helped to turn *Disappearing World* into an indelible record of tribal life watched by millions – anthropologists, film crews, film editors and, of course, all the many peoples who allowed us so generously to film them.

It's been ten years since I was involved in *Disappearing World*. So when Granada recently invited me to return to see two new films from the series – about the Kayapo of Brazil and the Basques of the Pyrenees – I cycled across London with some apprehension. As I got into the lift and went down to the preview theatre, my thoughts switched to another lift in Manchester eighteen years previously which had gone upwards to the 'Floor of the Gods'. I had been summoned then to see Denis Forman, the head of Granada Television, and David Plowright, the programme controller. They wanted to talk about a brief – titled 'The Vanishing Tribes of Latin America' – which I had written at the insistence of my then wife Caroline, herself an anthropologist, during an Easter week of immense frustration in Bogotá. We should have been filming the Pope's first visit to Latin America for Granada's *World in Action* but couldn't because of a union strike in Britain! The week had been well spent: the brief was accepted, Denis suggested

The Embera, a hunter-gatherer people who live along a remote river in Colombia, were the focus of one of *Disappearing World*'s earliest films.

Brian Moser, on location in South America.

9

'Let's call it *Disappearing World*', and David insisted that we should pay as much attention to the forces which were annihilating the tribal peoples as to the peoples themselves. We all agreed that we were not interested in making travelogues, nor did we want some omniscient commentator: rather, we would do everything possible to let people speak for themselves.

In the preview theatre, the Kayapo film began. The Indians were fishing (by bow and arrow) with effortless skill and tranquillity in a forest stream pierced by shafts of sunlight. Though I have never been in the Xingu National Park in Brazil, these images bore a strange resemblance to ones I had seen before. I was thinking of my very first film for *Disappearing World* on the Cuiva of Colombia, whom we had been able to contact through their trust in the anthropologist Bernard Arcand, even though they were in a constant state of war with the Llaneros – the cowboys who had taken over their land. The new film stirred vivid memories for me – of long night hours spent discussing Cuiva society and mythology and genocide, perched on moonlit mosquito and sandfly-infested sandbanks. We were all involved – Ernest Vincze the cameraman meticulously clean-

The Kayapo of Brazil are fighting to preserve their traditional way of life in the face of sudden and dramatic change.

'A shared commitment' under strain: a *Disappearing World* film team and anthropologist sample a Kwegu canoe on the river Omo in Southern Ethiopia.

ing his gear and reloading magazines, Bruce White recording Bernard's words of wisdom (which would later form the unpretentious commentary to the film), and myself worried whether there would be a film at all. That shared commitment has been for me the special quality of *Disappearing World*, with the onus, above all, on the anthropologist; without him or her, the rest of us had no possible contact with the people we were filming, since we did not speak their language or share their trust.

Suddenly, the Kayapo film took a new turn; a chief was filming a war dance with his own video camera. This, he said, was to ensure that 'our children and grand-children will never forget', and then he added: 'The Brazilians speak falsely, they break their promises. *Now* we have learned to use *their* technology, we can record what the Brazilians say for the Indians and Brazilians to hear, and so the Brazilians will be forced to act according to their words.' Ever since the arrival of

The Sakuddei of Indonesia are threatened by the large-scale exploitation of timber on their island territory.

the Spanish and Portuguese *conquistadores*, the vulnerable indigenous peoples of Latin America have been betrayed, enslaved and murdered by white invaders. The Kayapo, because of their unusual guile and determination, have managed to control their goldmine and may even halt the advance of hydroelectric dams planned for the Rio Xingu. Very few other tribes have managed to confront invaders in this way; certainly the Cuiva have not. When, in 1984, I revisited them shortly after they had given up their traditional nomadic life, only two of the original band of thirty in 1970 still survived; the rest had been murdered or had died of disease. Such terrifying facts alone justify *Disappearing World*; we had to record other peoples' ways of life before it was too late.

I suppose it was this sense of urgency, coupled with my personal knowledge of the appalling situation of Indian groups in Colombia in the late 1960s, which made *Disappearing World* start there. Some ten years before, I had made three small films in that area with Donald Tayler, now a curator at the Pitt Rivers Museum in Oxford, and Niels Halbertsma, a Dutch cameraman. We had lived among six different groups of Indians for over a year, recording their music. By 1970, on that same river in north-west Amazonia, we were aware of five different mission stations, and three anthropologists, Peter Silverwood-Cope and Stephen and Christine Hugh-Jones, at work. The opportunity to record a changing way of Indian life could not be missed.

It soon became apparent that the threat to the very existence of minority groups and tribal peoples was worldwide, and that *Disappearing World* should broaden its horizons. No longer could two Granada directors (Charlie Nairn and myself) cope alone. We were joined by Chris Curling, an anthropology graduate from Edmund Leach's stable in Cambridge, and after a further film about the Meo in war-ravaged Laos, the decision was taken that the series should acquire a more profound anthropological bent. We brought in four more anthropologists to be trained as

film-makers, Angela Burr, Melissa Llewelyn-Davies, André Singer and Pattie Winter, three of whom were nearing the end of their doctoral studies, and one who was fresh from university. We now felt able to go to almost any corner of the world in our efforts to understand the cultural identity of the peoples we were visiting. In André Singer and Melissa Llewelyn-Davies we had found academics who would go on to make films about societies of which they both had first-hand knowledge.

Since those formative years in the early 1970s, *Disappearing World* has established a unique archive of more than forty films made in every continent, and to the best available technical standards. As I sat watching the computerised subtitles on the Kayapo film, I couldn't help but recall the day when Chris Curling and I had sat in the same preview theatre entranced by the subtitled words of the Jie cattle herdsmen of Uganda in David and Judith McDougall's film *To Live With Herds*. It was this, above all else, which persuaded

us that the only way to understand ways of life so remote from our own was to *hear* the people speak. Why on earth should we denigrate another person's language by superimposing our own on it? Subtitles were obviously the answer, but at that time, in the early 1970s, they had to be burned on to the final print of the film with acid! To persuade a commercial television company that it should transmit an hour of Masai women or Mursi warriors speaking in their own tongues at peak viewing time seemed equally tricky; but somehow Jeremy Wallington, the executive in charge, did persuade Granada – and subtitling became a recognised trademark of *Disappearing World*. We all felt elated that through the anthropologist-translator and modern technology, tribal minorities could now have a voice not only on British television screens but on many other screens throughout the world.

The end of the Kayapo film left me wondering about the future of the series, the pastures still to be trodden, the new techniques still to be explored. I recalled

Filming Mursi crops devastated by parasites. The close cooperation between anthropologists like David Turton who has worked with the Mursi for twenty years and Granada film teams has always been the central feature of *Disappearing World*.

a letter I'd received once from Dai Vaughan, the film editor who shaped so many of the finest films in the series. 'We need to do a lot more thinking,' Dai suggested, 'about how wide the range of unexplored possibilities actually is.' I still feel that's true. Surely peasant societies, with the rapid changes that have been taking place in agriculture, deserve attention? But would it be possible to hold a television audience's attention with glimpses of the day-to-day drudgery of peasant life rather than tribal exotica? Only by the human relationships playing an ever more important role within the film I found myself thinking. To my delight, that was exactly what the second film at the preview did, in Leslie Woodhead and Sandra Ott's warm portrayal of two Basque shepherding families in the French Pyrenees.

Through that film, and the other films in the series, millions of people have been able to follow where only anthropologists went before, towards that 'final goal of which an anthropologist should never lose sight' – to quote Malinowski, one of the greatest of them – 'to grasp the native's point of view, his relationship to life, and to realise his vision of the world'.

Brian Moser
August 1987

INTRODUCTION

*'I often ask myself what advantages our "good society"
possesses over that of the "savages" and find, the more I
see of their customs, that we have no right to look down
upon them. We have no right to blame them for their
forms and superstitions which may seem ridiculous to us.
We "highly educated people" are much worse, relatively
speaking. A person's wealth should be judged by the
warmth of his heart.'*

FRANZ BOAS

One of the giants of social anthropology was the American scholar Franz Boas who, almost a century ago, realised that if we were going to understand how cultures work, we must go out and study other peoples. Only by learning their languages and living among them would we begin to gain insights into the way such people lived and behaved, and arrive at a better understanding of ourselves. Boas's pioneering work among the Eskimos and Kwakiutl Indians encouraged him to look at his own society, where he applied his field-work techniques to immigrants in the USA. Armed with detailed comparative information, he became the foremost critic of the racist notions prevailing in America during the first quarter of the century. He firmly refuted the belief that any race was superior to or more intelligent than another.

His travels and studies among the Eskimos and the Indians also made him acutely aware of how vulnerable and fragile those cultures were, and how important it was for him to record them (or as many vestiges of them as possible) before the inevitable changes of the twentieth century swept them away. His was not a call for the preservation of social institutions in some form of human zoo. Rather, he aimed to use the tools of anthropology to record what still existed and to trace what had existed in order to provide a permanent record of our human heritage. Those tools included face masks, written descriptions by field-workers, the language of a culture, photographs and – of growing importance – films.

Boas himself did not write or make films for the public; but he did not share the concern felt by many of his academic colleagues that the popularisation of anthropology was a potential danger to it as a discipline. He believed he had a duty as an anthropologist to 'impart systematic information' and provide 'healthy entertainment and instruction.' The contribution of anthropology to the public's eventual rejection of eugenics, the 'science' of human breeding, was an endorsement of

his policy. In 1906, a time when white Americans felt certain of their racial superiority over the blacks, Boas voiced his opinions publicly. 'The increasing antagonism between the white and the black races is not only a matter of concern from a humanitarian point of view,' he wrote, 'but entails serious dangers to the United States.' He continued to point out that despite anatomical and cerebral differences between races, 'there is no proof whatever that these differences signify any appreciable degree of inferiority of the negro'.

His stance over controversial anthropological themes often made Boas deeply unpopular with many academic colleagues. Matters came to a head in 1919 when he chose to address the American public by writing a letter to the editor of the journal *The Nation* concerning the use of anthropology as a cover for political spying in the First World War. The governing council of the American Anthropological Association censured him and stripped him of his membership.

Boas's colleagues were less outraged at his use of film and photographs as a research tool, although many leading anthropologists over the years have remained sceptical of the different media used to transmit their anthropological findings in relatively untechnical terms to a wider public. Until the early years of this century, public information about the work and findings of anthropologists or scholars of the human condition was derived mainly from travel books or popular novels, often first printed in journal form. The general public's knowledge of Africa and her inhabitants came from the books of H. Rider Haggard or Edgar Rice Burroughs. The Pacific was familiar because of Joseph Conrad and R.M. Ballantyne. Rudyard Kipling and A.E.W. Mason portrayed India, and Conan Doyle, after a holiday in Egypt,

popularised that part of the world. In their search for a common humanity, such distinguished writers sometimes expressed sentiments that contemporary authors should envy. Just over a century ago, for example, H. Rider Haggard wrote in *Allan Quatermain*: 'It is a depressing conclusion, but in all essentials the savage and the child of civilisation are identical. I dare say that the highly civilised lady reading this will smile at an old fool of a hunter's simplicity when she thinks of her black-bedecked sister. And yet, my dear young lady, what are those pretty things round your own neck? – they have a strong family resemblance, especially when you wear that *very* low dress, to the savage woman's beads . . . remember that in fundamental principles of your nature you are quite identical.'

Unfortunately, the majority of popular writers were guilty of the grossest exagge-

rations, offering stereotypes of the 'primitive' that were accepted and perpetuated wholesale by a thirsty public. The anthropologist Brian Street, in a recent study, pointed out how rarely the anthropological ideas of the time found their way into current popular literature. It was easier to adopt the outdated scientific theories with which the writers were more familiar and comfortable. The public had no access to anthropology, and it was rare for any of the anthropological texts to be written in prose suitable or interesting enough for wider reading. In England, the only exception was Sir James Frazer's classic *The Golden Bough* which influenced scholars and laymen alike. Yet Frazer had no direct experience of the societies he was writing about, so even here the public diet of information and theory was at third or fourth hand.

In America, Margaret Mead, a close colleague and student of Boas, and a committed field-worker, was one of the earliest and certainly the most famous of anthropologists to fall foul of her academic peers on the grounds of popu-

larising her material. She explained why she preferred to present her field-findings from the late 1920s in a more accessible form: 'In those days, anthropologists used to pepper their papers with language that nobody spoke. If I'd used words like "exogamy" and "endogamy" no one could have read the book. So I wrote it in English for the people I thought would use it, and if you write a book for people who are going to use something, you write it for the whole world.'

Her book, *Coming of Age in Samoa*, was a best-seller. Mead had a unique ability to put across to an interested public anthropological theory that became the subject of national debate. Childhood, adolescence, sex and marriage, breast feeding and parenthood were all discussed in relation to her field-work; and she made explicit comparisons with modern American experience in these areas.

She was not slow to see the potential of film either. With her third husband, Gregory Bateson, Margaret Mead took many thousands of still photographs and a mass of 16 mm film footage. This visual

material was not structured for popular viewing; it was intended to be a research tool. Nevertheless, partly as a result of her enthusiasm for new ways of reaching the public, film took on an ever greater importance in anthropology.

By the 1960s and 1970s, film was reaching millions in their living rooms through the spread of television, and anthropologists had an exciting new medium to use. Granada was one of the first television companies to take up the challenge. 'Our purpose is that of most anthropologists,' wrote Chairman Denis Forman in 1974, 'to show other cultures in such a way as to allow them to be understood. The film medium is in a special position to do for the public what academics do for each other – i.e to show the ways that societies survive and exist with values that might appear strange (in the context of our civilisation), but which are logical to them and should be respected.'

The *Disappearing World* series has become the most extensive forum yet devised for presenting anthropology to a worldwide audience, in a visual language which is truly international. More than forty hours of film have so far been seen by millions of viewers in more than twenty countries. But in order to give a satisfying and convincing response to those who query the success of this enterprise, both the anthropologists and the film-makers have been obliged continuously to examine their motives and their methods.

While working on one of the earliest and most influential of the *Disappearing World* films, about a group of Amazonian Indians, the Cuiva, the anthropologist Bernard Arcand wanted 'just to put the camera down and let it roll for the whole length of the film. What you would most likely see is a man just sitting in the sunlight, yawning, scratching his nose, laughing with his children and maybe shouting at his wife. Then maybe for the first time in history you could have seen these people as simply human beings, people who do scratch their noses and laugh at their children and shout at their wives. They are not always taking drugs and dancing, and running about naked.

A group of Cuiva listen to the film team's recordings.

19

That to me would be a "first" in history.'

Although *Disappearing World* shared Arcand's ambition to show such people as 'simply human beings', as film-makers seeking to communicate with a mass audience, we had to be a little more realistic. People scratching their noses for minutes on end makes for boring viewing; it may fascinate the academic anthropologist, but it hardly provides others with a more enlightening or sympathetic insight into Cuiva life and society. It was remarkable enough that anthropologists should have the chance to relay *some* of their experience and insights to millions of people; but to expect a peak-time television audience to become engrossed in the often tedious minutiae of everyday life of other societies was clearly unrealistic. What the films needed were the interpretative skills of an anthropologist, steeped in intimate knowledge of a people, to make sense of that society; only he could identify and select the themes that were most important and deserving of being 'translated' into a film. In fact, Arcand eventually adopted an approach that was even

more effective, setting a pattern for subsequent films.

He gave powerful expression to the anguish he felt for oppressed Colombian Indians. Backed by the skills of Brian Moser and his film team, Arcand clarified the relationship between the Cuiva and the Llaneros, the Colombian farmers who were causing their disappearance as a cultural entity. For the viewing public the plight of a completely unknown tribe in a distant land was both enlightening and moving; and for anthropologists the film was a vivid study of dynamic social change. It showed the workings of a society organised into small hunting bands and demonstrated how contemporary circumstances were unlikely to allow such a group to survive in its traditional form. This unique visual record of a society in crisis, in conjunction with Arcand's written reports, forms an important contribution to ethnography.

Style and content have both changed considerably since those early days. The first films, made between 1970 and 1972, had a strong social 'message'. They were

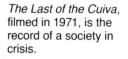

The Last of the Cuiva, filmed in 1971, is the record of a society in crisis.

based on stories that Brian Moser and his fellow director, Charlie Nairn, believed worthy of 'exposure': the clearing of the jungle in Venezuela; the impact of a road upon the Embera of Colombia; the influence of missionaries in that country on the Maku and the Barasana; the effect of the Vietnam war on the Hmong of Laos; and the pressures of drought, tourism and modern government on the Algerian Tuareg.

Moser and Nairn were strongly influenced by Granada's *World in Action*, the current affairs flagship on which they had received their training. The anthropologists they worked with were all young, fresh from their field-work and keen to tell the world about a situation they were helpless to prevent. Viewers were introduced to the social problems of remote cultures, and asked to share an understanding of what it meant to be controlled, pressurised, exploited and abused. The problems raised by the famous documentary drama *Cathy Come Home* were on their doorstep; *Disappearing World* was inviting them to look farther afield, and become involved with Colombian Indians in the same way.

The film-makers and anthropologists were portraying extremely unusual human situations and highlighting ways of life which were rapidly shifting. Five years

after working on the film *The Meo*, Jacques Lemoine could justifiably claim: 'As an anthropologist I had laid down as a principle with Brian Moser that the film should deal with the true situation and the exact feelings of the people. That is why our film is still meaningful today.' Andrew Turton of the School of Oriental and African Studies in London, when

21

reviewing *The Meo*, accepted that it was not a detailed ethnographic documentary, but acknowledged that it 'documented with considerable accuracy and skill a terrible chapter in the history of the Meo people of Laos'.

The first six documentaries in the series deliberately did not seek to achieve the visionary aims outlined by Boas. The film-makers felt that their most urgent priority was to explore the 'story' of changes threatening certain societies at that time. As Brian Moser points out in the Foreword to this book, the key, as ever with *Disappearing World*, lay in establishing links between the anthropologist with his years of field-work and the film-maker with his one-hour distillation of

The Barasana of Colombia have been the subjects of aggressive campaigns by missionaries from North America.

those insights. As Paul Henley, an anthropologist and film-maker, wrote of *Disappearing World* in his 1985 survey of British ethnographic films on television: '. . . the films were aimed, not at popularising topics that could be more effectively dealt with in a book or an article, but rather at reaching an understanding of what the way of life portrayed was like to those who lived it, either through encouraging some sort of empathetic identification with the people who were interviewed or who otherwise spoke directly to the camera, or simply on the basis of the clues provided by the sounds and images of them going about their daily business within their distinctive social and physical environment.'

Anthropology in Britain has been strongly influenced by the principles laid down by Bronislaw Malinowski, its undisputed 'king' at the London School of Economics until his death in 1942. Essentially, he insisted on the need to demonstrate, through intensive field-work, how the different elements that make up a society have a function in the whole. His own field-work in the Trobriand Islands, off the east coast of Papua New Guinea, became the example to be followed by the next generation of anthropologists.

Malinowski felt that without the understanding of another people that comes from living alongside them – learning their language, eating their food and participating in their daily lives – no one can come to grips with the real working of that society. It is often difficult and lonely work, as Malinowski recorded in his detailed diaries. 'I had periods of despondency when I buried myself in the reading of novels, as a man might take to drink in a fit of tropical depression and boredom.' But his perseverance paid incalculable dividends, and in much the way that Boas influenced American anthropology, so Malinowski laid the real foundations for anthropology in Britain.

When Brian Moser was setting off for the first *Disappearing World* films, the largest departments of anthropology in Britain were in the process of being vacated by some of Malinowski's most famous students – Sir Edward Evans-

On the man-made islands of the South Pacific Lau lagoon, the traditional 'Life of Custom' has been overturned by Christian missionaries from the West.

23

Pritchard at Oxford, Meyer Fortes in Cambridge, Lucy Mair and Sir Raymond Firth in London and Max Gluckman in Manchester. They had all insisted in their turn on the overwhelming need for long and intensive field-work as a prerequisite for any anthropological analysis.

While debate continued about the future approach and form of *Disappearing World*, two films were made which tackled new and very different themes – described by Forman as 'not so much deviations as irresistible subjects that are only slightly off centre'. *The Dervishes of Kurdistan* and *Kataragama* looked at two contrasting religious communities: an ecstatic Islamic order in Iran and a syncretic Buddhist festival in Sri Lanka. Rather than tribal societies under threat, these examined rituals that appeared bizarre, exotic and incomprehensible to a Western television audience.

Anthropologists Gananath Obeyesekere in Sri Lanka, and Ali Bulookbashi with myself in Iran, had the task of presenting Charlie Nairn and Brian Moser with an interpretation of 'alien' activities that would make them acceptable and intelligible to a television audience. Even so, the eminent Indianist Richard Gombrich called *Kataragama* 'a more accurate and

informative picture of religion in Ceylon than anything yet written'. But, such praise notwithstanding, the *Disappearing World* team, now expanded to six including both anthropologists and film-makers, felt that a correct approach was still proving elusive and that *Dervishes* and *Kataragama*, though interesting, had been merely a detour. The turning point came in 1974.

In an extraordinary experiment, a further six films were shown, in consecutive weeks at peak viewing time (9.00 p.m.). For the first time on British television, the films used subtitled translations and reflected the work of six anthropologists rather than relying, as previously, on the commentary of an on-screen anthropologist. Another significant departure was the subject matter. With the exception perhaps of John Sheppard's film on the Sakuddei of Siberut Island in Indonesia, the films concentrated not on processes of change (significant as these undoubtedly were) but on a single theme that gave coherence to each society portrayed.

The Mursi, directed by Leslie Woodhead with David Turton as anthropologist, looked at the decision-making process among a tribe of Ethiopian cattle-herders. Chris Curling relied upon the extensive field experience of Melissa

Masai women talked to anthropologist Melissa Llewelyn Davies about their daily lives and about their husbands, lovers and sons.

Llewelyn-Davies to examine the role of Masai women in Kenya. Carlos Pasini went with Thomas Gregor to the Xingu forests of Brazil to record the sexual divide among the Mehinaku tribe, and later climbed high into the Peruvian Andes with the anthropologist Michael Sallnow to observe Quechua religious practices. Finally, Charlie Nairn accompanied Andrew Strathern to the Papua New Guinea highlands where Andrew's friend Ongka, a Melpa 'Big-Man', was preparing to establish his authority by holding an elaborate and lavish feast – a *moka*.

These five 'studies' were parallels on film of the written research of the anthropologists concerned. Television was able to close the gap between anthropological ideas and public awareness of them. The lapse of several decades between the work of the earlier anthropologists and its introduction into popular literature could now be cut to a few years or even months. Each film in that 1974 series employed a device that has since become a standard and essential feature of any contemporary ethnographic film: persuading individuals to express themselves in their own language. Encouraging the Masai matriarch Nolpiyaya to relate her feelings about marriage and the role of women in her society stimulated an empathy for the Masai view of life which was unique and affecting; while Ongka, the Kawelka from Papua New Guinea, was able to describe his struggles

The anthropologist Reimar Schefold has studied how the Sakuddei of Indonesia are threatened by government plans to change their lives.

27

for status in terms that made his frustrations understandable and his seemingly extraordinary endeavours acceptably rational and logical.

John Sheppard with Reimar Schefold, on the island of Siberut found a society being devastated by the exploits of the logging companies who were systematically destroying the environment, and with it any prospect of the Sakuddei continuing their traditional existence. As with Brian Moser's earlier Meo film, the approach was shaped by external threats to the society. The resulting film ensured that the debate about a 'correct' anthropological approach to the material would remain unresolved among the team. Despite some negative reactions in the popular press, including the memorable 'see one rain dance and you've seen them all', the series was an unexpected popular success; and the critical acclaim that it received in 1974 justified the new direction in content and presentation. But some doubts remained, both among the film-makers and the academics, as to whether the wider conflicts which film could so dramatically expose, should be ignored.

Thomas Weaver pointed out to the anthropological world in 1973 that 'except on rare occasions, this discipline has not been directly or primarily concerned with social problems or social issues . . . . Anthropology, by its very existence and by the nature of the data it produces, is a

The Melpa of Papua New Guinea were filmed during elaborate preparations for a *moka* – a lavish feast to establish the status of an important man.

political activity. Failure to take a position – or the assumption of a neutral position by failing to face basic ethical problems – is a political action.' He and his co-author Gerald Berreman were concerned that the same mistakes that Boas had protested against two or three generations earlier would be repeated.

Eventually the series followed two distinct approaches. Most of the subsequent films concentrated on the internal aspects of the chosen societies and were not exposés of pressures being imposed upon them from outside. Only occasionally, as with films such as *The Eskimos of Pond Inlet* in 1975, *Afghan Exodus* in 1980 and *The Kayapo* in 1987, is the focus on purely external pressures.

Sympathetic programme management at Granada, particularly by the series executive Jeremy Wallington, ensured that 1974 to 1977 were fruitful years for *Disappearing World*. Rahman Qul, chief of the Kirghiz in Afghanistan, Ayang Anei Kur,

In an isolated wedge of Afghanistan, squeezed between China, the USSR and Pakistan, a small group of Kirghiz herdsmen survived under their chief Khan Rahman Qul until political pressures made them refugees.

'divine' king of the Shilluk of Sudan, and Mingma Tenzing of the Sherpas in Nepal joined the growing ranks of individuals who were given scope to tell their own stories; and the areas of the globe visited by the *Disappearing World* team included Arctic Canada, Morocco and Mongolia. A couple of films broke new ground. Mike Grigsby, with the anthropologist Hugh Brody, decided that the expression of people's ideas and feelings had come across so powerfully by means of translated subtitles that the addition of the voice of a Western commentator would be intrusive. The resulting film, *The Eskimos of Pond Inlet*, provided some information on caption cards, emulating the techniques of silent movies, but otherwise the only voices were those of the Eskimos speaking directly to the viewer.

The *Disappearing World* policy of encouraging remote peoples to speak to the camera in their own language and on themes of their own choosing, was in advance of much written anthropology where peoples were rarely given the opportunity to describe their own societies. Anthropologists almost always did it for them, using quotations from the peoples. One of the most interesting anthropological books to be published in recent years was Andrew Strathern's translation of Ongka's description of the working of his own Kawelka society; an example, in written form, of members of a society expressing themselves with as little outside intrusion as possible. While the Eskimos were pointing out to Grigsby and Brody how Canadian domination had changed their ways, Melissa Llewelyn-Davies, with the anthropologist Elizabeth Fernea, was also breaking new ground in Morocco by filming for the first time the women of an Islamic society, using an all-female film team.

Despite the success of individual programmes, a debate continued among the film-makers about 'where *Disappearing World* should be going'. Nancy Banks-Smith once wrote in *The Guardian*

that 'anthropology is the science which tells us that people are the same the whole world over – except when they are different'. Her words reflect the core philosophy of the film-making and research team at Granada, namely the desire to present other societies in such a way that an audience appreciated the similarities between 'them' and 'us'. The very individuality of each society ensures that a systematic approach remains elusive.

Brian Moser, in the last two films he made for the series, was obliged by political circumstances to adopt an unhappy compromise. These were the Mongolian films *On the Edge of the Gobi* and *The City on the Steppes*. Moser went with Owen Lattimore to a country which at that time (1975) was completely unknown in the West. The challenge was an exciting one, but access depended upon breaking a few of the rules Moser had introduced into the series, the most important of which was the editorial freedom of the film-maker to interpret his subject. Although Lattimore,

The Eskimos of Pond Inlet told the television audience about powerful pressures from modern Canada to abandon their traditional ways of life.

Some Women of Marrakech featured women in a strict Islamic society, filmed by an all-female team (left).

31

as a most respected Westerner with a lifetime of experience in Inner Asia, could gain permission for the first Western film team to look at Mongolian society, there were inevitable constraints over how the team could operate. Many of the social issues that fascinated Moser remained concealed from his camera. In deference to a society that manifestly was *not* disappearing, the visually stunning and unique documentaries he produced did not use the *Disappearing World* title; but they reinforced Moser's desire to concentrate on societies which he knew intimately and where he could allow the people in the film to express themselves freely.

To this end he embarked with his wife, the anthropologist Caroline Moser, on a project in the slum *barrios* of Guayaquil in Ecuador. Granada was denied the fruits of this endeavour by the temporary closure of the *Disappearing World* unit. In 1977 a dispute arose between the production team and the film technicians' union

about the optimum level of crewing for *Disappearing World* films. The original team dispersed and took their talents elsewhere.

Meanwhile in the universities, film was gaining credibility as a teaching tool. Peter Loizos, an anthropologist at the London School of Economics and himself a film-maker, set the seal of respectability on the series with a lengthy analytical article in *American Anthropologist*. After examining in detail the troubles and polemics surrounding the first twenty-four films in the series, Loizos concluded with a statement that echoed the ambitions many of us had always maintained for the programme and convinced us that we should sustain our efforts to revive it. He wrote: 'The *Disappearing World* series cannot, in the nature of things, stop itself being used by some people to strengthen their own sense of superiority. But had a well-developed study been done on the main effects of the series, I strongly suspect it would have

Brian Moser (along with the first Western film crew to look at Mongolia) found political obstacles to their attempts to record daily life in a Communist society.

shown a strengthening of sympathy for, and an understanding of, non-European peoples; no mean achievement.'

Aside from its popular appeal for television audiences, *Disappearing World* was also adopted by numerous individuals and academic departments as an integral part of their teaching – no longer merely as an entertaining adjunct to the discipline.

Film has never replaced text, but its value has been widely recognised and is growing. Paul Baxter of Manchester University succinctly expressed the relationship when reviewing Chris Curling's film *The Rendille*. Admitting that anthropologists and film-makers have different attitudes to the same subject, Baxter pointed out their strengths and weaknesses: 'Each seeks quite different aspects of truth and utilises quite different means of stitching scraps of culture together creatively. The analysis of ethnography requires the probing of a complex of minute particulars in a search for demonstrable connections; it is always tentative and demands detachment, openness and uncertainty. The bossy one-eyedness and distorting beauty of film, on the other hand, seeks to simplify, disarm and impose through the temporary suspension of disbelief. In some ways the difference between anthropologists and

film-makers is analogous to that between anthropologists and development planners. Film-makers and planners want life to be simple, whereas anthropologists are sure it is complicated. But Dr Baxter conceded that 'the sensory capacities of film can, if used perceptively and humbly enough, create a picture of and a feel for a culture better than almost any ethnographer has been able to do'.

The authors of this book remained inside Granada, working towards the re-establishment of *Disappearing World*. In 1979, with the making of *Khyber*, the possibility resurfaced. This was not a *Disappearing World* but a historical documentary examining the relationships between the British and the Pushtuns on the North-West Frontier, between Afghanistan and what is now Pakistan. With the cooperation of the anthropologists Louis Dupree and Akbar Ahmed, access was gained to the tribe in Afghanistan and Pakistan, and filming was extended to include a Pushtun village study that in 1980 was screened as *The Pathans*

(this being the popular name of the Pushtuns), becoming the first *Disappearing World* for nearly four years. Reviews in the British national press almost unanimously expressed the hope that it heralded the return of the programme on a regular basis. 'The series has always seemed to me one of the most valuable on television,' wrote Sylvia Clayton, 'for the way it peoples the world's map with living faces and I only wish *The Pathans* was the start of a series'.

Happily, her wishes were echoed within Granada and planning began on a new series of *Disappearing World*.

We decided for the first three films to concentrate on narrow themes of current anthropological interest. *Witchcraft Among The Azande* took as its starting point Evans-Pritchard's classic book on the subject, *Witchcraft, Oracles and Magic Among the Azande*, based on field-work done in the late 1920s. The aim was to examine the topics of witchcraft, magic and oracles with a view to 'translating' the thoughts and beliefs behind them for a sceptical public. In effect, it was the 'film of the book'. Despite the brilliance of his writings, Evans-Pritchard was aware of the failings of much contemporary social anthropology and in 1973, the year he died, he wrote that 'anthropologists have, in their writings about African Societies, dehumanised the Africans into systems and structures and lost the flesh and blood'.

It was therefore gratifying that two very different reviewers reacted similarly to the film. John Beattie, a student and close colleague of Evans-Pritchard, believed the film lived up to the standards set by *Disappearing World*: 'In doing so it meets,

Witchcraft Among the Azande looked at witchcraft magic and oracles in Central Africa.

The Sakuddei traditionally live together in clan houses, but today the Indonesian government insists that they move to new villages.

In China's communes, a consumer revolution in the the 1980s emphasises personal initiative under the 'Responsibility System'.

A peasant wedding in a commune in South-east China.

with outstanding success, a challenge not faced – at least in anything like the same degree – by earlier films in the series. The problem of how to represent as plausible, even rational, patterns of behaviour which looked at out of context must seem exotic, even bizarre, is at its most acute when what is at issue is magical behaviour. The Azande have indeed come to life in the new medium.' Nancy Banks-Smith wrote that 'what struck me most forcibly about the Azande was their vividly familiar "well hello there" kindred humanity. That they all believe and practise witchcraft seems beside that only incidental.'

The second film of the trilogy was given a similar reception. Claudia Milne, with the anthropologist Charlotte Boaitey, illustrated the way that Asante women in the markets of Kumasi, in Ghana, had established an economic independence within a polygamous society.

The final film returned to an area we already knew well – Mursi country in southern Ethiopia. Leslie Woodhead, working once again with the anthropologist David Turton, took as their theme the puzzle of patrons and clients. They looked at how the more powerful Mursi dominated a minority people called the Kwegu. This was a long way from the *Disappearing World* of the early 1970s. Rather than dwelling upon the disruption in tribal society caused by the intrusions of the West, Leslie Woodhead's film *The Kwegu* sought to explore the mechanism whereby one group in a society is able to dominate another. In addition to underlining the special relationship that existed between the Kwegu and Mursi, at the same time the film suggested how social inequalities anywhere might become part of an accepted order.

The following year we used a similar approach in China. Leslie Woodhead, with the anthropologist Barbara Hazard, tackled Han communes in south-eastern China in the film *Living with the Revolution* and *The Newest Revolution*, while I went with Shirin Akiner to the far north-west to look at the way an Islamic minority tribe had adapted to communism. Following that film, *The Kazakhs of China*, mounting financial and organisational pressures within Granada made prospects for further *Disappearing Worlds* appear bleak once again, and the remnants of the original team finally disbanded in 1983.

Fortunately *Disappearing World*, like the proverbial Good Dog, could not be kept down. Since 1985, under executive producer Rod Caird, a further five films have been made, and several new projects are being planned. Most innovative of the recent developments was the return to Ethiopia, for the third time, of Leslie Woodhead and David Turton. Driven by drought and famine, a quarter of the Mursi people had migrated to higher terrain, some fifty miles to the east 'in

search of cool ground', as they put it. *The Migrants* and the Mursi trilogy were the first substantial documentaries about social change to be produced by *Disappearing World*, for they span more than ten years and record the process of a people transforming their identity from pastoralists to agriculturalists. Rather as the Granada documentary series *Seven Up* has fascinated audiences by tracing how a group of British children have grown up over a twenty-one-year period, so the Woodhead/Turton films

themselves from the gold-hungry Brazilians who are mining their land, was a powerful 'social issue' story. In contrast, the gentler Basques film set in a Pyrenean valley, where Leslie Woodhead relied on the field research of Sandra Ott, presented an analysis of traditional social relationships in a changing but more familiar world. This film firmly acknowledged that Western and peasant societies have an important place in the latest phase of *Disappearing World*. Finally, working with Pierre Maranda in the Lau lagoon of the South Pacific, Leslie Woodhead depicted a people struggling to record and revitalise their hard-pressed traditional culture.

Mursi women of Southern Ethiopia are beginning to abandon lip cutting as a result of increasing contacts with the outside world

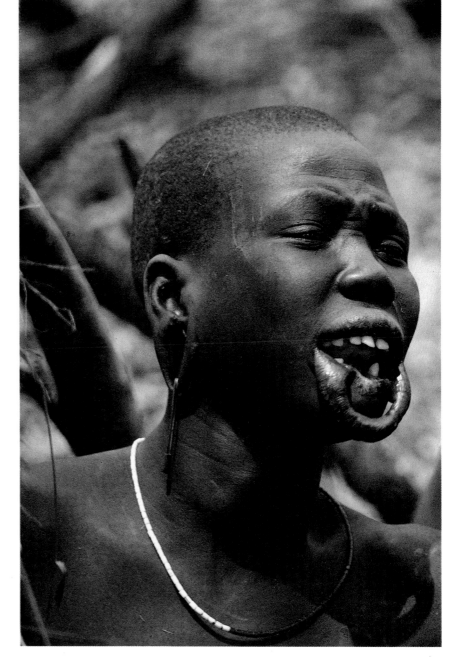

with the Mursi offer a continuing account of a tribal people in a remote part of Africa and of their developing contact with the outside world.

In 1987 Granada transmitted three more *Disappearing World* films, on the Kayapo of Brazil, the Basques of south-western France and the Lau of the Solomon Islands. Mike Beckham's collaboration with Terry Turner on the extraordinary attempts by the Kayapo to control their own future and protect

The Mursi have become familiar with the film teams who have followed their lives over three films since 1974.

Almost twenty years of experience in *Disappearing World* have shown that no single approach is right. The fact that audiences in their millions watch the programmes confirms that the film-makers and anthropologists involved with *Disappearing World* have a real responsibility to the public. The central purpose of the series remains to understand and empathise with other societies. When in 1884 Boas sat among the Eskimos and wrote to his fiancée that Western society had no right to judge itself in any way superior to so-called 'savages', he spoke from direct first-hand experience. Anthropologists continue to seek comparable experiences across the world, but few of us have the opportunity to encounter other cultures at first hand. In this respect Boas at the turn of the century, and *Disappearing World* three-quarters of a century later, have similar goals. David Turton, writing about the series, pointed out that it had the difficult task of being good television entertainment whilst at the same time providing academic anthropologists with a useful teaching aid. He concluded by asserting that 'the challenge these films offer is greater than this; it is to give those for whom anthropology is literally a closed book a feeling of familiarity with the lives and preoccupations of the people of another and very different culture; it is to

help an audience make a journey of its own, to reach what the philosopher Gabriel Marcel has called "the familiar at the heart of the remote . . . an elsewhere that is also a here"'.

It may be that this collaboration between the film-maker and the anthropologist has worked to the extent that these roles have coalesced. The film-makers have had to become anthropologists, and Evans-Pritchard's words strike a familiar chord in us all: 'In social anthropology you are studying not just as an observer but also as a participant, you are not just a member of the audience, you are also on the stage. The anthropologist is in a very peculiar position, because you are trying to interpret what you see, not just with the head, but with your whole personality, with your heart as well.'

We have endeavoured, through the television series and now with this companion volume, to encourage that journey of discovery, to convey that experience of 'an elsewhere that is also a here'. At the same time even a brief glance through some of the stories recorded here shows how the fears expressed in the early 1970s, when *Disappearing World* began, have been tragically fulfilled today. Brian Moser has pointed out that of the original nomadic band of Cuiva filmed, only two are still alive; the Kirghiz of Afghanistan

A film on the island of Lamalera in Southern Indonesia records the lives of fishermen who still hunt for whales from open rowing boats.

fled their homeland and after many deaths have become refugees in Turkey; the Hmong of Laos have suffered continuous warfare and persecution; and the Kurds are embroiled in the current Iraq/Iran conflict. The catalogue of change is long and often painful. The *Disappearing World* films provide unique images of a part of our human heritage. Our hope is that this book may allow more time to look, to read and to absorb.

It was always obvious that *Disappearing World* ought to make a book as well as a series. The key to a book's structure seemed to be, as in the case of the series, the visual material. A library of transparencies collected from more than forty film expeditions had been built up over the years. Although some had been used in magazines and books, the vast majority of them had, until now, formed an untapped reservoir of unique images.

When we had made some twenty-five films, we began serious plans for a book. Initially, we debated the possibility of organising the material in some sort of geographical order – a chapter on Africa, another on South America, and so forth. There were too many gaps. Where, for example, were films from North America, eastern Asia or India? After a further ten years many of the regional gaps had been filled, but by then we were not convinced that a geographical breakdown had any real logic. A reader with an interest in central Africa, for instance, would hardly get a comprehensive background to that area and the societies living there by being offered a section on witchcraft among the Azande.

We then considered whether we might instead copy the conventional themes used in introductory texts on anthropology – with separate chapters on religion, economics, politics, kinship, etc. That made a little more sense, considering that anthropologists, in their attempts to understand the working of human societies, used detailed examples from these different areas for purposes of comparison.

The Mursi material would then have been an example of the way tribal societies wield political control – much as Edward Evans-Pritchard used the Nuer of the Sudan in anthropological texts a generation earlier. But several problems remained. The *Disappearing World* films were not planned to fill the needs of a comprehensive anthropology course. Several films dealt with politics, none with kinship; economics was an element in a few films but was treated in detail by none. Furthermore, whereas much contemporary anthropology tackles the social structure of tribal society without analysing or describing the process of social change, many of our *Disappearing World* films focussed on such change without analysing the social structure of the tribe or group.

These difficulties could have been overcome by using the society described in each film as a trigger for each section, and then resorting to other writings and research to flesh out the chapter. *Witchcraft Among the Azande* could then have formed part of a broader chapter about tribal politics, provided there was suf-

ficient data available concerning Azande chiefs to give it adequate anthropological interest. But then the book would not have matched the films; this, we felt, was the prime consideration and ultimately dictated the structure we adopted. It is our hope that the book is useful in its own right; but it should equally be seen as a detailed record and extension of the films.

The themes it covers are those covered by the films. The script and contents of each film determined the breakdown of chapters. The first three chapters, *Winds of Change, Clash of Cultures* and *A Matter of Choice* all relate to the theme most often tackled by the series: social change. There is, of course, change in every one of the films; but the ten societies examined in these chapters, and to some extent also in *Behind the Curtain* (Chapter Four), are extreme examples of what the developed world is doing to its tribal heritage. Some of the changes are taking place without total disruption of the traditional way of life of a people; other cases should be cause for both concern and shame. A chief of the Kayapo tribe in Brazil (Chapter

Basque shepherds at their summer pastures in the French Pyrenees – the pivot of a way of life which is rapidly changing.

Two) expressed the tribal dilemma forcibly: 'The Indian is not like an animal in the forest – he is not a pig or a dog. The Indian is a human being too . . . I, chief of the Gorotire, have only one way of talking, not three or four. The problem with the white man is that he has more than one way of talking.'

But savage stereotypes live on in the public mind; so it seemed important, too, to examine the varied and complex mechanisms whereby tribal groups control and order their lives. *Order, Order, Order* and *Gaining Control* (Chapters Five and Six) describe these mechanisms in eight such societies. The sophistication of religious beliefs and practices among a further six appear in *Christians and Pagans* and *Celebration* (Chapters Seven and Eight). Finally, there is the relationship between the roles of men and women, which was

the dominant theme in four of the films, in *Men and Women* (Chapter Nine).

The most significant innovation in *Disappearing World* has been to allow people from other cultures to talk directly to Western viewers. In the book we try to follow that practice too; quotes from the indigenous people have been woven into the narrative. In addition, the work and words of directors, researchers and, in particular, anthropologists all make important contributions to the text. We thank them all and hope they feel justice has been done to the effort they put into the films. First and foremost though, we owe a debt to the many societies we visited, who tolerated us poking our cameras and waving our microphones at them and allowed us to expose their lives on screen to the gaze of millions around the world.

ON LOCATION
filming *Disappearing World*

I was having a drink the other day with an old hand of *Disappearing World* when he showed me his tattoo. The elegant blue crab, precise as a watchmaker's gear-wheel, was inscribed on his forearm and a good story went with it. John Sheppard had received the tattoo from the Sakuddei people when he was filming a *Disappearing World* on the island of Siberut off the coast of Sumatra in the Indian Ocean. 'The Sakuddei saw it as confirming the special friendship between themselves and the film team,' John recalls. The sound recordist and the cameraman got their own mementos: 'They were tattooed with little darts so that their arrows would always fly straight in the future.'

Although few of us carry such striking souvenirs, all of us who've worked on the *Disappearing World* films seem to have received some special imprint from the experience. There is, I suppose, nothing quite like it anywhere else in television. It's a curious business, spending weeks, even months sometimes, out of contact in some of the world's remotest places alongside people who often share almost none of our assumptions about ways of living, while trying at the same time to make a film with those people. It can be memorably uncomfortable, but the stories are as plentiful as the insect bites. The *Disappearing World* store of bizarre anecdotes, gleaned from the collective experience of more than forty films in exotic locations is rich and varied. Crew tales of blood for breakfast compete with horror stories of surviving on wood grubs and roast armadillo when the food has run out;

hundred-mile treks through the bush in search of non-existent rituals vie with breathless hikes in the Andes or the Himalayas. We've collected a rare cocktail of tropical diseases between us over the years; we've got lost, become stranded, been accused of murder. But somehow at the end of it all, though it's been touch-and-go on occasions, we've always returned with a film. And for me at least, the *Disappearing World* films I've been involved with have become the most absorbing business of my life.

A Melpa man in Indonesia makes his first acquaintance with a film camera.

47

In Mursi country, Leslie Woodhead samples cow's blood for breakfast..

It all begins where it must – with the anthropologists. Their experience and insights have always been the basic fuel of *Disappearing World*, the vital ingredient through which we can hope to move beyond the level of travelogue towards something more revealing and lasting. New projects usually start with a research trawl through university departments of anthropology in Britain and abroad. The latest trilogy of films resulted from visits by researcher David Wason to almost fifty universities throughout Europe and America.

But projects discussed and plans laid in tidy offices can seem pretty unreal in the bush. A few weeks in a squalid tent can test the chummiest of relationships and there have been some memorable flare-ups. One anthropologist got fed up and went home. Another reached a wordless impasse with the crew and reported them as criminals to border guards. It is, after all, an improbable marriage, this alliance of film-makers and anthropologists, and might seem doomed for divorce from the outset. We television people are trying to make films and tell stories which will entertain and inform a peak-time audience who may have switched on expecting *Dallas* rather than a film about a symbiotic relationship in East Africa. The anthropologists have different priorities, of course. After a decade or more of working with their people in the field, they are looking to make a film of record which will have meaning and value for an academic audi-

ence for years to come, as well as for the people themselves and their children.

It's perhaps surprising and certainly satisfying to find we've managed to rub along together productively for almost twenty years.

For the film people, the weeks before lift-off for the location are crammed with lists and logistics, an obstacle course of budgets and complicated inoculations. There are thousands of questions, and a worrying amount of guesswork: How to get there? Where will we live? What will we eat? How will we move around? Whose permission do we need? Questions about the actual content of the film are temporarily parked as we fret about moving our cumbersome caravan to that distant dot on the map.

Most *Disappearing World* films have been made 'short-crewed'. This means that we've worked with a minimum number of people, far fewer than would be usual for documentaries in less remote places. The impossibility of reaching many of our locations (which can require chartering small boats or light planes) with a full crew of eight people, together with the need to be as unintrusive as possible, has necessitated special negotiations with the television unions. But even short-crewed – just four people, camera operator, sound recordist, producer and researcher, plus of course the anthropologist – even then the lists of items needed are surpringly daunting.

Brian Moser recalls wallowing away

Filming *The Migrants* in Mursi country, the team walked a total of 200 miles or so.

49

Getting to locations can be difficult. To reach the Kwegu, on the remote southern edge of Ethiopia, the team chartered a military helicopter.

from the Granada car park for an early *Disappearing World* in Colombia, driving a ludicrously overloaded Landrover. 'As well as 20 kilos of glass beads,' Moser remembers, 'I had a thousand 12-bore cartridges, four shotguns, an inflatable dinghy, fish-hooks galore and living essentials for the next three months.'

I still have in my files the lists from three films I made in southern Ethiopia. They're full of boy scout curiosities like 'waterproof matches' and 'snake gaiters' and 'whistles', page after page of freeze-dried food, medicines and film gear. One item reads like something from a nineteenth century traveller's tale: 'bead gifts for tribe'. And the memories of hauling those twenty-six packing cases through distant airports, and onto an army helicopter before finally portering them through the bush remain vivid and exhausting.

Getting there, in fact, can be almost the hardest thing. Whenever possible, a researcher goes on ahead to smooth the way with the authorities and to sound the alert about possible problems. Most

Disappearing World producers become familiar with the crackling 3 a.m. phone call from some distant exchange bearing unwelcome news: the charter plane will cost twice as much; the road is swept away by floods; the Minister is unavailable to sign the permit; most of all, 'It's going OK, but send more money.'

Sometimes, the location is so remote, it's just not possible to do a reconnaissance. Then we have to rely on the anthropologist's experience, contacts and memories and cross many fingers. The night before departure is always full of 'what ifs'.

In the end, the travelling can be anything from disorientingly quick to despairingly protracted. Just after Christmas in 1981, I dug my way out of a Cheshire snowdrift to leave home and within seventy-two hours found myself scorched and panting alongside a remote African river complete with crocodiles. In 1974 it had taken two agonising weeks of route marches through a tribal war to reach more or less the same place. Brian Moser remembers running out onto a primitive South American airstrip waving

Brian Moser receives decorations from the Barasana.

André Singer and his team heading for Kirghiz country 15,000 feet up in the Afghan Pamirs. Many films have involved lengthy approach marches and unorthodox transport (below).

peso notes to stop a DC3 as it was taking off, and persuading the reluctant pilot to take his crew and piles of equipment. Other colleagues tell of panting after yaks laden with film gear up into the Himalayas, of days in canoes ploughing up Amazonian rivers, of Eskimo sledges and Saharan camel caravans.

And at the end of the journey, there's often anti-climax. 'Our main informant for the Rendille in Kenya immediately went off goat-herding,' producer Chris Curling recalls. Again, when Chris finally reached the location of the Shilluk in southern Sudan to film the installation of their king, 'nothing happened'. They waited in punishing heat for the vital ceremony, but still nothing happened. In the end, the cameraman had to leave for another job, observing that his closest similar experience had been solitary confinement in a South African gaol.

It's been a familiar frustration. 'We went to film a camel journey, but it never happened,' Charlie Nairn remembers of the Tuareg. Filming with the Kawelka of Papua New Guinea in 1974, Charlie spent almost three months waiting for a ceremonial distribution. Ongka, the film's leading character, was assembling a massive array of gifts from pigs to motorcycles in order to impress his neighbours with his generosity. The crew waited and waited, but finally they had to come home before the great hand-out took place. In 1987, Mike Beckham's waiting had a more successful result. After weeks of hanging around with his crew in an Amazonian settlement, the Kayapo hunting party arrived home at last bearing spectacular racks of live turtles for an important ceremony.

I reckon it's the essential *Disappearing World* experience, waiting for something to happen. Over the years, it's what I mostly remember: expecting the crop-ritual, anticipating the canoe-launching, hoping for the ceremonial duelling. It's the waiting that really tells me I'm back on *Disappearing World*.

The pace must be almost unique for television; some of our projects have taken a decade to mature, surviving problems of access and much else before finally coming to fruition.

On location, crews become accustomed to unfamiliar rhythms where cooking and water-purifying and surviving fill the

Cameraman Laurence Jones with the whale hunters of Lamalera. After weeks of waiting, the Lamaholot have got their whale and he has his film.

days while the business of film-making becomes almost incidental. For people familiar with reorganising reality to fit tight schedules it's an instructive experience, being required to curb our impatience to match the lives of the societies we're recording.

For a film-maker like myself who'd spent a decade making current affairs documentaries for Granada's *World In Action* series, working alongside anthropologists meant changing the habits of a professional lifetime. After the enjoyable years of being encouraged to work simultaneously as producer, director, investigative reporter, interviewer and script writer, I found myself relying on a close collaboration with someone who knew far more about the material than I ever could. I shared my new dilemmas with my diary when I was shooting my first *Disappearing World* with anthropologist David Turton

in southern Ethiopia: 'A lengthy chat after dinner about how I'm going to edit the film. I'll just have to work closely with David or an inferior film is going to result. I simply can't know enough about what we've shot. After my weeks of loading film and portering the tripod, it's hard to work out what my contribution as director will have been.'

The need to live alongside the people we're filming has provided us with some strange lodgings. *Disappearing World* crews have become familiar with successive generations of tent technology, from the cramped pyramids of the early 1970s to today's more spacious domes. All of them, I remember, become equally slummy and resistible after a few weeks' occupation. I made a list in 1985 of the litter which had somehow found its way into the little pocket of the tent I was sharing with the researcher. It seems to

Mike Thomson films vivid evidence of China's consumer revolution. This lavish dowry in a peasant wedding reveals the new wealth in the rural communes.

summarise the daily sleaziness of a filming safari: 'two fractured health-food bars, crushed sleeping pills, an old elastoplast, a mysterious key, congealed insect repellent, a broken cassette box containing vitamin tablets, an assortment of dead insects and one muddy sock.' The nightly hose-down with insect repellent followed by the crawl into the throat-clogging darkness is one of my least fond memories of *Disappearing World*. And the puncture of an airbed at 3 a.m. seems to locate with unfailing accuracy the rock in the small of the back.

Sometimes, of course, we opt for local lodgings. André Singer speaks with fondness of his weeks in a *yurt*, a Kazakh herder's felt tent in north-west China. 'It was wonderfully warm and weatherproof, if somewhat aromatic,' André recalls. John Sheppard lived in a Sakuddei palm-leaf house and tells how the crew gained

privacy by declaring the place taboo, a restriction understood and respected by the islanders. I have undimmed personal memories of my time in a Sherpa house, nearly 14,000 feet up in the Himalayas. Huddling breathless in the freezing gloom alongside a couple of munching yaks, I remember my bedroom had a distinctly biblical feel.

Charlie Nairn has more alarming domestic memories of his time in the Sahara with the Tuareg. Sleeping out under the stars, he awoke frozen and in need of a pee. 'I wandered off a few yards into the desert and then found I was completely lost. It looked like the surface of the moon and it was four chilly hours before I could locate our camp again.'

And then, of course, there's a film to be made. The aim always is to try and communicate through individuals, to offer a television audience an insight into other

ways of life from the viewpoint of those who live them. We seek, through the anthropologist, to get as close as possible to a limited number of characters, following their daily lives and encouraging them to speak directly to the camera about the things that matter to them. It's been our experience that this is the most effective way to make accessible to a television audience lives which seem remote from their own. Coming to know those individuals, the viewer may gain a sense of their special 'vision of the world'.

I know that, for the anthropologists, the film-makers' search for character and story can set off alarm bells about distorting realities to serve television priorities. I'm aware too of how frustrating it must be for my anthropologist partners that a single page of text can convey more detailed information than 25 minutes of film. At the same time, they have relished the layers of content that can be derived from a single sustained shot in an apparently unremarkable sequence. I recognise the investment of trust that the anthropologists have made in us film people. For the television professional, it's another film – often unusually absorbing – but still an incident in a career. For the anthropologist, the film may draw on a life's work, and could prejudice relationships and understandings built up over years in the field. Somehow, we've managed a workable compromise, for all the cumbersome necessities of documentary filming and the unavoidable fact that we can never be as unobtrusive as a lone anthropologist with a notebook.

At their best, we hope the films can begin to substantiate the claims of one of the founders of anthropology, Franz Boas, who wrote:
'The value of anthropology is its power to

The anthropologist Sherry Ortner interviews Sherpa Mingma Tenzing in his Himalayan village, the centre of her field work.

55

The anthropologist Sandra Ott hears Basque shepherding stories from Ambrosi Junet, her friend and guide during ten years of field work in a Pyrenean village.

Embera children get to know the strange goods imported by the film crew. Familiarising a people with the equipment is an important part of making the films (below).

impress us with the relative view of all forms of culture. When we recognise the shackles that tradition has laid upon us, we are also able to break them.'

Inevitably, over the weeks, a strange and intense relationship develops between the invading film folk and the people they're recording. David Turton told me how it had been for him, alone with the nomadic Mursi of southern Ethiopia for more than a year, learning their language a word at a time. 'They asked me about my home and whether white men were cannibals, shedding their skins like snakes.' Charlie Nairn found the same curiosity in Papua New Guinea. The Kawelka were inquisitive about the crews' fathers and

their work. A locksmith and a professor weren't of much interest, but Charlie's own father was something else. 'As a Scottish clan chief, he carried a sword on special occasions,' Charlie revealed. 'They were really impressed by that.'

Carlos Pasini tells how his Mehinaku 'brother' in the Brazilian rainforest was baffled by his concern when a unit sack, containing film and pen and ink, fell into a river. 'Why are you so worried, brother?' the Mehinaku asked. 'Why don't you make some more ink and some more film?' When Carlos explained, the man said, 'It must be very sad to be a man and not to be able to make the things you have need of.'

Brian Moser tells of following a wild boar hunt through the rainforest with the Maku. 'The trip was almost a disaster. We couldn't carry enough food, so for three days we existed on fried flying ants – you just pluck off the wings, put the bodies in a pan and they cook in their own fat tasting like succulent bacon in butter. Luckily, it was the ant-swarming season.'

The cattle-herding Mursi pitied us for our lack of cattle and hopeless feet. One evening a man asked me if I'd been to the moon.

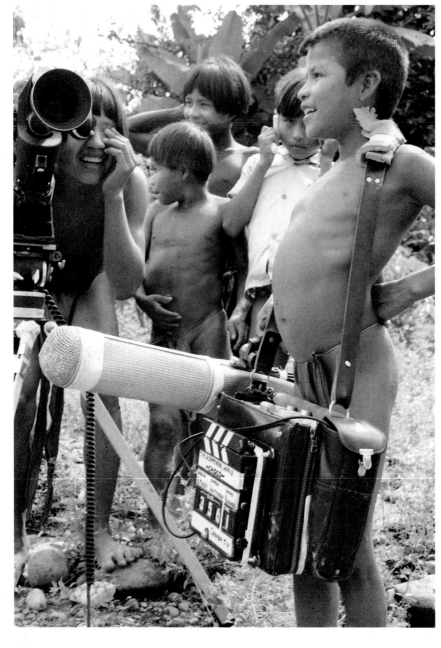

The Panare

In his study of the Panare tribe, Jean-Paul Dumont wrote of his first day among them. 'I was submerged in a tropical ambience; heat buzzing under high-noon sun, the atmosphere refreshed only by the clear sounds of running waters. I was full of naive enthusiasm as two men began to ferry my boxes and myself across the river Turiba. The jerking of the rough dugout canoe did not stop my wonderment. For the moment, even that was exotic.' Three years later, the anthropologist was hardened by his experiences. 'I have lived among the Panare for two years, but I cannot say I really know them. You cannot pretend to know these people and I do not know how they are going to react to us as a film team. Ultimately the Panare reject everyone who is not one of them.' It was an inauspicious way to begin the very first *Disappearing World* film in 1970 called *A Clearing in the Jungle*.

He wanted to concentrate on the religious beliefs of the Panare; but where societies such as the Azande of the Sudan or the Umbandistas in Brazil were open about the beliefs that pervaded their everyday life, Jean-Paul Dumont in the Venezuelan Amazon, was faced with a harder task. 'The Panare Indians have always resisted my penetration of their culture and they have always refused to tell me anything about their myths or their religious beliefs. If you ask about their beliefs, they don't answer at all, or they tell you to go to hell.' His study and the film, faced with such a barrier in the field; concentrated instead on everyday life

and survival in the jungle. After three weeks the Panare began to avoid the film team: 'In their kinship structure, we had no place, and it wasn't long before they started the process of rejecting us, and hiding themselves from us. After three weeks it became almost impossible.'

Time and again, we've been moved by the patience and generosity of the people we've descended on. We arrive uninvited, obtrusive, demanding, but on many occasions we've been received with rare friendliness.

I have fond memories of our crew swapping vocabulary with smiling Mursi warriors, ending inevitably with 'bum' and 'dick' and gales of laughter. And I can still see the image of the crew teaching a couple of Mursi girls to play pat-a-cake in a downpour, while Charlie Nairn cherishes the recollection of his cameraman teaching a group of Panare Indians to whistle pop songs.

It's true, of course, that we often bring things people want. John Sheppard remembers the enthusiasm of the Sakuddei for the beads he'd imported. 'They scrutinised each one with the critical eye of a diamond dealer in Hatton Garden. And they were almost as keen on the Grateful Dead T-shirts we left behind.' The Azande of the southern Sudan were equally fond of the Charles and Di T-shirts they gleaned from the film crew. Many of us have been chastened to realise how casually we squander our resources when even a cast-off box is valued by people who recycle our throw-aways in a score of ingenious ways.

Some of our imports are more mystifying. I recall the Mursi fascination for our digital watches and how they'd concluded from the pulsing blip marking the seconds

that the watches must contain a tiny animal and the blip was its heartbeat. But far more important, of course, than our second-hand clothes and trinkets have been the tools and the money we've been able to distribute.

It's only recently, though, thanks to lightweight video players, that we've been able to give back something else – the

films we've made. In 1985, we were able to show the Mursi the films we'd made with them in 1974 and 1982. It's not an image I shall forget, as some 200 people, entirely innocent of the very notion of television, gathered in a forest clearing to peer at the strange box. We'd had some concern that people in the audience whose dead relatives would be seen walking and talking might conclude we'd somehow raided the spirit world. In the end, it seemed that television's newest audience was divided on the issue.

One man asked: 'What's the use of it? I can't eat it or tie my bull up with it.' Another was more encouraging: 'It's good,' he said, 'because now that our life is changing, our children will be able to see how we used to live. We can use this to teach them about our traditions and our history.' In the same way, the Kirghiz, now refugees in Turkey, are making a collection of films and photographs as their own record of a vanishing way of life.

Carlos Pasini remembers with special affection an incident late in his filming with the Mehinaku in Amazonia. 'There was an eclipse, a fearful time for the Mehinaku who believe a monster has

The film team swelled to record numbers in a Chinese commune in 1982. Eight officials accompanied the crew throughout the filming.

Television's latest audience. In 1985 the Mursi saw themselves on TV in the films *Disappearing World* had made with them during earlier visits. They call television 'a box of spirits'.

Mursi children queue up for a first encounter with the film camera.

The film crews make special efforts to familiarise local people with the equipment.

60

Moser tells of an unforgettable parting with the Cuiva. 'The Agua Clara group, who had absolutely no previous contact with white men, very gently touched our hands and then just disappeared into the burning grasslands. I'll never forget the gentle beauty of that, especially when you remember they were at war with all other white men.'

'I am sad because I know I'll be dead before I see you again,' a Mehinaku said to Carlos Pasini who recalls, 'the last image of all, those Mehinaku waving goodbye, half-emerging from the tall grass. It will stay with me as long as I live.'

Charlie Nairn has his own, rather more ambiguous memory of leaving the Kawelka after three months in the highlands of Papua New Guinea. 'Thousands of people were there to wave goodbye,' Charlie remembers, 'but it wasn't quite what we'd expected.' It seemed people had learned what they took to be a white man's goodbye from a visiting Australian magistrate. 'There were all these people on the hillsides, flapping their hands dismissively and yelling "piss off!".'

Cameraman Jon Woods, dressed for a wedding in the South Pacific Lau lagoon.

devoured the sun and the resulting blood may turn you into a horrible creature.' The only protection, say the Mehinaku, is to run to the village and cover your body with protective black paint. 'Finding that the crew were filming away in the forest, a young Mehinaku man risked his own soul to run and rescue us.'

The moment when we leave for home seems to stay with all of us. I remember sailing away from an extraordinary artificial island in the South Pacific, our boat laden with pineapple gifts, our stomachs crammed with a farewell banquet which stretched for a hundred yards along the village square. Across the water we could still hear the goodbye serenade composed and sung by a choir of local girls and featuring all the crews' names. Brian

1 THE WINDS OF CHANGE
TUAREG, ESKIMOS, BASQUES

The changes that most of us have witnessed and are still experiencing in our lifetime are unparalleled since the Industrial Revolution of the nineteenth century. Advances in science and technology alone, which shape all our lives, occur with such frequency and rapidity that many of us are scarcely aware of them. Yet the changes brought about by shifts such as the decline of rural life and the drift to urban centres, and by the fierce competition to adopt technological innovations in our everyday lives are creating social and cultural gaps between one generation and the next, the long-term consequences of which are incalculable.

The influence of the Western technological revolution on more remote societies has for the most part been more gradual and limited. Yet even those geographically isolated communities so beloved of anthropologists are no longer immune. The allegation that anthropology does not recognise or pay heed to the process of change has never been true. Anthropologists have always been deeply aware of the implications of change in every society; and the impact of one culture upon another remains the modern anthropologist's prime concern.

Most of the films in the *Disappearing World* series illustrate aspects of change. Some societies have themselves chosen to adapt and to make conscious decisions about their future, embracing new habits and attitudes whilst retaining an outward allegiance to established values and beliefs; some have been swept along on a swiftly flowing current that leaves them few options of their own; and others reject change completely, and find themselves engaged in conflict, often tragic and bitter, with strange people and new ideas.

The three societies described in this chapter – Tuareg, Eskimo and Basque – could not be more sharply contrasting. The camel nomads of the Sahara, the hunters of the Arctic and the shepherds of the Pyrenees have different livelihoods and inhabit different worlds. Yet they are all affected by change. Although some members of these societies regard that change with suspicion and face it with reluctance, while others cautiously or even openly welcome it, the process itself seems remorseless.

The Tuareg
In the heart of the Algerian desert live the nomadic Tuareg, the 'blue men' of the Sahara. Their reputation is based partly on their dramatic appearance, for the blue veils make them look mysterious and somewhat sinister, and partly on their past history, for these once-formidable warriors, like most nomads, know how to exploit to the full their inhospitable environment. The Tuareg, who are descended from the Berbers, were described by travellers in 1903 as 'marauding nomads, who on account of their impious character, have been named by the Arabs *Tawarek* or "God-forsaken"'. Less than half a million Tuareg, controlling more than a million square miles of territory extending into Algeria, Libya, Niger and Mali, managed to keep their traditional enemies, the

The Saharan homelands of the Tuareg offer scant support for their camels and goats. They must move their tented settlements regularly to seek out fresh grass.

eating one another. For twenty years no other European dared set foot in Tuareg country.

In 1902 the French had their revenge, defeating the Tuareg at the battle of Tit. The nomads submitted to the control of the better armed, better organised French army. Under French hegemony they were permitted for more than fifty years to continue their traditional camel-herding existence unhindered, travelling many hundreds of miles to trade salt for millet.

To Westerners the nomad has often been seen as a figure of romance, even though an observer as experienced as T.E. Lawrence described nomadism as 'that most deep and biting social discipline'. Nevertheless, the romantic myth persists, perhaps because those whose lives are regimented by the clock envy people who can move about as they please and who

The blue robes of the Tuareg convey an air of romance at odds with the reality of their lives as desert nomads (above).

Arabs, out of the Sahara for centuries. The French, who were the first Europeans to encounter them, discovered the Tuareg's hostile nature to their cost.

In 1880 they decided to build a railway 2,000 miles across the Sahara south through Tuareg country, sending out a reconnoitring armed column, consisting of 105 men carrying 25,000 bullets. The Tuareg who offered to guide the French colonel led him ever deeper into the desert; there they poisoned his water supply and his dates, persuaded him to split his column and, when they had him alone, killed him. Struggling back, his desperate and starving men ended up seem to be far closer to nature. Anthropologist Jeremy Keenan, who lived among the Tuareg in Algeria for over seven years, observed the flood of Western tourists, who came in search of mysticism and romance, with bemused cynicism. 'There are those,' he wrote, 'who come to the Ahaggar to immerse themselves in a "Tuareg culture", to escape from the pressures of civilisation . . . and to search, as if on a pilgrimage, for their ancestral heritage – to experience, temporarily and impossibly, a philosophy and way of life that has been destroyed and denied them – the "freedom", "tranquillity" and "naturalness" of nomadism. The trappings and symbols of civilisation, except those that ease the process of immersion (the sunglasses, Ambre Solaire, Enterovioform, and wrist-watch – and of course the camera, which provides the "proof"

The Tuareg always had a reputation for fierceness; in the past they were much feared (left).

Nomads are often sentimentalised as symbols of a lost way of life, freer and more relaxed than the pressurised urban existence of the West (below).

The reality of Tuareg life is a punishing sequence of scorching days and bitter nights, when anyone left without a tent or fire risks death from exposure.

of experience) – are discarded self-consciously for the blue *gandora*, *chech* and sandals, which, like Polynesian grass skirts, have no meaning outside the tourist culture.'

In reality a way of life based upon finding fresh pasture for herds is far from tranquil and relaxed; and like gypsies in our own society, who are both envied and rejected, nomads are feared and despised by those who govern them. People who cannot be confined to one place throughout the year are difficult to control for purposes of education, health and, most important of all, taxation. Thus they are regarded as politically unstable. Add to this official suspicion and natural catastrophes such as recurrent drought and famine, and it is hardly surprising that the Tuareg nomads are being transformed beyond recognition.

Nomadic people are often hit harder than others by change because any threat to their means of survival, namely their herds, is a threat to their entire social fabric. Herds are more than a source of food to pastoral communities; they possess a wealth of social and symbolic significance for their owners. The erosion of the nomadic existence which once provided the Tuareg with their economy is also creating a cultural vacuum which they are powerless to fill.

The landscape of the Tuareg, typically the stony, barren Ahaggar Mountains, is varied but everywhere harsh and menacing. As Jeremy Keenan wrote of his first visit: 'I was a complete stranger. I had a certain fear of becoming lost . . . or possibly even dying of thirst. But to these people it is home. Each mountain has a name, it is male or female; the mountains marry, they divorce, they move away; it is part of their mythology and the land itself reflects the social order.' Sidi Mohammed, Keenan's closest informant and friend among the Tuareg, illustrated how dangerous the terrain was by relating how his own small daughter wandered away from camp one winter night, wearing no clothes, and was found next morning dead of exposure.

The Tuareg are attached to their landscape; even their mountains can marry and divorce.

67

The Tuareg nuclear family, consisting of parents and children, lives in a single tent; and the extended family of brothers, cousins and their families usually inhabit the same camp. This camp often journeys more than 1,000 miles to trade in salt, animals and animal produce. The camels, sheep and goats which are the mainstay of their nomadic life are highly vulnerable and render this traditional existence precarious. But the Tuareg have an intricate web of debts and obligations, so that in times of real need families can rely on relations to provide help.

There has always been a close interdependence of nomads and settled agriculturalists. The former require staple crops and the latter need access to animal produce and other goods acquired from distant markets. Despite frequent antagonism and friction (because the farmers tend to regard the nomads as predators) the economic bond is important.

Change has been painful for the people of Sidi Mohammed's camp. He himself (in his fifties at the time of filming in 1972) had an arrangement which provided him with crops and allowed him the freedom to take caravans across the desert. He owned gardens which were tended on a contract basis by *Harratins* – black Africans descended from freed West African slaves or members of trading caravans from the south who remained in the north. The contract system permitted the Tuareg

Families live together in a single tent; extended families share a camp.

Sidi Mohammed and his family rely on a web of relationships to survive in bad years (right).

to retain at least four-fifths of what the *Harratins* produced. The Tuareg employed the *Harratins* as hired labourers but also operated a slave system known as *Iklan*. The slaves were brought back from journeys south, from countries such as Niger, or captured from slave caravans heading for the ports of North Africa. They were the property of individual owners, and could be sold or exchanged at whim. Descriptions of the system admit that the Tuareg usually treated their slaves well and that the men often took slave women as wives. The slaves were often made to dig underground aqueducts, some up to two or three miles long, for irrigating the land contracted out to the *Harratins*.

In 1962, with the arrival of Algerian independence, the systems of slavery and contracted labour were both terminated. The Tuareg lost their slaves, the land previously worked by the *Harratins* and one of their principal sources of food. But the older men like Sidi Mohammed refused to surrender the principles of 'social discipline' which had guided their

fathers and grandfathers. Some of the younger Tuareg, however, realised that survival depended on their adopting a new way of life and accepted the need to cultivate their own crops as part of the process. Sidi Mohammed's cousin, Elwafil, for example, left the hills and began working in the village where Sidi Mohammed once had his private garden. He also swallowed his pride and started helping to maintain the aqueducts dug by the former slaves.

Yet, as Elwafil explains in the film, the values of pastoral life have not been rejected even by the new generation: 'It is many years since there were good rains in Ahaggar. The pasture and the goats are dying. In the past, when there were rains there was pasture – the grass sprang up. Now there is no rain. While such conditions last it is better to live in a house. There is water at Hirafok, and the gardens are reliable. If there were camels I'd go on caravans rather than work in the gardens. When there were camels in the camps they went to Amadror to mine salt and then to the Sudan to get millet, but

Slaves belonging to the Tuareg were freed after 1962, but many continue to live with their old masters.

now there is very little. But I prefer to live in the camps. The house is good, but only while such conditions last.'

Those who struggle on as nomads refuse to believe that the traditional ways cannot be re-established. When Sidi Mohammed lost all his camels in the drought, he found the means to buy more. Nothing was more important to him than to maintain prestige by continuing his traditional lifestyle. Jeremy Keenan, when working on the film, saw this as a paradox. 'Sometimes when I sit here with Sidi,' he recollects, 'it all seems so strange. We know that this way of life is rapidly disappearing. . . . But Sidi doesn't see it that way, he sees it in terms of a day-to-day problem of how he can get grain up from Tamanrasset and how he can provide for his family next month – he certainly has no conception of this way of life coming to an end.'

The Eskimos

In their very different Arctic environment, the Eskimos (or Inuit) face similar dilemmas to the Tuareg. They too have been confronted with radical changes in the outside world sweeping across their Canadian homeland. The strains introduced by these changes are so intense, and the alternatives to change so bleak, that they have only an illusion of choice.

In the past the entire economy and survival of the Eskimos depended upon hunting – of seals, caribou, wildfowl, walrus, whale, bear and the arctic fox for its valuable fur. 'In the old days we Eskimos used to live only on wild animals,' one man explains to the anthropologist Hugh Brody in the film. 'The old people were brought up on wild country foods. Their stomachs are used to that and even today there are many who still prefer to eat the wild animals with the blood and everything. They get weak on store food.'

Most Eskimos used to live in camps of two or three families. These camps were the permanent bases from which the hunters set out on long treks that often lasted several months, although for much of the year game was available nearby.

North of the Arctic Circle, off the east coast of Baffin Island in Canada, live the Eskimos of Pond Inlet. The influence of white Canada on them only began to bite in the 1920s. Traders, trappers, whalers, missionaries and explorers had previously established contacts and attempted to introduce changes – for economic or religious reasons – but only then did the Eskimos become dependent upon the Hudson Bay Company and their centuries-old traditions begin to die. The Company issued a warning in a paternalistic book entitled *The Eskimo Book of Knowledge*: 'Take heed, Inuit, for the future will bring

Only a few Eskimos on Baffin Island in the Canadian Arctic still survive by hunting and fishing.

Outboard motors give the Eskimo speed over the polar bear and make fishing easier.

From the 1920s, many Canadian trappers came to the Eskimo territories in search of valuable furs of bears, foxes and seals (above).

our Traders have learned to bestow the care of a father upon you and upon your children.'

By the late 1930s the Eskimos of Pond Inlet no longer lived as self-sufficient hunting groups, but depended fully on trade. They were deliberately encouraged to become trappers rather than hunters. Traders and missionaries systematically eroded Eskimo traditions and converted the people to a lifestyle better suited to Western needs. Many traditional practices were abolished, and by the 1950s most Eskimos were Christians, encouraged to abandon their camps and transfer to larger, permanent settlements. 'Those whites they had all the power,' explains Anaviapik. 'They were extremely frightening. Yes, they were feared. We always followed whatever rules they made. Even the adults were afraid of whites. The whites seemed to be the real bosses. Even when Eskimos were told to do things against their tradition, they would never say no. In the old days we were easily scared of the whites.'

even greater changes than have taken place in your country in the past twenty years. There will be white trappers who will trap the foxes out of your country; strange ships will come among you seeking only your furs. Many white men will explore your lands in search of precious rocks and minerals. These traders and these trappers are like the drift-ice; today they come with the wind, tomorrow they are gone with the wind. Of these strangers some will be fairer than others, as is the nature of men; but whosoever they be, they cannot at heart possess that deep understanding of your lives through which

As in colonial Africa, Asia and South America, along with the settlements and the white administrators, came disease. Measles, poliomyelitis, influenza, scarlet fever and mumps, followed by tuberculosis, ran rife, compelling the Eskimos to depend on the white man's medicine and

Christian wedding on Baffin Island. Missionaries have converted almost all the Eskimos in the area.

technology. Pond Inlet exemplifies the speed with which change overtook the majority of Eskimos. In 1955 there were only 37 Eskimos living in the settlement area, whereas 230 others still lived in their traditional hunting camps. Ten years later the Canadian government introduced a housing programme, urging the others to move to the settlement. By 1975 they had succeeded and no Eskimos lived in year-round camps any longer.

'We were urged to move to these new homes,' says Utuva, the wife of Anaviapik. 'They said we got sick living in sad houses. They said that ice always formed inside our houses; that if we had new houses, we'd be less sickly. That's what we were told. We were told to move. We were going to be less sick if we had nice warm houses and had an oil stove instead of blubber lamps. But we just got sicker and sicker, because we were too hot probably!' Utuva also thinks that when they used to be hunters and lived in camps, they were healthier and fatter. Her husband agrees. 'When I see Eskimos who live away from whites, beautiful! They have good blood. They're fat too. Whenever I visit Pond Inlet, the Eskimos here seem white, bloodless and thin, as if they'd been ill!'

The latest agent of change is wage labour for an oil company. Inukuluk, another Pond Inlet Eskimo, worked for Panarctic Oil for two years, but found the experience both worrying and depressing. Later he refused, when asked, to work for the company. Similarly, he went to school at an Adult Education Centre, but was far from impressed by the experience. 'I even began to think: whites are amazing. They do so much work that doesn't look like work at all. In fact, it's very tiring indeed. That writing, just using that little pencil is very hard going. So I got more and more tired. Sometimes it was very difficult. Having to try to speak English and getting it all wrong. I began to think I'll never become a real white man. And even the schooling I've had seems to add up to nothing.'

The greatest change affecting Eskimo life is the gulf which is developing between the generations. Thanks to the new education, and with only the experience of settlement life, the young strive to be more like the whites and less like their parents. Already many of them speak English more fluently than their Eskimo mother tongue. Boredom, alcoholism, drug-taking and, most tragically, a growing suicide rate reflect the breakdown of traditional values. As one parent expresses it: 'The children did not cooperate because they have been away at school. They have never really heard of hunting the way we know about hunting. I worry about it, because the young people do not hunt; maybe it is because they do not want

Today, the Pond Inlet settlement is a permanent home for Eskimos who have abandoned the traditional hunting camps. Many young men work for oil companies and speak English; hence an ever-increasing gulf between generations.

Anaviapik and his wife Utuva recall that the hunting community of their youth seemed healthier and happier.

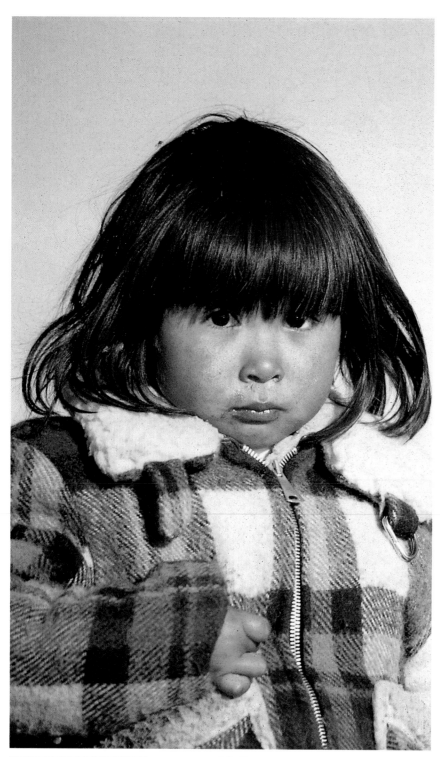

The Basques

The changes experienced by the Basques who live in the south-western corner of France may appear less dramatic than those affecting the Tuareg or Eskimos, but they are nonetheless unrelenting and irreversible. The special sadness is that the Basques are believed to have lived in their area longer than any other European cultural group, and although their origins are unknown, their traditions are rich and unique. The Basque language has no root in common with other European tongues and is so complex that an eighteenth-century French abbot decided that it must unquestionably have been the language spoken by God.

Older Eskimos are concerned about the future as their children grow up amid rapidly changing values.

to get cold. Some of the young people help their parents and some do not. They think they are living like the white man; they think it is better not to help because they have learned the way whites live.'

Many Eskimos, like the Tuareg, accept change reluctantly. It is not that they hanker to return to the hunting camps and the hardships and uncertainties of their earlier subsistence, rather that they see all around them change over which they have no control and which is removing from them their unique Eskimo identity.

As early as the twelfth century the Basques were recorded as being pastoral people, with some agriculture, who were 'thirsty for blood and ferocious as the wild beasts with which they live'. Today some Basques are still prepared to employ that ferocity in a separatist struggle to establish political independence. Basque nationalism is at its fiercest in the three Spanish Basque provinces south of the Pyrenees. In the three provinces north of the border in France, the struggle for autonomy is much less insistent, though the sense of Basque identity remains strong.

The Basques of Santazi, a community studied by Sandra Ott, have maintained that strong sense of identity and a social

Until recently, the Basque village of Santazi was isolated at the end of a steep valley in the French Pyrenees (above).

Today, a new road links the shepherding community of Santazi to the outside world; many young people now work in the French lowlands (left).

The Goillart family herd their sheep on some of the steepest pastures in the valley.

and geographical isolation that is only now being broken down. Many of them pessimistically accept that their way of life as they have known it is doomed – a situation reflected in the fact that over the past century the Santazi population has dwindled from almost a thousand to a mere 390.

The village of Santazi, identified on the map by its French name, Sainte Engrâce, lies in a secluded valley a few miles from the border with Spain. In this basin, surrounded by the Pyrenees, Basque shepherding communities like Santazi have survived through sheep-farming, cheese production and some agriculture. The people also raise cattle, pigs and poultry, hunt wild boar and doves, and gather apples and nuts.

The Basques of Santazi have always therefore been reasonably self-sufficient, needing just bread, coffee, salt and sugar to be brought in from the outside. Only when a road into their valley was completed in 1932 was a new market opened up for them, enabling them to supplement shortages of food at home by selling animals, wool and the cheese they make from sheep's milk.

One family who have weathered the changes of recent years are the Goillarts, whose forebears have lived in the same home for more than 200 years. Madgi and Felix Goillart are fortunate in having two sons, one of whom has become a dedicated shepherd and will, therefore, maintain the family interest in their farm. Although they are one of the most isolated of the local families, change is already affecting them. But for the Goillarts it has been beneficial.

Change was heralded by a road which reached their farm in 1977, enabling them to bring in feed for their hundreds of sheep. The Goillarts admit that life is now much easier than it was for the previous generations. 'People from the old days ought to come back,' Madgi tells Sandra Ott in the film. 'Looking down on us from the sky they could see how our life is now.' Her enthusiasm extends to a passion for television soap opera. Madgi, much to the irritation of her husband and sons, has become a *Dallas* addict. 'Funny thing about television,' she says, 'always lots of beautiful people. On TV there are never ugly people, just pretty and handsome. With JR you just have to watch out! He's

Madgi Goillart remembers a much tougher life in Santazi when she was a girl. The road reached the family house only in 1977, but today she enjoys watching 'Dallas' on TV (left).

Ambrosi Junet has been taking his sheep to summer pastures in the high Pyrenees for more than thirty years.

77

sneaky – just fancy all those women! He's
only a film actor. I get a laugh out of that
kind of madness.'

The changes in the valley have been
less happy for the Junet family, living a few
miles from the Goillarts. They have only
one son, Jean Pierre, and he is working
away from home during the week as an
electricity linesman and earning a good
salary. He feels he has no alternative,
pointing out that one farmer at home is
enough. His own son, still a small boy, has
also announced that he does not want to
be a shepherd like his grandfather
Ambrosi. The continuation of traditional
Basque life, as represented by Ambrosi
Junet, is thus far from secure: 'I've seen in
the past ten years that there are far fewer
shepherds; many houses here have ceased
to exist, many are collapsing and many will
collapse soon.'

Ambrosi insists that the local school is
partly to blame, for it teaches the children
in French instead of in their native
Basque. 'They can learn French later,' he
says. 'If they don't learn Basque now,
they'll never be able to speak it.' In fact,
because of the dwindling population, the
little mountain school which used to be
such a thriving little community is now
attended only by a handful of children and
is threatened with closure.

The focus of the traditional life that
Ambrosi Junet feels is so important for his
people is the annual move to the high
pastures in early summer. For centuries
the Basque shepherds have collaborated
in syndicates called *Olha* to work with
their flocks in the summer pastures; and

The Sami
In 1986, a wind blew over the Sami reindeer herders of Norwegian Lappland
that changed their lives forever. It came
from the damaged nuclear power station
at Chernobyl, and it brought deadly
radioactivity, poisoning the pasturelands
of the Sami and threatening their whole
means of existence. As a result, Tomas
Renberg, a Sami herder featured in the
film *An Invisible Enemy*, had serious
doubts about the survival of his people's
traditions into the next generation. 'In our
work we Sami reindeer herders have
faced up to many tricky situations,' he
explains 'and we have solved all of our
problems over the years, predators, poor

grazing, and all kinds of dangers for reindeer. Conflicts of interest with farmers,
fishermen and the power industry – these
are all things that we can do something
about. You can see these things with your
own eyes. But with this we can see
nothing, so we call it an invisible enemy.'

for some thirty years Ambrosi has taken his sheep up to the *Olha* hut known as Ligoleta which he shares with a group of his fellow shepherds. High in the mountains, in their all-male world, they enjoy a brief companionship whilst milking and making cheese. Ligoleta is also the name of the syndicate to which the shepherds belong and which is responsible for sharing out the workload of milking and herding.

The syndicate meets at the end of March for an annual dinner at which they plan the next season's schedule. Shepherds eat and drink well, and it is an occasion when men who spend much of the year apart on their remote farms can get together for a good gossip. But it is also the most important business meeting of the year when they must agree on the work-sharing up at the high pastures. Milk from the combined flocks will be distributed equally in the form of the prized mountain cheeses, valued far more than the house cheeses made in the village. After milking the flock, each shepherd at the *Olha* will take

The shepherds take turns to stay with the syndicate's combined flocks in the high pastures, milking twice each day and making the prized mountain cheeses (above).

his turn in making cheese which will be a symbol of his status as shepherd and family provider, even of his sexual prowess.

The Ligoleta syndicate's discussions in 1986 focussed on the need to preserve the shepherding way of life, no easy task with so many of the younger men being tempted towards alternative means of employment and so placing an additional burden on their elders. Long after midnight, Ambrosi Junet spoke sadly about the threats to his traditional ways. 'After all, what have we got to look forward to?'

Ironically, the attempt by some people in Santazi to improve their conditions has actually contributed to the unravelling of traditional ways. The local priest, Father Joseph Arhex, has been an important agent of change in the community. 'It was a hard life, a difficult life,' says Father Arhex as he recalls Santazi in the 1950s, when he first arrived in the valley. 'The people were all very nice and the place was beautiful. So I said, and the mayor said as well, we had to make a road and we did make a road. We made roads to every house. After that life really changed.' Father Arhex is also the town hall secretary and the main link between the local people and the French government. His skill in raising funds from the European Economic Community in order to push through changes has undoubtedly increased local prosperity; but he has also

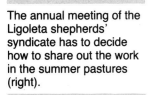

Santazi's eleventh-century church St Engrâce has a dwindling congregation, and even special festivals, like Palm Sunday when laurels are blessed, have become less spectacular.

The annual meeting of the Ligoleta shepherds' syndicate has to decide how to share out the work in the summer pastures (right).

80

transformed the community's religious life.

Father Arhex remembers Mass as an important occasion for bringing the community together. Now his church is largely empty except on special occasions such as Palm Sunday. For this he may himself be partly responsible, as he has done away with confession and certain other rituals, to the dismay of some older people. Madgi Goillart laments the passing of religion as an important element of community life. 'In the past you went to Mass every Sunday, you always went. In Holy Week we'd go out to show respect for our good Lord. . . Now there are even some people who work on Sunday. I don't think that's a good thing at all. On Sundays I only do vital work with the animals and in the house. . . I don't often go to Mass, but I still have my religion inside and a relationship with God.'

Not only are some of the Basques from the valley moving away to Paris or Bordeaux and marrying out of the community altogether, but French families are gradually moving in. Several couples have bought houses in the valley and there is interest in other properties as potential holiday homes. The Basques used to be indifferent to outsiders and tourists. Today, the newcomers and the visitors are regarded increasingly as a source of income.

Until 1986 Santazi lay at the end of the road, isolated under the ramparts of the Pyrenees in a steep cul-de-sac. Today there is a new road linking the valley to the Spanish border and beyond; and in 1987 Santazi even found itself on the route of the Tour de France cycle race. The Goillarts, the Junets and their neighbours have to come to terms with the fact that their lives will never be the same again.

Herding the flocks up to the high pastures is the central event of the Basque shepherding life.

The Cuiva of Colombia have been reduced to a handful of survivors as a result of their clash with a more powerful culture.

CLASH OF CULTURES

CUIVA, KAYAPO, SAKUDDEI, MAKU AND BARASANA, MEO

Margaret Mead once wrote: 'We live in a world which is so haunted by the destructive powers which have been released in the twentieth century that it is of vital importance that we keep a reasoned belief in the future of human living.' One of the earliest rationales behind *Disappearing World* was to try to influence that future by showing how horrifying the destruction has been that has swept through unprotected tribal societies in their remote settings.

Many *Disappearing World* films tell stories of pure greed and thoughtlessness. The urge to build a road, to cut down trees or to search for gold was, as a rule, far more important than the welfare of the local inhabitants. And when the needs of the locals were considered, it was often with a view to saving their souls or using them as cheap labour. Practically all the societies we explored revealed tragic signs of cultural warfare. The most tragic of these were the remaining 600 Cuiva Indians filmed by Brian Moser in 1971. They provided some of the most moving images and most clear explanations as to what happens when two cultures with different ambitions for the future meet.

The Cuiva

The Cuiva Indians are a group of nomadic hunter-gatherers who in the nineteenth century are believed to have roamed the plains that run eastwards from the Andes mountains to the Orinoco River. Today the few survivors live in a far more restricted region of Colombia, hemmed in by two rivers, with a smaller scattered population across the nearby border in Venezuela. They live in small bands of about forty people, surviving on the wildlife and natural crops of the grassy savanna plains. With spears and bows and arrows they hunt small animals such as wild pig, catch fish and gather fruits and roots. When the hunting becomes difficult they pack their possessions and move on to a new site.

The Kayapo of Brazil found themselves with a vast goldmine on their territory, worked by thousands of Brazilians. They now control the mine and have used their share of the gold to buy video cameras with which they are preserving their rituals.

The Cuiva are ceaselessly on the move; they like to shift camp every four days.

The Cuiva are ceaselessly on the move; they like to shift camp every four days.

This continual wandering was one of the central preoccupations of the anthropologist Bernard Arcand in his fieldwork. Since it would have been quite possible for the Cuiva to live adequately by remaining in one location, Arcand was puzzled not only by the fact that the bands travelled from place to place, but also that they moved around so frequently. 'In one month,' he noted, 'we made forty-seven camps and slept in twenty-seven different places. I made a list of the reasons they gave and probably the most beautiful one to me was when they said: "Oh, we've seen this camp for too long, let's go and see somewhere else."'

Over two years, Arcand calculated that one band would move every seven days or so. One explanation, he concluded, for their rolling up their hammocks and seeking a new home was to try a change of diet. Someone might suddenly suggest, 'Oh, it would be good to eat another fruit,' and then, within only five minutes, to Arcand's astonishment, everyone would pack up and move on.

At the time of filming, the self-sufficient life of the Cuiva was already being threatened by the activities of the Colombian cattle ranchers known as Llaneros, who recognised that the tropical forest lands were ripe for exploitation. The growing demand from urban South America for beef, and the insatiable hunger in the United States for beefburgers, made ranching an increasingly profitable business. Llaneros were creating grasslands for their herds by destroying vast areas of forest, leaving the land susceptible to erosion. Waves of ranchers were soon eating away the homeland of the Cuiva and wiping out its wildlife.

The Llaneros regarded the Indians as a source of cheap labour and were angered when the Indians objected to their land being taken over. In response they either shot them or seduced them with alcohol, money and jobs. Gabriel Gouzdez, a successful rancher, explains in the film that 'they are just like animals, they don't wear a stitch of clothing. I've seen them completely naked like a horse or a cow. The Cuiva Indians should be put on a ranch of their own. They should be given a piece of land so they can work.'

The Cuiva had memories of the harsh methods used by the new settlers to drive them from the land. Many were killed out of hand, others forcibly kidnapped. As recently as 1967 a Llanero rancher was put on trial by the government for inviting sixteen Cuiva to a meal and promptly massacring them. He and fellow settlers admitted their crime and confessed to having killed at least forty other Indians as well. They were acquitted on the grounds that because they had not regarded the

Cuiva as humans, they should not stand trial for murder. The government implicitly concurred.

'They killed my father and took away my brother,' explains one Cuiva woman, in a horrifying account of a massacre that occurred while the family were in their canoes. 'My father drowned, he was covered in blood. They caught my brother and he cried, "Daddy, they've got me." I don't know where he is now. The whites then killed my uncle, they killed Cinaru my husband. They cut up his body. Cut his arms off, opened his belly . . . They chopped off one leg then the other. I was shot. The bullet stayed in my skin and it hurt for many days. They hit me on the head; I was crouching down at the bottom of the boat, trying to protect myself.'

It is hardly surprising that the contempt felt by the Llaneros for the Cuiva is

Colombia cattle ranchers known as *Llaneros* justify the kidnapping and killing of the Cuiva because they regard the Indians as animals.

The Cuiva have had many terrible experiences of exploitation and massacre (left).

85

wholeheartedly reciprocated. The Indians view the settlers as people who break all the normal rules of society, who are brutal, mean and selfish. The Cuiva have an interesting myth to explain the origins of the 'non-Indians':

'A man came to his shelter and placed his son in a hammock. The next day, the son said to his father, "Build a fence and bring the timber to build my house." "All right," said the father. So the man built a long fence and a house. After many days of work, his son said, "Father, do the cooking. And then go kill the Indians who steal my cattle." The father went and killed the robbers. The next day, the son jumped on his horse and went to check his cattle in the savanna. He had horses, cows, guns, cooking pots, machetes, mosquito nets, cloth hammocks and trousers. When he returned from the savanna, he scolded his father: "You never do anything. All you want to do is eat my nice fat cows." The father was shy and did not dare look his son in the eye. Then the son took his gun and killed his father. The following day, the father came back to life again and began to laugh. "My son," he said, "you have become a 'non-Indian'." The son left taking his belongings. And that is how "non-Indians" were created.'

The Cuiva have found it increasingly difficult to survive. Formerly, when the men were not out hunting, everyone lived as a close-knit family unit. As Arcand reports in the film: 'Cuiva traditionally spend something like fifteen to sixteen hours a day just sitting at home chatting to neighbours, joking about, singing. Their work day is really very brief . . . To live well, eat well and feed the whole family well, the Cuiva on average need only to spend around twenty hours in a week in food production, leaving sixteen hours out of twenty-four lying in their hammocks! A way of life we should envy rather then destroy.'

Arcand realised that the only option for the Cuiva was to work for the Llaneros and become third-rate citizens in an alien environment. This has destroyed their traditional pattern of close family life, and created malnourishment, prostitution and alcoholism, but there is now no turning back; the Cuiva, like other Indian groups in South America, have succumbed.

The traditional patterns of life of the Cuiva have been destroyed.

The Cuiva used to share a relaxed and contented way of life. Today, it has been devastated by contact with an alien culture.

The Kayapo

Unlike the Cuiva, the Kayapo Indians living in the Xingu rainforest of central Brazil have been fighting back. Their clash with other Brazilians stems from justifiable mistrust and fear of being exploited and slaughtered, and has assumed extraordinary proportions. Ropni is a prominent Kayapo chief in the battle to retain an identity and autonomy for his people in the heart of the rainforest. He takes an uncompromising stand: 'Brazilians who try to get in here will die – die by my own hand. I say it and I mean it. So I'm not going to give the Brazilians gold from our land. None of our timber. None of our forest. None of our land. When the Brazilians first pacified us, they gave us coffee, sugar and all the food they eat. The Brazilians slept with our women. Our men slept with Brazilian women and all this weakened us. I don't like it.'

Ropni has good reason for his mistrust. In 1897 the Kayapo population was estimated at around 5,000 (although since they live away from the major rivers, surveys are approximate, and the figure could have been higher); today only about 2,000 remain. Contact with Europeans in search of Brazil nuts and rubber brought fatal disease; warfare and extermination further reduced their numbers.

The Kayapo have access to a wealth of natural foods. Maize, sweet potatoes, sweet manioc and yams, which are easily cultivated, provide the staple diet which they supplement with fish, fruits, nuts, deer and tortoises. In the rainy season they occupy permanent village settlements; but during several months of the year they become nomadic hunters.

The anthropologist Terry Turner, who was with the team filming the Kayapo in 1987, explains that Ropni's people have always been engaged in a continuous struggle to prevent rival tribes and Brazilians from exploiting their land: 'All his life he's had to fight off Brazilian incursions . . . Some fifty Brazilians have died in the skirmishes he has fought over the years. He is also an intelligent political leader and diplomat. It was he who persuaded the Brazilian authorities to grant his people the legal title to the land bordering this stretch of the Xingu River.'

Such a concession is all the more important because the vast area once controlled by the Kayapo has recently come under a new threat. In the course of the 1980s a new situation arose which could well jeopardise all Ropni's efforts to keep the Kayapo unified. Gold has been discovered on Kayapo land, though not in the part where Ropni rules.

In 1982, 3,000 determined Brazilian miners invaded Indian territory. In 1985, the Kayapo, unprepared to accept such a violation of their land, retaliated. They devised a simple and effective plan. Seeing that the only access to the gold mines of the Gorotire region was by light aircraft, they occupied the airstrip and refused to allow any planes to land. Dressed in traditional battle paint and feathers, and armed with war-clubs, bows and arrows and rifles, they cowed the miners on the site with a calculated exhibition of savagery. Meeting no resistance, they established effective control over the region. Today, employing only four warriors armed with war-clubs, they successfully police the mine and have imposed their own 'customs', searching the miners and their baggage to prevent any gold being smuggled out of the territory. As Turner points out: 'All of this represents a conscious use by the Kayapo of their reputation among the local Brazilians as savage killers.'

The Kayapo have therefore become businessmen; they even keep their wealth in a Brazilian bank. Furthermore, they have every intention of protecting their investment by all possible means. These include buying themselves a light aircraft and hiring a Brazilian pilot; the Kayapo are thus the first Amazonian tribe to possess an airforce.

Kayapo society is paying a price for this success. Many traditionalists, like Ropni, would prefer to abandon the mining of gold altogether, and maintain their culture as it was. 'Before the Brazilians made peace with us,' he reminds the men of his village at an important ceremonial occasion, 'our forefathers performed this beautiful naming ceremony. They went off on the hunt and came back and feasted and were happy together. And then the Brazilians pacified us. Some of your brothers have become fascinated with

Although their share in a goldmine has brought some of the Kayapo wealth and new territory, they insist that they will not surrender their customs and essential values.

89

understand me? Let me hear you thunder! Yes! Yes! Yes!'

Even more astutely, Kanyonk has realised that his tribe can make use of Brazilian technology to preserve the tribal culture. 'We Indians, we understand our own things and we know how to teach each other. But we also see the Brazilians' video recorder and we like that. We saw how it was used to record our ways. The Brazilians speak falsely. They break their promises. Now we have learned to use their technology we can record what they say to us and force them to act according to their words.' This policy was successfully adopted when a group of pilots attempted to break the contracts they had with the Kayapo for flying to and from the gold mine. The Kayapo had taped the original negotiations on video and were able to play back the recording afterwards to prove their case.

Other changes have affected Kayapo accommodation. New rows of houses similar to those in the towns of Brazil are replacing the traditional circular village layouts. The new houses tend to accommodate single families rather than the old-style extended families. Most son-in-laws, for example, no longer live with their wife's parents as they were expected to in the past. Even more significant is the dwindling importance of the men's house at the head of the street. This used to be the centre of male social life, where the young learned from their elders. But

Brazilian ways. No! Do not betray yourselves . . . You should follow the ways of our fathers – only the ways of our fathers.'

Ropni sent a similar message to the group of Kayapo who actually control the gold mine. 'Do not have this desire for money, do not seek for gold! Do not allow the Brazilians to get concessions for gold on your land. Let us stand together with one another. Let us rub our culture back into ourselves.'

His words were not universally approved. The Kayapo of the mining region at Gorotire claim that they have turned the tables on the Brazilians without destroying their own culture. Kanyonk, another Kayapo chief, rebuts Ropni's accusations, pointing out to a gathering in his village that they have not copied the Brazilians by trying to raise cattle. 'We are true Kayapo of Gorotire,' he claims, 'who only kill wild game in the forest. We Kayapo do not wait to ask Brazilians for permission to fish. Every day all of you men catch fish for us to eat. Do you

Although some Kayapo have abandoned their village housing and significant features such as the man's house, they still perform important rituals – like this ceremony to give a child a 'beautiful name'.

young boys and bachelors no longer sleep there; instead they live with their parents until they are ready to marry and set up their own households.

Changes such as these do not necessarily mean, as Ropni believes, that when the Kayapo are 'touched by gold' they abandon the old ways. Terry Turner points out that rituals like the naming ceremony, are, if anything, being celebrated even more enthusiastically than before. Nor do the Kayapo themselves accept that they have rejected their own culture. Kupranpoy, one of the 'new breed', explains: 'we don't lust after money. We don't lust after Brazilian things. We all still go to the forest and hunt animals. We all still go fishing. Our wives still go to the gardens to get food for our children. We do everything just as before.' Although boys and young men do hanker for novelties introduced by the

Brazilians, he predicts that this urge will be short-lived. The older men wear shoes only reluctantly to protect their feet from thorns; most of them are still proud of their body paint and the beads in their ears.

The Kayapo were particularly worried, however, by a rumour that the Brazilian government wants to build dams that will flood their land. Chief Kanyonk journeyed to Brasilia to find out whether there was any substance in this rumour. He met with no success and on his return summoned the men to discuss strategy.

'My dear ones,' he announces, 'my ritual kin. Listen! I have gone to Brasilia, but in vain. I went to see President Sarney, the chief of all Brazil, but in vain. We Kayapo don't want our land to disappear under the big dam. We don't want our fish killed, nor the animals we hunt. We Kayapo don't want this! The Brazilians

Chief Ropni is totally committed to keeping the Brazilians from taking Kayapo land. 'They will die by my own hand,' he says. And he urges his people: 'Let us rub our culture back into ourselves'.

kill us! They lay waste to us! We don't deserve this. We Kayapo must determine our course independently. I am a chief, and all the Kayapo chiefs speak the same way.'

Terry Turner hopes that the Kayapo's earlier adaptability may help them survive today. During the crisis over the gold-mine they displayed a pride and solidarity which Turner saw reflected in their performances of a war dance, in which the men dance with their arms spread protectively over the women and babies. And it may be that they will assert their identity by reverting to the shows of strength displayed prior to the arrival of the Europeans, when they formed raiding parties against neighbouring peoples. No matter what happens, it is impossible not to feel admiration for the achievement of the Kayapo – a David and Goliath story that occurs all too rarely in the twentieth century.

The Sakuddei

Another rainforest society on the other side of the planet has been less adaptable to the pressure of exploitation by outsiders. Siberut is a small, remote island off the coast of Sumatra. In its heartland live the Sakuddei people who, like the Cuiva of Colombia and the Kayapo of Brazil, used to enjoy a leisurely and highly organised social life. For some years the Indonesian government have been systematically destroying it, advancing the familiar argument that they are helping the Sakuddei people by providing education and health facilities, and bringing them 'civilisation'. In the film the island's governor claims that his intention is 'in the shortest possible time to uplift the social conditions of the people concerned, and of course without shocks . . . and bit by bit to bring them into contact with the general development of Indonesian society'.

In 1974, when filming took place, the Sakuddei were already unhappy at these changes which related primarily to the structure and organisation of their villages. The Sakuddei live together and have no real leaders. All decisions are made

92

collectively, though some individuals gain more influence and power than others by strength of character or ability to express themselves well. Traditionally the people live in a clan house called the *Uma;* as many as eight families, often comprising more than forty individuals, may occupy three large rooms under one roof.

The complex social relations within Sakuddei families revolve around their clan house. The government decided to change this social structure by creating new villages. Such attempts have caused deep unrest. The men at one of these new villages, Pasakiat, were outspoken. They explained that only one family could fit into the new small houses, often not even that: 'The children sleep out on the terrace. It is like a chicken coop, or a house for pigs. Our hearts dislike these small houses, so we will build a new house ourselves.'

The official view of Sakuddei life is somewhat different, as the governor explains: 'Their economy is scattered, you know. They have their coconut field somewhere and they have to go with a small boat for a couple of hours and then

Sakuddei life revolves around the clan house. Indonesian government plans to move them to new villages have aroused deep resentment.

93

back again in the afternoon, and so on. It makes things very difficult for us to regulate. It's impossible to execute a good system of government, except by having a reorganisation of the villages. Then it is much easier for us to give our guidance, to bring them up so that they can go to school in one hour or an hour and a half. Then school has meaning, a polyclinic has meaning, education has a meaning.'

Some Sakuddei also have welcomed the idea of schooling, but not at the cost of totally abandoning their traditional values. Since these are so heavily dependent upon the clan house and close family ties, they were unhappy at having to send the children 'away' to the new government schools. 'With school nearby,' one villager explains to the film team, 'the children could live with us and see our ceremonies. When we made feasts they could join in. They could know school *and* our customs. Your world *and* ours, our work with pigs and trees. But once they go away, they will only see the work of other people. We would rear the pigs, look after the trees, do everything, but they wouldn't care.

They wouldn't see. As to this writing, we want our children to learn it. That is good. If we all knew the meaning of writing we would know together what is strong and good.'

By imposing compulsory education, the government is also aiming to do away with the Sakuddei forms of religion. The Sakuddei believe in a spirit world where everything has a soul. Communication with the spirits is provided by medicine men who use holy plants to bridge the gap between man and the world of souls. This elaborate and intricate religion offers particular solace in time of illness. Amandu-matkerei, one of the most famous Sakuddei medicine men, tries to explain: 'It's like your doctor. It means life. We call the ancestors. We dance with the souls, then we wear our beads and our headband, our Toggoro loincloth, flowers in our hair, beautiful flowers, and chicken feathers. These are the signs of a medicine man. We know much, we medicine men. We are men of knowledge.'

One of his fellow medicine men stressed the importance of maintaining their benefits: 'Our religion is old. Our fathers' religion – a good religion, one we know. They made no iron and we can't either. We can't make cloth – in this we are ignorant. We can't make knives. We don't know machines. But our fathers' ways – we know *these* things. The rituals for pigs, how a house is built, the ways to hunt game. We won't give them up.'

The government considers these traditional beliefs to be uncivilised and that the people should choose one of the officially approved religions – Christianity, Islam or Buddhism. The island's chief of police has therefore banned the medicine men, alleging that their taboos are a waste of time and that they do not properly examine the sick. Nor does he believe that Sakuddei beliefs are deeply rooted in their society, claiming that without evidence of real praying, such beliefs cannot be

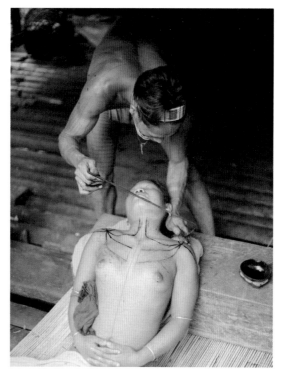

Sakuddei medicine men and their religion are considered uncivilised by the government (left).

As many as eight families may live in one Sakuddei clan house.

classified as a true religion. He proceeds to arrest and fine anyone found practising the old ways.

The Sakuddei have been bewildered by the choice offered to them. 'The new religions are strange to us,' confesses one old man. 'These new things are not of our world. If we had the choice and we were not afraid, most people would follow the old ways. Even those who are "Christian" call the medicine men when they are ill. They believe in them. But when the government hear about it, they punish us.'

The clash between cultures on Siberut has been intensified by commercial priorities. Outsiders are keenly interested in the trees growing on Sakuddei land. This lies inside the boundaries of a vast logging concession granted by the Indonesian government to a Filipino company. In theory there are controls over the area of forest land the loggers are allowed to cut. In practice the controls are lax, and the Indonesian government benefits from the considerable sums of money handed over by the company. Freed of any effective restrictions, the loggers are determined to exploit the Siberut resource to the full. The only sufferers are the Sakuddei.

'We have a target production of 20,000 cubic metres a month,' explains a logging representative. 'That is around 6,000 trees a month.' At that rate it was clear in 1974 that the raw materials used by the Sakuddei to build their long clan houses would soon have vanished.

The Maku and Barasana

Ron Metzger is an American missionary with the Summer Institute of Linguistics. While working among the Maku tribe of Colombia, he tells *Disappearing World*: 'Civilisation is coming and it's going to come in more and more. It's our desire to bring up their standard of living, to adjust them to the onrush of civilisation. The scriptures tell us to thirst after the spiritual milk that we might grow thereby. Without that spiritual milk, without the Word in their own language, it's just like a baby without milk . . . We want to be able to provide them with that source of spiritual milk – the scriptures . . . If they don't believe, well, they'll be cast into a life of fire. They'll suffer eternally, they'll go to Hell.'

This attitude has bewildered the Maku and provoked opposition from anthropologists working in the region. Peter Silver-

The Maku of Colombia are bewildered by the campaigns mounted by determined American missionaries.

wood-Cope explains that the Maku are puzzled by the missionaries: 'The Indians look at missionaries – they see guys who manipulate and control the economic source of white trade goods, they see them as being very rich people, they see them as people who give orders, the people who forbid. There are various government organisations, missionaries and foreign charities all considering the Indian problem. But what is the Indian problem? The Indians have managed to live in this forest without poisoning it, without exhausting it and without overcrowding it. For me the most serious problem which faces us is not the Indian problem. The problem is white.'

The elaborate system of beliefs of the Maku has endured for centuries. Their isolation in the Amazonian forest, with only the nearby Barasana as trading

Until recently, the Maku have maintained their elaborate system of beliefs without outside influence (right). The Barasana, who live downriver from the Maku, have lost their beliefs and myths under the proselytisation of aggressive Catholic missionaries (below).

partners, kept outside influences at bay until the past few decades. They are hunter-gatherers for whom animals play an important role both in everyday and spiritual life. One of their shamans explains: 'There are animal houses above this world. In these houses live pigs, tapirs, *magutee*, howler monkeys, spider monkeys and black monkeys.' The role of the shaman is to persuade the animals to come down to earth so that his people can hunt them. He does this by blowing tobacco, as part of a complex ritual.

Such beliefs are anathema to the missionary. Ron Metzger complains: 'These people are in another world, they might as well be on the moon. They're in another world culturally, in another world linguistically, and I think our goal, in this group, is to bridge that gap.'

In 1971, isolation had spared the Maku from the missionaries; but their river neighbours, the Barasana, who inhabit large clearings that are easily accessible to boat travellers, had been less fortunate. Catholic missionaries in the early 1950s had initiated change by burning Barasana ritual objects and artifacts and throwing them in the river. They had also taken the tribe's sacred trumpets, traditionally to be seen only by men, and shown them to the women, thereby rendering them valueless.

The anthropologists Stephen and Christine Hugh-Jones, who lived among the Barasana, found very few who still knew about the beliefs of their forebears. Even their myths were dying out, leaving only the essential myth of their origin. This says that under a certain waterfall hundreds of swallows made their nests. Every evening they flew out through the falling water and fanned out all over the jungle. They were the first people distributing themselves all over the land. The cave where they lived was both the Sky Mother and also her womb. When she gave birth to humanity, her natal blood poured over the rocks and mixed with the waterfall, which is why the water appears so red. The Sky Mother made the world, but at first there was no earth and no trees – just hard stone. The first people wandered around on this stone frantically seeking water to drink. The Sky Mother told them they would find water in a tree. They felled tree after tree, leaving the stumps, which became the mountains. Eventually they came to the water tree which was the tree of life, and they chopped and chopped at it for two months with stone axes. When at last it crashed to the ground, its branches made all the rivers.

The loss of their traditions and beliefs has made a vacuum in the lives of the Barasana; but it is too easy to blame every-

The loss of their beliefs has left a vacuum in the lives of the Barasana.

thing on the missionaries. Stephen Hugh-Jones admits that the missionaries are sincere and that many of their activities are of great benefit to the Indians. They provide them with medical services and protection against the rubber-gatherers. Their education policy is more controver-

The Barasana have benefited from the medical services provided by the missionaries, but both Indians and priests remain bewildered by each others' motives.

sial. 'The Barasana now want change and if you remove the missionaries you remove part of their life. Both sides show a complete ignorance as to the basic motivation of the other. The missionaries' ideas about Indians plagued with fears of devils and demons are matched only by the ideas of the Indians about Catholic priests who can't reproduce because they can't have wives.'

Meanwhile the missionaries continue their work. Through the spread of schools and teaching, health care and economic progress, they believe they are winning their particular battle. A prayer at the annual conference of the Summer Institute of Linguistics spells out the strength of this conviction:

'We thank you for the assurance that the work we are doing here in Colombia is not in our own strength, that it is a supernatural work empowered by your holy spirit, and we thank you that we stand on victory ground; the victory has already been won for us, we go forth to claim it, Lord, we go forth to claim it for the Indian people of Colombia and not only for them, but for all those many varied groups of people with whom we come in contact day after day.'

The Meo

Probably the most devastating clash of cultures recorded by *Disappearing World* occurred in Laos among the Meo people or Hmong, as they call themselves, where warfare led to the virtual destruction of the entire tribal community.

The Meo were once aborigines in north and central China, and are mentioned in some histories as having fought the Chinese as early as 2700 BC. Over the last 3,000 years they have been forced to migrate southward to preserve their own way of life. They came to inhabit villages scattered over the mountains of southern China and south-east Asia. Until recently, 400,000 of them were living in Laos. The French anthropologist Jacques Lemoine spent thirteen years living there, much of them with the Meo. He witnessed their decline in numbers from 400,000 in 1960, to less than 250,000 in 1972, the year he and Brian Moser filmed them. In Lemoine's words, 'The film turned out to be a testimony to the desperate struggle of this

The Meo of Laos have
been devastated by the
war in South-east Asia
over the past thirty years.

Over 3,000 years, the Meo have been forced to migrate southwards from northern China to preserve their identity.

people for survival. 'This was not our choice, but the direct result of circumstances.' The highlands of Indo-China where the Meo live had seen continuous fighting for over thirty years. In Laos the mountainous region in the north was the battleground between the American-backed Royal Lao forces and the communist Pathet Lao with their North Vietnamese allies. By 1972 the Pathet Lao controlled most of the highland area, and those Meo who opposed them had been compelled to leave their homelands and flee to areas ever farther south.

More than 100,000 Meo refugees had crowded into camps in the last unoccupied

Refugees

War is the ultimate expression of cultural conflict. In Afghanistan the different tribes have struggled against outsiders for centuries, and most recently against the Russians. Turkmen, Hazara, Kirghiz, Tajik, Uzbek and Pushtun have been forced to flee to Pakistan and Iran. They represent the greatest refugee influx (five million people) in the modern world.

Obidullah from the the Popolzai tribe fled to Surkhel camp in Pakistan. His story has been repeated thousands of times. 'We came to Pakistan because of the non-believing Russians. They were killing and imprisoning us. I took my family and fled with my children. We all had to leave, even those who were ill. My own granddaughter died here and my wife is still very sick.'

102

Rice is the prime subsistence crop of the Meo.

highland zones before reaching the plains of Vientiane. 5,000 were living in the refugee camp at Phou Phai Mai. Most of them had spent the last ten years moving from camp to camp as the war rolled backwards and forwards over the mountains. For some this was their fifteenth home in that time.

Traditionally they had been hill farmers practising a 'slash and burn' economy. Their work would begin with the first rains of the wet season on their fields. In the hills, land is no problem. Every year the Meo would burn off different areas of forest to make new fields. Their main crops were maize and rice for subsistence, and the opium poppy as a cash crop. They also raised pigs.

When Lemoine first wanted to study them, he searched for a zone untouched by war. He chose a remote village across the Mekong River and befriended a village elder and shaman named Chu Yao. Yet even this small community had some experience of war. The elders told Lemoine how in 1962 they had been given American guns so that they could become part-time guerillas, but had given the guns back and tried to ignore the war. For a long while they managed to avert threats to their neutrality by diplomacy; they succeeded in making soldiers from both

sides aware that they were not welcome in the valley. Eventually they faced the menace of conscription, and Chu Yao toyed with the notion of telling the Royal Lao authorities that all of his men were opium addicts, unable to fight.

They were in an impossible position. When the Pathet Lao or North Vietnamese soldiers forced them to cooperate, the Royal Lao airforce retaliated by sending T28 bombers to strafe the area. The villagers were compelled to flee into the surrounding forest, which meant they could no longer tend their fields. 'We had to leave our village,' explains Njuan Nzai, a Meo farmer. 'The Pathet Lao and the

Despite Meo efforts to remain neutral, both the Americans and Communist guerillas have pressurised them to become soldiers. Many Meo boys have found themselves in uniform.

North Vietnamese came very close to it and fighting broke out between them and Royal Lao soldiers. Bombs exploded in our fields and shells fell on our houses.'

Jacques Lemoine later reported that in the year after *The Meo* was filmed, there was a ceasefire in Laos, and many Meo returned to their land. But after 1975 the excesses of the Laotian Democratic People's Republic in 'reorganising' village life added a new burden to Meo society. Lemoine told of 'children and adults being uprooted and enrolled in different collective occupations, not the least repressive of which was the apparently gentle folklore organisation, whose only purpose was to introduce new styles of dancing, singing and playing music based on Chinese and Vietnamese models'. Crops were taxed, contributions of food had to be 'volunteered', and the exchange of goods for profit was abolished. The village hierarchy was transferred to revolutionary committees run by cadres in their late teens, and denunciation became a powerful political weapon.

Since Laos became Communist in 1975, the Meo have been subjected to intense political pressures and the fundamental restructuring of their lives.

A MATTER OF CHOICE

LAU, SHERPAS, MURSI MIGRANTS

Many isolated tribal communities have been sadly exploited, disrupted and all but destroyed by the bruising advance of Western technology. There are those who believe that such societies can only be adequately protected by encouraging them to stay secluded. Yet this insidious pattern of events is not inevitable; such romantic notions of hermetic survival fail to allow for peoples who are determined to make their own choices and initiate their own changes.

The three societies described in this chapter are all facing outside pressures just as powerful as those confronting the Eskimo or the Tuareg. But each of them has chosen to adapt rather than succumb, to absorb new values, to utilise new technology and to face the consequences of a new social situation. In a Pacific lagoon, in a Himalayan valley and in a remote region of southern Ethiopia, each of these very different societies is adapting to change in its own fashion, seeking at the same time ways of preserving some of the traditions that make them unique.

The Lau

In a lagoon off the island of Malaita in the Solomons, the Lau people have lived for hundreds of years on an extraordinary scatter of some sixty artificial islands. Built up from coral rocks gathered from the floor of the lagoon, these island homes have traditionally afforded the Lau protection from enemies and disease. But in the late twentieth century the 5,000 Lau

are having to defend themselves against a new, creeping form of attack. For centuries every aspect of Lau existence has been shaped by a system of beliefs and values known as 'The Life of Custom'. But over the past thirty years Christianity and new ideas from the outside world have challenged the ways of 'Custom', leaving the

The Lau of the Solomon Islands live on extraordinary man-made islands in a South Pacific lagoon.

'Sacred Mouth' Ratu is one of the last remaining Lau priests still following their traditional religion (right).

On the island of Foueda, the priest's house has lain in ruins for years since he committed ritual suicide in despair at the spread of Christianity in the Lau lagoon (below).

In 1986, the men of Foueda built a House of Culture to preserve and perpetuate the traditional 'Life of Custom' (far below).

Lau in confusion and turmoil. In the film, *The Lau of Malaita*, Ratu, a priest on Funafou, the oldest of the Lau islands, tells the anthropologist Pierre Maranda that apart from himself there is only one other traditional priest left in the entire region. 'The men of Custom – they are almost gone,' he says. 'Custom is no more.'

The two priests remaining on the island of Foueda committed ritual suicide in 1983. Despairing at the rapid spread of Christianity in the lagoon, one of them broke a fierce taboo by swimming under a woman's canoe, the other knowingly made an error in ritual. Within a week both had died. No one had dared to enter their ruined houses to retrieve the sacred objects for fear of being killed by spirits angered at the intrusion. But in 1986 the realisation that soon there would be nothing left of their traditional beliefs and lifestyle galvanised the islanders into action. The men of Foueda decided to create a 'House of Culture' to preserve and perpetuate some of the old ways, and *Disappearing World* was able to film this happening.

The islands of the Lau lagoon already have innovations such as Western clothing, cassette recorders and even a video player. These have had an impact, but it is religious practices which have been really transformed. Christian missionaries have brought more than their message to many of the islands; now only on Foueda and on a few other islands does the Custom life survive, including belief in the power of dead ancestors and in a vast array of spirits inhabiting virtually every corner of the Lau world.

A striking example of the confusion created by the new existing alongside the old on Foueda is apparent in the household of a highly traditional 'Man of Custom,' Dede To'ou. To men like him the spirit world is an ever-present reality. 'The Goosile is a thing that eats people. He snatches people and pigs . . . The wild spirit is a spirit that lives in the jungle. He touches someone and they die . . . Killilea makes a woman hang herself . . . The spirit of the net watches over fishing nets . . . The spirit of the armies – if we're going on a raid, we will kill many men.'

Although electronic equipment and T-shirts have arrived in the lagoon, some young men are determined to revive Lau culture through older activities such as dances (above).

Dede To'ou is a skilful fisherman and a dedicated 'Man of Custom'. But his son has become a Christian convert.

109

Dede To'ou has no one to whom he can pass on his traditional knowledge, such as how to make your garden prosper through spirit power. His own son Tuita is a convert to Christianity, and as a man in *Sukulu* (a Lau word which embraces the effects of Christianity, schooling and technology), he is barred from inheriting his father's ritual knowledge. Tuita is in fact a devoted member of the church on Roba, a tiny island off Foueda, built expressly for Christians to worship without polluting Custom areas. 'For those of us in *Sukulu*, they are forbidden,' explains Tuita. 'We don't take that spirit power. We pray to the Lord above. We put our trust in him.' This accords with the teaching of the sect who converted this part of the lagoon: that traditional Custom practices are sinful and must be abandoned. Dede's response to his son's conversion is outspoken. '*Sukulu* has destroyed my boy. Custom ends with me.'

Despite the bleak prospects for traditional religious practices, the men and women of Foueda continue to observe Custom in their daily relationships. At the end of a day's work, Dede still likes to join

Spans of money made from seashells are an essential part of Lau wedding dowries.

his friends in the *Maanabeu*, the men's area. Lau Custom says that the way for men and women to be happy is to spend plenty of time apart. By tradition, even married men and women slept apart. Although on many islands the strictly separated areas of taboo for each sex have collapsed, on Foueda they are still maintained. The men's area is the political and spiritual hub of the island; a woman must stay outside the little wall that marks its boundary. Conversely, the women's exclusive space, the *Maanabisi*, is guarded by fearsome taboos; any man who sets foot there risks death from the spirit.

Custom demands that a woman should live in the *Maanabisi* for four days during menstruation and for thirty days after childbirth. But even on Foueda there is an increasing tendency for some women to escape to taboo-free Christian islands where they can have their babies in more comfort. 'They don't want to stay here. They prefer a Christian place where life is easier,' admits Sousou, a woman of Foueda. 'Life here's not very comfortable. Sitting on those rocks for thirty days, it isn't nice at all.'

A great divide between the sexes exists in the Lau lagoon. Even in their canoe, Dede's head must remain higher than his wife's, although she does the steering. Women are seen as low, but dangerously powerful; men are regarded as high, but vulnerable. A woman of Foueda explains: 'For us it's not the woman but the man who rules the house. If a woman wants to go somewhere and a man says "you don't go", then the woman stays put. It's only if a man permits it that the woman will go. If a woman's more important it wouldn't be nice in the home. They'd quarrel day in and out.'

Elsewhere the sexual divisions sanctioned by the spirits are shifting, and on many islands the women's area has fallen into disuse. Funafou now has a generator and a video cassette player. A canny islander charges his fellows a few pence each to see the videos he brings in via the ship which visits the lagoon every week from the Solomon Islands' capital, Honiara. Audiences seemed a bit baffled by *Grease*, he says, but *Rambo* was a big hit.

There are islanders who try to retain Custom alongside new ways. At one

A bride on the island of Foueda.

On her wedding day, the bride wears a Western-style white dress, along with her shell-money dowry.

wedding on Foueda, for example, the bride wore a western-style wedding dress along with traditional shell money, dolphin's teeth necklaces and a crown made of Solomon Island dollars. More intriguingly, despite their obligations to abandon Custom, many Christians in the Lau lagoon recall their upbringing and are anxious that traditional life should not vanish entirely. Hatley Toata, one of Foueda's leading Christians, points out: 'I'm a man of *Sukulu*, but I knew all the Customs from my father when I was small. Never mind that I went to *Sukulu* – village Custom stays with me. *Sukulu* came later.'

The plan by some of the young men on Funafou to build a 'Cultural Institute' was one of the most ambitious recent attempts to arrest the loss of Custom, the focus of their determination to preserve traditional objects and ideas. They hoped to display the ritual items from Custom ceremonies, such as pan pipes and food bowls, although they also admitted to some rather less spiritual motives. 'Tourists and people who drift this way can see it and pay if they want to see the culture of Malaita. Things in that house will be the ancient things, and things from our origins . . . And they may want to buy for money when they see the things inside.' For the time being, though, these bold plans are in ruins. Not long after an official opening by the Solomon Islands' Prime Minister, the

The Lamahalot

The Lamahalot people live on a group of islands off the Eastern coast of Indonesia. They are largely agriculturalists, although the people in one village, Lamalera, on the island of Lembata, are fishermen. The villagers of Lamalera are the last Indonesians to hunt the powerful sperm whale in rowing boats. Although Christianity and Western technology have transformed the lives of the Lamahalot, when it comes to whaling, the old ways persist. The boats have to be built according to set rules, and 'any violation will be immediately spotted by a whale which will always stroke the boat', explained anthropologist Robert Barnes. The fishermen believe that the whale tests the boat and is helped in so doing by their ancestors. The whales are harpooned by one man standing on a platform which extends in the front of the boat. The fishermen use no motors and rely on their skills as rowers and harpoonists to avoid being killed by the whales. The danger is considerable and a flick of the whale's tail can be lethal.

A harpoonist demonstrates his skill.

The Sherpa village of Thami in the spectacular approaches to Mount Everest.

Cultural Institute collapsed. People on Funafou told us it was flattened by a recent cyclone, but it may have had more to do with local clan rivalries and disagreements over money.

The Lau on Foueda want to ensure that the same thing does not happen to the House of Culture they are building to keep Custom alive. While the *Disappearing World* team with Pierre Maranda were on the island, the Lau made a special effort to complete the House so that it could be filmed and the film kept as part of their preserved traditions. Risking the anger of the spirits, ritual objects belonging to the two dead priests were rescued from the ruins and placed reverently in the House of Culture alongside other objects the islanders had assembled. 'If we look at what's happening today,' one man remarks, 'and look at what's going on around us, we see there's still something alive today. The old ways aren't over, it's not at all the end of everything. There are things that have changed. Nowadays, if someone thinks right about our Custom, he'll be able to keep it alive and make it live again.'

Kalabeti, the Christian son of one of the most influential of the old traditionalists, makes a revealing statement about how the Lau are choosing to adopt the best of two worlds. He explains that he can take the things from Custom that suit him and also those from *Sukulu*. The things that make life too difficult for him, he rejects. 'It doesn't matter if we're in *Sukulu* or not. We want our things, the customs of the village to live on. Then, people coming to Foueda will see our things that are still alive. That's why we want the House of Culture built here.'

The Sherpas

The village of Thami, 12,500 feet up in the Nepalese Himalayas, is the birthplace of Sherpa Tenzing who, with Sir Edmund Hillary, conquered Mount Everest in 1953. The forces of change there are no less pressing than in the South Pacific. The Sherpa homelands are remote, but their location on the spectacular approaches to the world's highest mountain has brought a stream of visitors, along with new technology, ideas and opportunities.

113

Purwa Tenzing has chosen the life of a Sherpa farmer (right).

Three Sherpa brothers who have followed very different lives: as farmer, Buddhist monk and mountain guide (below).

For the 25,000 Sherpas, change has been very recent and very sudden, since the Kingdom of Nepal was opened to the outside world only in 1952. The new policy brought not only foreigners into Sherpa country; it also introduced reforms from the capital, Katmandu. Every aspect of Sherpa society was affected, most strikingly through the state education system which has lured away many young people from the mountains to Katmandu or Darjeeling in India.

Despite their distant mountain location, the Sherpas have always had contact with other societies. Originally a Tibetan people until they migrated into Nepal about 450 years ago, through trading they have maintained links both with Nepal and with Tibet, though the process of change resulting from these earlier contacts was much less dramatic than the impact of the tourist boom of the past thirty-five years.

As with the Lau, change for the Sherpas is not all conflict. They have found different ways to adapt. In the village of Thami, the anthropologist Sherry Ortner was able to explore the choices open to Sherpas within a single family. Three brothers had responded in three very different ways to the influences that were sweeping through Sherpa society.

The first, Purwa Tenzing, was a farmer and had chosen to remain in Thami. There, as in all Sherpa villages, the family survives on subsistence farming and yak herding. Each family can produce what it needs to live, and so it does not have to cooperate in harvesting the only crop – potatoes. Such features of Sherpa life are reproduced in the appearance of the village itself. Each family's house is separated from the next and the boundaries of each family's fields are precisely defined. All property is privately owned, and no leaders exercise power over people's lives. Every family keeps to itself, responsible for its own welfare. The inevitable corollary is a lack of cooperation and community feeling. 'Our land is separate,' explains Purwa Tenzing. 'Our own fields are separate. We build houses on our fields, we live separately. And so we live spread out. If we build the houses too close, people fight. It's better to be separate.'

Purwa Tenzing's annual round is gruelling. Spring and summer are the busy months for farming, when potatoes and a little wheat are cultivated. Autumn is the season when fuel has to be collected for cooking and warmth, and the precious dry wood brought from far away. The nearest suitable trees are more than two hours' climb away, and since growth is very slow at heights of 14,000 feet and wood has been gathered here for centuries, there is a desperate shortage of timber in the region, and controls on woodcutting are strict. Purwa Tenzing and his wife Ai Kami set out shortly after sunrise, five times a week throughout the autumn, carrying home loads of more than a hundredweight of wood on their backs. Sherpas also make trading expeditions into Tibet at that time of year. Since the Chinese occupation, the routes are more tightly controlled; only a handful of older men still make the arduous six-day journey over the 19,000-foot Nangpala pass.

Purwa Tenzing's way of life differs little from that of his father before him. But his brother, Dorje Tenzing, has abandoned farming and chosen an equally traditional occupation, that of a Buddhist monk. Both brothers follow the Buddhist teaching that every individual must seek his own salvation, that daily life is partly a preparation for reincarnation, and that meritorious actions and the avoidance of sin are ways to ensure a better life next time. But Dorje, being a monk, has withdrawn from village life to pursue a salvation unconnected with worldly success. For Purwa, and indeed most Sherpas meritorious action will obtain a favourable rebirth; for Dorje and his fellow monks, it will allow them to escape the cycle of death and rebirth altogether. 'I have renounced the cycle,' explains Dorje. 'The cycle means your soul is attached to your possessions. Your soul keeps thinking: "I like my things so much" . . . Then later you grow old and die. That is all suffering. Even when you're dead, your soul is not lost. It is born again. You could be reborn as a worm or a smelly black beetle – an insect in the house that really stinks. Oh! we might be reborn as those things!'

Only two or three Sherpas in every hundred become monks. Boys training for a religious life may begin as young as six. It is a powerful source of merit for Sherpa parents to have a son who is a monk. Another advantage for Dorje in choosing the religious life is that he avoids what he

Collecting scarce firewood from steep mountainsides is a gruelling autumn task for Sherpas (far left).

Buddhist monks like Dorje Tenzing seek personal salvation and an escape from the cycle of death and rebirth.

The re-incarnate Lama of Thami monastery is at the centre of the autumn Fire Ceremony. He was discovered as a baby when he was able to identify the belongings of the previous Lama.

116

considers to be the drudgery of his elder brother's farming routine. 'When I studied religion, I didn't have to work. If I wasn't a monk, it would be "cut wood, go up, go down, go and trade", so many orders. But if you do religion, nobody gives you orders about work. It's high, it's bliss.'

The third brother in the Tenzing family, Mingma, has chosen a completely different life as a mountain guide. His story of rejecting the ways of previous generations is revealing: 'I used to stay alone on the hill. I was afraid; maybe a Yeti would come. I used to hear Yeti cries. I was really scared. When the yaks died my parents shouted at me. So my heart was sad. Then I saw some people who went off to do *sahib* work. They had nice clothes and good shoes and watches and radios. I was very keen. If I had those things and I could speak English I'd be happy . . . So I ran away to Katmandu.'

The capital of Nepal is more than a hundred miles from Thami, but for thousands of Sherpas like Mingma, it has become home. It is where the tourists arrive and where jobs are to be found. Mingma and his family moved there ten years ago. Since then he's been away for much of the year on treks and climbing

expedition, but he has a home on the ground floor of a house in the Sherpa district of the city. His wife, Pasang Hlamu, has made her front room available to any Sherpa from Thami who is in Katmandu looking for work. In this way she can provide hospitality and make a little money selling beer to her guests.

The Fire Ceremony is one of the few occasions in the year when the people of Thami have a personal involvement with the monastery which overlooks their village.

As a boy, Mingma Tenzing longed to escape from his village to the Nepali capital of Katmandu and find work as a mountain guide (left).

117

Education is leading many Sherpa children away from the mountains and from the life led by their parents.

The possibilities for schooling are one reason why Mingma and his wife prefer to live in Katmandu. The illness of their son, Ang Tsultim, is another. He was a baby when his parents arrived in the city, and within months he caught polio. It left him unable to walk without crutches – an impossible handicap on the steep mountain tracks around the village. For Pasang Hlamu the move was essential and good: 'In Thami it's difficult. You have to carry loads, you have to work in the fields. In Katmandu you needn't work.'

The keys to Sherpa prosperity in Katmandu are tourist trekking and climbing expeditions. It is a dangerous and competitive business, but it gives Mingma Tenzing status – he is a *sirdar* or expedition leader, which allows his family to live much better than in Thami. He has few regrets at having chosen a 'modern' lifestyle, and is not overly concerned as to whether certain aspects of Sherpa culture, including their native tongue, are lost. 'If our language is lost, it doesn't matter,' he asserts. 'Small villages and many languages are hard for people.' His wife, however,

disagrees: 'It's better if the Sherpa language isn't lost,' she argues. 'If our language is lost, the Sherpa name will go.' 'Then I'll be happy,' replies Mingma. 'What is the Sherpa name anyway? We eat by carrying loads. Is that big?' But Pasang Hlamu has the last word: 'Mingma is no good. When Sherpas carry loads, they don't steal, they don't tell lies. Even if they carry loads they have a good name. If our language is lost, the Sherpas won't exist.'

The Mursi Migrants

The pressures which induced many Lau and Sherpas to adopt a different way of life came from outside. But in a remote part of southern Ethiopia, a radical change in an entire way of life has been initiated and carried out by a community without any outside influence whatsoever.

The Mursi are a society of about 5,000 cattle pastoralists constantly on the move in pursuit of a hard living (Chapter Five). Until recently they were virtually untouched by the ways of modern Ethiopia. They live in inhospitable territory close to the borders of Sudan and Kenya, hemmed in

by mountains, isolated by the Omo River, and far removed from any accessible roads or airstrips. Mursi country, like most of Ethiopia, was badly hit by drought and hunger in the 1970s. The scorched East African landscape of Ethiopia has become grimly familiar across the world, but the territory of the Mursi lies hundreds of miles south of the highland famine areas in Ethiopia's greener and more fertile lowlands.

Even in their traditional land along the Omo, however, the Mursi found life during the drought years of the late 1970s increasingly hard. In 1980, starvation finally compelled almost one-quarter of them to set out on a desperate exodus to higher and better watered ground in the Mago valley, some fifty miles to the east. This mass migration, 'in search of cool ground', as the Mursi put it, took approximately one thousand people to a new homeland. It also brought the Mursi for the first time into sudden and bewildering contact with modern Ethiopia, in the form of a nearby highland market village called Berka.

Drought and hunger in the late 1970s drove the majority of cattle-herding Mursi off their lands along the river Omo in Southern Ethiopia in a mass exodus – 'in search of cool ground'.

The Mursi migrants have made a new home in the better-watered Mago Valley; but the move has also meant problems for the Mursi cattle.

The 'Cool Ground' of the Mago Valley has provided the Mursi migrants with better harvests. Their new home also brings them into regular contact with the outside world for the first time (right).

House-building is traditionally a woman's job among the nomadic Mursi. With the loss of their cattle, Mursi migrants are becoming farmers living in permanent settlements.

At first, the migrants were able to combine their two traditional subsistence activities. They took along some of their cattle to the Mago valley and also grew a good harvest of sorghum. Some of the grain was bought by their new neighbours, the Ari people, who had long lived in the region around Berka. But although initially the move was very successful, with no sacrifice of the values that were so important to the migrants, things soon took a turn for the worse. The cattle began to die and subsequent harvests were poor. Instead of selling sorghum in the market at Berka, only a few hours' walk away, the Mursi were forced to exchange goods in order to buy it. Tension with the Ari arose over stolen honey. Some of the migrants were tempted to return home, but the majority stayed in the valley; for even with these setbacks, life was still better there than it had been along the banks of the Omo.

Things did eventually improve for those Mursi who remained, although their pattern of life has altered. The major drawback to their move is that the Mago region is infested by the tsetse fly and so is unsuitable for cattle. Cattle produce milk, meat and blood for hungry people; but for the Mursi they are additionally a source of deep conviction and pride in their own identity. The tsetse fly and sleeping sickness are destroying their few remaining cattle. The migrants still hope that vaccines available in highland villages will protect their herds; but inexpert vaccination is likely to reduce their resistance and accelerate their extinction.

Though they are reluctant to acknowledge it, these harsh facts are compelling the Mursi to abandon the cattle-oriented way of life and move towards cultivation and dependence on the market. In their new home the Mursi migrants can grow sorghum with greater reliability and security than was ever possible in the lowlands beside the Omo. Furthermore, because they are so close to the market, in the event of grain being in short supply, they can exchange honey, animal hides or tobacco for their staple diet. For the first

The highland village of Berka, only a few hours' walk away for the Mursi migrants, is transforming their lives. For the first time, they are encountering a cash economy in the Berka market.

time, the Mursi migrants are also becoming part of a cash economy. 'This for the Mursi is something quite new,' comments the anthropologist David Turton, who has spent almost twenty years working with the Mursi. 'They have emerged from a situation in which they hardly knew that Ethiopia existed, to become aware of their position within Ethiopia and more and more a part of it.'

The loss of the cattle and the proximity of the Berka market are also altering the traditional roles of Mursi men and women. In the past, men herded the cattle while women cared for the crops. Only the men had contact with the outside world, buying and selling cattle and rifles in the highland villages. Nowadays it is the women who visit Berka most frequently, buying grain and other foodstuffs in times of shortage and selling grain when there is a surplus.

One striking result of the women's growing contact with the outside world is a renewed debate about whether to cut their lips or not. Mursi women have traditionally adorned themselves by cutting the lower lip and wearing a lip plate. The Ethiopian government frowns upon this custom, and already some of the Mago Mursi no longer allow their daughters to do it.

As women find new power by buying and selling grain in Berka, the men, having lost their traditional role as cattle-herders, may well seek a new role, by taking more interest in cultivation and commerce. Should this happen, Mursi women might become more, rather than less, economically dependent on their men.

There are other new factors affecting the men. Ulikuri, one of the migrants, was also one of the first to be enlisted in the Ethiopian army. 'First I went to Somalia,' he tells David Turton. 'Then I went to Eritrea. That's how it was. I saw everything – the Red Sea and Asmara and Sudan. It's our country. It's all Ethiopia. We're one people. Then I came back here.' Because of his travels, Ulikuri is aware of other forces which will bring change to his people. The migration was a conscious response to hunger. Further developments, such as road-building and education, will be outside Mursi control.

'Our customs will in the end disappear,' Ulikuri predicts. 'We'll become highlanders. That's it. It'll take a long time, but our customs will go.'

Many of the Mago Mursi do not share Ulikuri's fatalism and regard the traumatic shift from one form of subsistence to another as only temporary. Nor would the majority accept that by making the transition they are necessarily abandoning or sacrificing their traditional values and customs. In fact, some of the real traditionalists in Mursi society, like their priest Komorakora, strongly favoured the migration. David Turton sees a social mechanism in this that enables communities such as the Mursi to adapt to upheavals in their lives. 'People who hold to traditional ways,' he notes, 'can take advantage of opportunities for useful change by smuggling in new ways under the cover of pursuing established values and beliefs. Indeed, it may only be by insisting that they're employing these new ways for traditional ends that societies can allow themselves to accept that they've really embarked on radical change.'

Mursi women have always regarded lip-cutting as a special mark of their identity.

The Mursi lip plate is disliked by Ethiopia's revolutionary government, and some migrants are abandoning the practice.

BEHIND THE CURTAIN
MONGOLS, KAZAKHS, HAN

The greatest overland trade route the world has ever known linked the ancient civilisations of the East to Europe. It was known as the Silk Route, made famous in the West in the late thirteenth century by the travels of the intrepid Venetian, Marco Polo. Along the network of roads stretching from eastern China across central Asia journeyed merchants and caravans, missionaries and explorers; they carried with them not only goods, some of them precious, but also their languages, values, religions, technology and art. Warriors too swept across the steppes from Peking to the Caspian Sea; and in these expanses of forest and mountain, desert and grassland, Scythians, Huns, Mongols, Turks and Chinese created societies sharing many cultural features.

A curious mixture of the traditional and the modern in Mongolia inspired another great traveller, Owen Lattimore, to turn his attention away from commerce towards exploration. 'I remember one day,' he recalls, 'seeing a caravan of camels loaded with wool being led into the station yards at a railhead and the camels grunting as they kneeled beside the railway cars and the loads being taken directly from the animals into the railway wagons. And it struck me dramatically that there was the age of Marco Polo meeting the age of modern steam and industry. I thought right then that I would abandon my job and go travelling into that distant background to find out what it was all about.'

Disappearing World followed the trail of Marco Polo and of Lattimore to three communities along the ancient Silk Route. Although they speak different languages, observe different religions and have different economies, these societies today have an important feature in common; they all lie inside a Communist state. Within one generation, they have had to adapt to a similar imposed political ideology.

The herding Khalka of Mongolia, the pastoral Kazakhs of Xinjiang in northwest China and the agricultural Han from Wuxi in the Kiangsu province of eastern China live well over 1,000 miles from one another, but they all exist under Communist hegemony. Many cultural traditions have been lost as a result; but humans are ingenious, and each of these diverse societies has found ways of preserving certain traditions or incorporating them into the new order. Far from being swamped by an alien, overwhelmingly powerful political regime, they have willingly assimilated those outside innovations that have proved to their own best advantage and pretended to adopt others.

The Mongols

The Mongolian People's Republic is the size of the whole of western Europe. It was once the centre of one of the greatest land empires on earth. Today few areas of the world are so little known. One reason is that the population is very small – under one and a half million. Another is that the climate in a country situated on average more than 4,000 feet above sea level, is often inhospitable. Northern Mongolia is a land of forests and mountain ranges,

For a thousand years, trading caravans have followed the Silk Route between Europe and China through the spectacular landscape of Mongolia.

interspersed with vast grassland steppes. The south is dominated by the Gobi Desert which spreads southward into neighbouring China. This beautiful but rather forbidding land-locked region gave birth to the most successful and feared conqueror of all time – Genghis Khan. The empire he established in the thirteenth century, which lasted for more than 150 years, owed its foundation to the mobility of these horse-warriors from the steppes. Centuries later, the herding of horses, yaks, sheep and cattle remains the basis of the Mongolian economy, but as a result of collectivisation and of modern methods of raising livestock and managing wealth, today's economy would be quite beyond the comprehension of Genghis Khan.

For sixty years the explorer, traveller and anthropologist Owen Lattimore observed the impact of the Communist revolution on Mongolia (left).

Horses are central to Mongolian life. In the past, they gave the Mongol armies speed and mobility; today they remain important for transport, for their milk which is the basis of the traditional drink, and for sport.

The Gobi desert dominates southern Mongolia. Oases provide vital water and rest for the camel trains which cross the desert.

The collective, or *negdel*, is the key to contemporary Mongolian life. It developed as an integral part of the socialist state established between 1921 and 1924, which modelled itself on its neighbour and ally, the Soviet Union. Collectivisation aimed to destroy the power wielded previously by the ruling religious houses and princes. The struggle to overthrow them was long and bitter; not until the 1940s could the country lay claim to be successfully launched in a new direction.

Owen Lattimore is one of the few Westerners with an intimate knowledge of Mongolia. He was a welcome guest there both before and after the revolutionary changes. 'In the *negdel*,' he explains to Brian Moser in the film, 'as everywhere else in Mongolia, the transition from the old method of pasturing animals under the authoritarian control of nobles and clergy was a transition with a human cost. People knew that they wanted to get rid of the old before they were quite sure about the methods of the new, and like every country that has gone through the process of collectivisation, there was an early period in which the enthusiasts went too far. And this resulted not only in losses, but in actual uprisings.' But the extremism of the 1920s and early 1930s eventually gave way to a policy known as 'The New Turn', and the key to successful collectivisation of the country became education and persuasion, rather than force.

The state began by confiscating privately-owned herds. Land and animals were divided among the new cooperatives. Each member of the *negdel* was paid according to an elaborate work-points system, with a bonus for exceeding the normal production rate. At the same time, a measure of private ownership survived. Some families were permitted to buy and own horses, cows and their livestock. It persisted largely because the members of the collectives, who drew pay and had a share in the yearly production, enjoyed a good deal of purchasing power.

Between the 1950s and the 1970s there was a radical change in the style of housing. Until that time most Mongols lived, like their ancestors, in felt tents called *yurts*. These highly mobile homes have today given way to houses and apartment blocks, thus removing one vital element of the nomadic way of life.

By and large, claims Lattimore, although many important traditions have been lost, the people enjoy many compensations. 'In the old days, practically everything they produced was taken away from them, either by the nobility or by the clergy. Today everything they produce goes into the common fund of the collective and from it they draw wages as they go along and also a share of the profits at the end.' The system, he maintains, has removed the iniquitous gap between rich and poor, has helped to eradicate serious disease and has immeasurably increased the everyday standard of living of many Mongolian peasants.

The changes have not obliterated all traditions. The Mongols still enjoy their old sports of horse racing, wrestling and archery. Horse racing has always been popular, with races sometimes covering distances of over twenty miles. Jockeys include women and children; indeed, the average age of retirement for a jockey is twelve years old! The horse remains, as ever, a vital pivot of Mongol society. The

In remoter areas of Mongolia, people still live in 'yurts', felt tents on wooden frames which would have been familiar to their ancestor Genghis Khan.

Children in today's Mongolia are taught the values of modern life, and the nomadic existence of their parents and grandparents is rapidly being forgotten.

fermented mare's milk, *kumis*, is a popular traditional drink, and at every festival there are songs and poems in honour of the horse, particularly the winner of a race:

'Gelding great with our mother's glory!
Gift of happiness he gives this day.
Foremost and famous among all horses.
Fine are your treasures beyond description.
Fair is your form beyond compare.
Fleet of foot in the skill of running.
Fond and gentle to handle.
Fastest of all in the race today.'

Where change does appear to be irrevocable is in the towns. Mongolia, until the mid-twentieth century, was an almost totally rural, herding nation. Nowadays more than half the working population is in non-pastoral employment. The capital, Ulan Bator, has attracted labour for its booming industrial development. The necessities of a modern urban existence have made many of the older practices and customs redundant. The townsfolk still retain their language, but other symbols of traditional Mongolian life, such as costume, religion and ritual, are either being forgotten or repressed. The townspeople talk with nostalgia about the joys of country life. But the drift from the country to the town is daily increasing, with no immediate sign or prospect of the trend being reversed.

Sporting contests are very popular in Mongolia, with wrestling, archery and horse racing especially keenly pursued.

Though they have lost many important traditions, Mongolia's peasants enjoy a healthier and more prosperous life.

The Kazakhs

To the south-west of the Mongols live a related people, some of whom still live in felt *yurts* and still depend for their survival on a mobile lifestyle. They are the Kazakhs, descended from Turkic and Mongol tribes who have inhabited the Tien Shan mountain regions since before the first century BC. Their homeland is dominated by the peaks of the Tien Shan range which rise majestically to more than 16,000 feet above sea level. Although some grain, fruit, beet, potatoes and cotton can be grown in the valleys and the lowlands, the Kazakhs are traditionally animal herders, using the vast grasslands to raise their sheep, yaks and horses.

Of the approximately eight million Kazakhs living in the Soviet Union and China, only a tiny proportion today retain any vestige of the nomadic life led by their forebears; and this remnant is to be found in Xinjiang on the Chinese side of the border. Although related to the Mongols, the Kazakhs speak a Turkic language that could be understood by a citizen of Istanbul; but, in common with their Mongol cousins, they have had to accept Chinese-style collectivisation, originally modelled on the Soviet type. After the Communist Party took power in 1949, the Kazakhs were forbidden to practise Islam, prevented from owning their herds privately and compelled to witness the abolition of their traditional political hierarchy. Communist China had to make minorities such as the Kazakhs accept the new kind of world that Communists were fighting to create. This was particularly important for the Chinese because about half of the country's land mass is inhabited by some fifty-five minority peoples. In many cases force was used, and some people fled abroad to the Soviet Union, or even as far as Turkey, taking with them as much personal wealth as they could carry. The majority stayed, but were compelled to hand over their possessions to the newly formed collectives.

Today, the Kazakhs have adapted to Communism in a way that many of them believe gives them the best of both worlds. A good example of a Kazakh who inhabits 'two worlds' is Abdur Qair, known as an *Aqsaqal* or 'white beard'. A respected elder, he is a member of the local Communist Party and, like all Chinese Kazakhs, belongs to his local collective organisation.

Before the Revolution, Abdur Qair and his father herded their own sheep, horses and cattle. It was important for them to show off as much of their wealth as they could. The annual family migration meant taking all the goods needed for the six or seven months spent in the spring and summer pasture lands. Yaks, horses and

sometimes camels were loaded with felt tents, carpets, bedding, boxes of utensils, clothes and food. Finery such as embroidered felts and decorative carpets was draped ostentatiously over the animals for all to admire.

Abdur Qair still makes the annual trek from winter to summer pastures, setting up the family tents in a lush wooded valley at an altitude of 10,000 feet. His reasons for choosing this location are strictly practical. 'We live here because there is good pasture. Secondly, water is close. Thirdly, the wind doesn't blow, and fourthly, the sun rises early and sets late.' But since private wealth is no longer officially countenanced, he has to hide his most valuable possessions in the middle of his bulky loads.

In the past the main economic unit was the family, and today Abdur Qair still travels as a member of a family group, even though he is part of the larger, all-embracing collective. His team consists of about a hundred families who share common grazing ground. Four such teams are organised into a brigade of more

than 2,000 people, and three brigades make up the commune.

Abdur Qair still thinks of himself first as a Kazakh and is proud of his heritage, but he has also adapted to the new commune structure. A member of the same East Wind People's Commune who has not adapted so well is his neighbour, Mukai, an individualist who prefers his traditional clothing to the newer Chinese outfits adopted by most of the younger Kazakhs. He is the last member of the commune who still uses eagles to hunt rabbits and foxes, a skill for which the Kazakhs were formerly renowned. 'Instead of doing other work, some Kazakhs still go hunting,' he explains. 'It is a job like any other. But it is very skilled work. I take an eagle and train it to understand human speech. Then it can hunt valuable animals, and earn me money. It is a skill learned from my father and will be passed down to my son.' But few younger Kazakhs wish to take up this particular skill. During the Cultural Revolution, between 1966 and 1977, hunting with eagles, along with other Kazakh customs, was suppressed

Before the Chinese revolution abolished his title, Abdur Qair was a Kazakh chief or Khan. Today, he is a respected elder and member of the collective committee which orders the affairs of the commune.

131

because it represented a form of minority self-expression and private enterprise.

Although Kazakhs may be able to dispense with their eagles, like the Mongols they regard their horses as essential for survival. They call the animals their 'wings' and they learn to ride from childhood. Their proverbs say that a Kazakh prizes only four things – his horse, his gun, his birthplace and his wife – in that order of importance. Horses are treasured for their milk and as a measure of wealth, and, just as of old, because they give the Kazakhs mobility in the mountains, which affords them some independence from the Han Chinese.

In spring, families come together to round up the newborn foals so that the mares can be milked. This is the first stage in preparing *kumis*, the mildly alcoholic fermented mare's milk. Once it is ready for drinking, its first tasting provides everyone with an excuse for family gatherings and parties. A sheep, later to be sacrificed and eaten, is brought into the tent and celebrations begin. 'Powerful Father,' prays one old woman, 'come down from the mountain! Enter the *kumis* bag! Give from the stone! Come into the tent. May the *kumis* spurt out! God is great.' As Muslims, the Kazakhs are not accustomed to any alcohol during the rest of the year, but now the bowls of *kumis* are drained dry, and although the drink is not very strong, everyone rapidly becomes tipsy.

Since families and teams are no longer isolated self-contained units but part of the brigade, this organisation controls many everyday matters. It has an administrative centre, a school, sheep-shearing facilities, storage houses and, most importantly, a shop. In the past, men found it difficult to buy necessities, such as shoes, cloth, teapots or even grain, and it was impossible for women to do so. Nowadays, standing below a sign exhorting commune members to struggle together to improve production, they can buy a wide range of household articles – from kettles to sugar and sweets. The goods have come to the people, who no longer need travel to the towns.

The tribal elders, who once exercised sole authority, now have to accept that all important decisions are made by a committee, which includes a Communist Party Secretary, chosen at commune headquarters, and four other members elected every four or five years. Very few women become committee members, despite recent emancipation, but for the first time many of the younger men now have a say in policy matters. It is hard for the elders to accept the new committee structure. In the past, for example, they would not have allowed their juniors to use the term *yoldas*, meaning 'comrade', as a form of address, since it implied a lack of respect towards them. Today, it is an accepted term of address.

Kazakh communes have devised an elaborate method of paying members. Each individual, whether he attends the herds, patrols the grasslands or serves in a shop, is allotted points on a scale. At the end of the year these points are traded in for goods and animals. The principal commodity produced by the brigades is wool, which is sold to the government. After careful weighing and packing, the wool is sent by lorry to Urumchi, the capital of Xinjiang province. The money earned finances such necessities as an electrical generator or the transport of goods to the capital. It may also be banked to help members survive in harsh winters. In years when herdsmen do exceptionally well and increase the brigade's income above the expected level, some animals are returned to them for private ownership. If output has failed to reach the allotted target, they may have to deplete their private flocks and herds in order to maintain the brigade's income. The brigade committee monitors output and meets regularly to discuss the welfare and progress of the production teams.

The Kazakhs have always been renowned for their wool, which goes to make carpets and high-quality garments sold all over the world. In Urumchi this booming industry is controlled by the Han Chinese who make up almost three-quarters of the local population. Due to the government's present policy of giving the national minorities more autonomy,

and the valuable contribution they make to the economy, the Kazakhs unexpectedly find themselves better protected than members of other nationalities in the lowlands or even the local Han Chinese.

The team committee is also responsible for education. The schooling of Abdur Qair's children and grandchildren is even more dogmatic than in other parts of China. It is utterly divorced from everyday life, and one wonders how much the children can understand or appreciate. What, for example, can they have made of the following history lesson, taught them by Kaziza, Abdur Qair's daughter?

'Chapter Three is called "The Great Friendship",' she announces. 'Marx and Engels were good friends. They studied social science. They led the Proletarian Revolutionary Movement. They wrote the famous Communist Manifesto. Marx was expelled by his reactionary government and lived abroad in exile. His life was very hard and he often had to go to pawn brokers to leave his clothes so he could buy bread . . . Despite his hard life Marx carried on the Revolutionary struggle. Engels supported Marx and helped him.'

To Abdur Qair, however, the importance of this education lies not so much in the contents of the lesson, as in the new

Even in the remote mountain communes, Kazakh children receive education in maths, history and Chinese – though its highly politicised content must often be bewildering.

During China's Cultural Revolution, the Kazakh Islamic religion was banned and all religious objects were ordered to be destroyed. Today, Islam is again permitted, but religious leaders like this old man are rare and few young Kazakhs are learning to take their place.

status it gives his family. 'I have worked for others since I was nine,' he claims. 'I used to have no shoes, so stones cut my feet. They were hard times. Since Liberation my children have all had an education. Because it was Party policy I became a Party member and now my children work for the government. Only one child is now at home. The rest work for the people. Things have changed, as you can see.'

Religion has also undergone radical change. During the Cultural Revolution, when indigenous religions were forcibly discouraged, Korans and other holy books were burned and open prayer was forbidden. Today the people are being encouraged to practice their faith once again. The Kazakhs never had the reputation of being devout Muslims. Some of the older people still pray, but there are very few Mullahs left. Yet it was over Chinese attempts to destroy their religion that some of the bitterest opposition to the government broke out. Kazakhs like Abdur Qair adapted to the new regime, believing that their isolated location would protect them from too many other drastic changes.

It is the alterations to marriage customs that have affected Kazakh society far more than it expected. Kazakh weddings were traditionally arranged by parents. But Kaziza, Abdur Qair's daughter, and her fiancé made their own decision to marry. Her father followed tradition by going to the groom's family for formalised discussions, but the meeting was largely symbolic. Even so, the couple decided not to get married officially until their parents had completed all the ritual meetings to discuss the merits of the match and the characters of the young people.

The women at Kaziza's wedding discussion were forthright in their view that the break with tradition was a good thing. 'We've seen the old and new,' says one old woman. 'Our children live in happier times. In the past, a woman had no choice. She went wherever her mother and father sent her. Most of the girls went unwillingly and were sold in return for horses. In the past we lived with pots and pans, were whipped and couldn't speak out. Today, we women have more equality. When I was twelve years old I was sold

to an old man of fifty-four. He died when he was seventy-four. Nowadays the young can fall in love and everyone is happier.'

The Han of Wuxi

One thousand miles from Xinjiang, in Kiangsu province of south-east China is a commune called Hola. Situated near the city of Wuxi, some seventy miles inland from Shanghai it lies in one of China's most fertile regions. Today the area is also becoming highly industrialised. The members of Hola are Han Chinese, who constitute the overwhelming majority of the Chinese population; the terms Han and Chinese are virtually synonymous. The wedding of a young peasant couple, Chen Liping and Zhu Guozong, both from a Wuxi commune, which *Disappearing World* filmed, contained elements of the traditional life of the Chinese countryside but also hinted at the great changes which are underway in the 1980s. The couple's lavish dowry, worth more than £700, was vivid evidence of the latest stage in China's revolution.

Within a single lifetime, millions of people in China have experienced feudalism and starvation, the brutal Japanese occupation of the 1930s, the arrival of the victorious Communist armies in 1949 and the turmoil of collectivisation during the 1950s. Then, in the 1960s and 1970s, they saw the frenzies and pitched battles of the Cultural Revolution. Today they are living through what may prove to be the most far-reaching changes of all.

On their wedding day, a young peasant couple can look forward to a more prosperous life in China's countryside than their parents.

One of the most senior members of the Hola People's Commune is Mrs Ding. She is a member of the Communist Party and her husband and elder son are commune accountants. Her daughter-in-law works in an electronics factory and her younger son is a university engineering graduate. Throughout their lives, the Ding family have lived in what is now called Big Ding village. It used to be a feudal community of landlords and peasants. Today it is one of ninety-one production teams that make up the commune. More than 400 people live in the village: peasant farmers, factory hands, silkworm cultivators and office workers.

Mr Ding recalls a harder life as a youth in the village in the years before Liberation. 'In the 1930s I must have been only seventeen years old . . . I lived alone with my mother. The rest of the family had died . . . She made a living by raising silkworms. I went to school to study and at that time we suffered. We had no other income at all.'

The 1937 Japanese army occupation of their region left Mr and Mrs Ding with vivid memories. 'When they came,' recalls Mrs Ding, 'the Japanese policy was extermination. They came to China to kill, to burn and to rape the women. I must have

been seventeen. So I hid and father fetched wood. When the Japanese came I ran to hide in the wood-pile. I was shut up inside, hidden by the firewood. For this, the Japanese beat my father. I was afraid. Once a Japanese thrust a bayonet into the pile. It cut off the end of my finger. It was very frightening.'

Peasant families like the Dings were more likely than most to welcome the Communist Revolution. Indeed, Mrs Ding regarded them as liberators. 'At that time they said the Communists were bad. Why? Because they would herd us all in communes. Then it was said if you had any property they would take it away, that two people would share one pair of trousers.' But when, in 1958, the communes were established in the countryside, Mrs Ding joined the Party; she felt that it would liberate her as a woman. She became a commune leader with special responsibility for women's affairs.

She failed to persuade her husband to join the Party too. He argued that one leader in the family was enough. Their son Ding Zhi Hong was more enthusiastic, however. Today he is an accountant in the village's brigade office and an active Party member. In 1966, when he was sixteen, he became one of Chairman Mao's Red Guards. Teenagers like himself, consumed by ideological fervour, left school and travelled all over the country, dedicated to creating a new revolution and to overthrowing old Party members like his mother.

The Cultural Revolution brought profound confusion to the Ding household. Unlike her son, Mrs Ding was critical of Mao and the growing unemployment caused by his new policy, but for ten years she dared not voice her opinions except within the family. There also she came up against the objections of her husband. 'Mr Ding and I had a big argument,' she remembers. 'Old Ding said, "This is good." I said, "It can't be good." He said, "How do you know? Mao said the Cultural Revolution had many merits and the losses were small." I said, "Factories stop work, workers are idle. Is this small? Mao must be a bit muddle-headed."' When Mrs Ding tried to speak out at a team meeting, she encountered more hostility. She was accused of getting old and senile. Frightened when other members of the team got angry with her for insulting Mao, she decided to keep quiet.

The Ding family today are living through another revolution, the 'Responsibility System'. In effect the commune structure, the mainstay of millions of rural Chinese, is being dismantled. Under the slogan of 'The Four Modernisations', the new system emphasises individual enterprise and aims to encourage material wealth. The words of a song young girls in the commune sang to celebrate China's National Day in 1982 reflects the new wave of materialism that has swept across the country:

'The granary is full, the grain shines like gold.
The rivers teem with geese, each one like a cloud.
The Party's policy is better than dewdrops.
Work makes us rich and everyone is happy.
The new system composes a new melody.
We will climb to the peak of happiness step by step.'

The 'Responsibility System' has transformed the patterns of the countryside. Fields in the commune are now divided into strips, each worked by a single peasant or household. The more the peasant produces, the more he or she earns. Material incentives have replaced moral pressures or physical coercion. This is the new face of China's countryside. A brief experiment with a similar policy some twenty years ago was violently opposed by Chairman Mao, who was convinced it would lead to inequality and divisiveness. But today's commune leaders, like Mrs Ding, do not accept that a new gulf might develop between rich and poor. The communes now have their own street markets. Once they have provided their quota for the state, the peasants are permitted to sell their surplus produce for cash, another major shift from Maoist policies towards private enterprise. The dilemma faced by the government is how to preserve the cooperative basis of the Revolution and keep together a billion people, while still encouraging individualism and the pursuit of prosperity.

One of the ingredients of success is to permit commune members a say in resolving their own disputes. Cases are no longer referred to officials and a court system, but discussed by a team of mediators from the commune. Mrs Ding spends much of her time on disputes. 'I have experimented with my own family,' she explains, 'and it's made me more effective in my work.' Her 'experiments' consisted of goading her husband into believing bad things of his mother and then pointing out how gullible he was.

Mrs Ding has strong views about the role of women in commune affairs.

The recently introduced 'Responsibility System' in China's countryside emphasises material incentives; the more the peasants produce on their individual strips, the more they earn.

A commune fishing team harvests a man-made fishpond. The government's dilemma is how to preserve the cooperative basis of the Revolution while encouraging individual effort.

'Women relied on husbands to live,' she points out. 'Husbands would come home with some money, but women just stayed in and cared for the children. Men said, "You'll get money, stay at home, light stoves, watch the babies", so women's brains died.' She believes that women now play an effective part in the everyday affairs of the commune. There is of course a price to pay. Mr Ding does not consider that her mediating duties should interfere with her responsibilities as a wife and mother. But the cases take up her evenings and often continue into the night. 'There was one occasion,' Mrs Ding recalls, 'when I mediated a conflict until one in the morning. Old Mr Ding was really furious, saying "You're better than the Party Secretary now, and your work has become more vital than his." He was being sarcastic with me. I got very angry so I started to argue with him, but my son said, "You're home, so let's forget it."'

Right across China the commune structure is undergoing rapid change, and the Hola commune is one of those most affected by reason of its location in the affluent south-east. Mrs Ding is convinced that, despite many difficulties, these changes are for the better. Other communes in other regions are experiencing a harder struggle for prosperity than the Hola commune, but the desire for the new values is shared by millions. Young office workers echo the general feeling in this song:

'We exchange our chickens for a tape recorder,
We exchange our chickens for a TV,
We exchange our chickens for a camera,
We exchange our chickens for a washing machine.
A recorder, a TV, a camera and a washing machine.
Don't you think this is wonderful?'

ORDER, ORDER, ORDER

MURSI, PUSHTUNS, SHILLUK, KIRGHIZ

The spectacle of a Prime Minster hurling invective at a heated group of senior politicians and listening politely in turn while opposing ideas and insults are thrown back has become an accepted part of everyday political life in many countries. It is difficult to imagine what a New Guinea highlander or an Amazonian Indian seated in the Visitors' Gallery of the British Parliament would make of this eccentric version of democracy.

When *Disappearing World* reverses the process in order to look at the way tribal societies handle *their* politics, we employ a secret code-breaker – an anthropologist – who can make sense of the seemingly bizarre goings-on in remote places. The abiding feature of our investigations into other peoples' ways of life is how essentially recognisable many of their institutions are; behind the elaborate rituals are practical and effective mechanisms to ensure that society runs smoothly. Debate in the Ethiopian bush is really no more strange as a political process than Western parliamentary rituals.

But most of us continue to think in terms of 'them' and 'us'. The colonial stereotype of tribal organisation, taken from the pages of *King Solomon's Mines*, depicts an African chief wielding autocratic power over his compliant subjects, maintaining his authority by physical force. Alternatively, tribal society is seen to have no organisation at all – merely a collection of 'savages' living in a state of wild anarchy.

The more information anthropologists have gathered about organisation of societies, the cruder such stereotypes have appeared to be. They now know them to be quite invalid. But assembling data behind the walls of universities is one thing; communicating such facts to the general public is another. Notions which have been exploded and are today wholly unacceptable to anthropologists still get an airing outside the discipline, often reinforced by images from feature films of the *Tarzan* genre.

When order in a society appears to be maintained by unfamiliar rituals, it is easy to dismiss that society as irrational. Even if that were true, the words of the American anthropologist Clyde Kluckhohn should give pause for thought. 'The fate of our western civilisation and perhaps of civilisation in general may hang upon humanity's gaining some orderly and systematic insight into the non-rational and irrational factors in human behaviour.' But in fact, field-workers have been showing more and more the opposite: that apparently non-rational and irrational behaviour is, set in its proper social context, logical, rational and effective.

The Mursi

The Mursi, a people living in the far south-west of Ethiopia (first discussed in Chapter Three) have no chiefs, no elected officials and no obvious political institutions. How they could survive without any visible political organisation, was a puzzle that much intrigued David Turton from the beginning of his field-work in 1968.

Young men are not allowed to take part in Mursi debates, but they are expected to listen and learn from their elders (right).

Among the leaderless Mursi, debating in groups is a way of ordering their lives; they make decisions about their problems, hand on news and pass down traditions.

Turton from the start noticed that the Mursi men spent an inordinate amount of time in group discussions. Gathered under a shade tree, they would listen intently while an orderly succession of speakers paced up and down, debating with controlled passion. Fascinated by these proceedings, Turton felt that once he had mastered the language, he would get some of the answers he sought to his questions. But much to his frustration, he then discovered that speakers used a special language in their debates, a variation of everyday speech, but more complex than it. For Turton it was rather like learning the English language so as to study the British parliamentary system, and then discovering that its debates were conducted in Elizabethan English.

Eventually Turton became fluent enough to understand the debates of the Mursi, and came to appreciate what an integral role they played in the ordering of their lives. As he comments: 'For the Mursi, debating is not something you do only when there is a particular problem. It's something which should be going on all the time. You might even say that a community which debates together, stays together.' Turton recognised that the debates were not only a means of making decisions but also of communicating news; additionally they provided a way for the elders of the society to pass down oral traditions. Although there was no chairman and no rules of procedure, speakers were expected to be brief and to keep to the point.

The mechanism of public debating, Turton believed, could present a film-maker with an interesting perspective on Mursi society. 'My main thought, however, was that I would get a visual record of meetings, in which the non-verbal behaviour of speakers was likely to be not much less important than what they actually said. I saw it as an effort to present the Mursi as understandable human beings to the television audience. I wanted the audience to say, "That's like us".'

The device that director Leslie Wood-head adopted, of following the process of decision-making by filming a series of debates, was a courageous choice. It's not often that a Western television audience is offered a film that consists mostly of tall, naked tribesmen pacing up and down in the bush, gesticulating with spears and arguing about cattle. Yet the debates were dramatic, and through them the tensions and problems of everyday life were vividly revealed.

In June 1974, when filming began, the Mursi were at war with their northern neighbours, the Bodi. This meant that their all-important cattle were vulnerable

Although there are no rules and no chairmen, speakers in Mursi debates are heard in silence in an orderly succession of speeches (above).

The ceremony of 'Spearing the Priest' strengthened the Mursi at a time of war with a neighbouring people.

141

to attack and needed protection. The Mursi were facing a dilemma; should they hide their animals in the south as far away as possible from the enemy or should they keep them in the north, near their crops, where they could defend them more effectively? In a society with leaders, that kind of decision would be made by a hierarchy; among the Mursi it is arrived at by debate, a kind of bush democracy, but involving only men past their twenties, and no women.

A Mursi debate at a time of crisis. Even if a man is not ferocious in battle or rich in cattle, skill as an orator gives him great status.

The Mursi Priest is a focus for the community.

In the summer of 1974 a debate took place after a Bodi raiding party had stealthily slipped past Mursi men in the north and found cattle in the south guarded only by herd boys. They had killed two of the boys and returned to their own territory. Following this shooting, Mursi men gathered beneath a tree. 'Here we are debating,' said a man called Ngokolu. 'Some people want to leave the cows down south. They say, "If the cows had been up here, the Bodi would have got them long ago." That's what people are saying. If we had built proper compounds down south and all of us had watched over our cattle, there's no way the Bodi could have got us. As it is they've killed our children – young children – in their sleep. This area round here is hard to defend. The bush is so thick it gives the enemy good cover. Let's go and debate with the people in the south and build compounds.'

His advice was scornfully rejected by the next two speakers. The first, Komoro-kibo, said: 'Your words are empty. You don't know the Bodi. But I have lived with them . . . They don't think like us. I know the way their minds work. If they're going to attack us, they will have built a more secure settlement with stakes. Once their women are safe inside it after harvesting, then they'll attack our women. How can you be so short-sighted? They're about to attack us now. I know how the Bodi think. This is what you should say: "Let's bring the cattle up here." There's plenty of water here at Moizoi.'

The next speaker was Charlongtonga: 'Those were the words I wanted to hear. Let them come and attack us in our homesteads. Let us drive the cattle close to here. Who said this country is hard to defend? When this bush is trodden by the cows, won't these clearings open up like a plain? Let us go now and sleep. I've heard all I wanted. Do as the last speaker said.'

For the Mursi, Turton points out, the resolution of a debate has nothing in common with the parliamentary process. 'There is no voting, because they have time to go on talking until some kind of consensus emerges, time to go on so that they can avoid the split which inevitably takes place the minute you ask people to raise their hands.'

Although they have no chiefs, the Mursi do invest one individual with ritual and symbolic significance, like a kind of priest. He has the role of mediator – what Turton calls a 'permanent conductor of absolute power'. He explains: 'The priest is the means by which the community can plug itself into supernatural power. He's a symbolic head, a focus around which the community can unite.' Although he has no authority over his fellow men, at the end of the debate he summarises the argument and reflects the general feeling. In the debate about whether or not to move the cattle, having gauged the prevailing sentiment of the gathering, the priest said that talks should continue with other people in the south so that an even wider consensus could be reached. 'Let's go to the south and make compounds and debate with the people down there,' he tells the men. 'If we decide that we should all come together, then let the cattle sleep in one place. That's what I have to say. Tomorrow, let's look for a safe place for the cows and make compounds.'

With their cattle safely installed in the new compounds, there was more debating. Men from the north of Mursi country were accused of leaving the cattle in the south without adequate protection, abandoning them to the mercy of the Bodi who were able to sneak up and kill the herd boys. A celebrated veteran called Mitatu mounted the most scathing attack. As a *jalabai*, an influential man, Mitatu was listened to with special attention. Such a man need not be particularly rich in cattle or ferocious in war, but when he speaks, people say 'his words stick'. So for the Mursi, skill as an orator can give a man something of the status of a leader. Mitatu continues the attack on the young men who in the opinion of certain elders, have not defended the society well. 'Have I not looked after you? I've told you about war, and how you should defend the elders. Do you hear me? You who have left the cows with children. What's wrong with our people? What's wrong?'

Again, the priest summarises the new consensus. 'Boys have died. If we had stayed together, it might have been all right. As it is, we're scattered, and the Bodi slip through unnoticed. Calm down, Mitatu. Don't point your finger so much. They have done wrong. But leave off now.'

The outcome of a Mursi debate is seldom a surprise to its participants. Its real function is to mobilise action and gather maximum public support for an already understood policy. 'This is done,' Turton suggests, 'by connecting some proposal with an ultimate Mursi value which can't be publicly contradicted.'

Such reliance on group discussion to help maintain order in society is not, of course, unique to the Mursi. The political structure of the ancient Greeks is perhaps the most celebrated example of a system based upon decision sharing. Western-style democracies pride themselves on offering each citizen a voice in political decision making; but it is often hard to determine whether that voice is really significant in affecting government policy, as it is with the Mursi.

The Pushtun tribesmen who live in the mountainous areas of eastern Afghanistan and western Pakistan have fiercely defended their code of living for centuries.

The Pushtuns

On the borders of Afghanistan and Pakistan lies the homeland of the Pushtuns, who are better known to the West as the Pathans – twelve million people living across one of the great trading routes of Asia. Apart from a warrior tradition, they appear to have little in common with the small tribal community of the Mursi. Yet their social organisation relies upon a similar kind of group discussion, and the ability to speak fluently and persuasively is greatly valued.

This enormous tribal confederation has somehow maintained its cohesion and identity over many centuries, exhibiting a strength and unity of purpose against powerful invaders throughout history, including the Greeks under Alexander the Great and, in the last 150 years, the British and the Russians.

The political organisation of the Pushtuns has long been a puzzle to anthropologists: so in 1979 *Disappearing World* explored how political decisions were made and how the Pushtuns had managed

to survive in the face of overwhelming military odds.

The whole venture presented special problems because the Pushtuns are an orthodox Islamic society with a suspicion of film rooted in their prohibition of graven idols and images. They also adhere strictly to purdah, whereby women from puberty to old age are secluded from the sight of men other than close relatives, which obviously meant that foreign males wielding cameras would be anathema. Furthermore, the tensions created by continuing political upheavals ruled out easy access to tribal villages, whether in Afghanistan or in Pakistan.

Fortunately the Pakistani anthropologist Akbar Ahmed was able to provide unique facilities and information. His knowledge of Pushtun society stemmed from a long-standing and intimate association. He was also a government administrator of the tribal regions and could thus combine his role as a political liaison agent between the tribe and state with his academic interests – following a tradition from the nineteenth century established by the British in that part of what is now

western Pakistan.

There are no leaders or chiefs with real political authority among the Pushtuns. Certain individuals achieve a measure of influence by virtue of their fighting prowess, wisdom, debating skills or adherence to a tribal code of honour, but their authority tends to be transient, stripped away as readily as it is granted. If this suggests that Pushtun society is unstructured and anarchic, the evidence of the *Disappearing World* film suggests the opposite; it is in fact highly elaborate and rigidly organised.

The actual subjects of our film were the Mohmands, a Pushtun tribe living in Pakistan along the mountain frontier with Afghanistan, who have a long reputation for bitter and successful warfare against neighbouring tribes and against the British. Their history as told through their oral tradition is rather inaccurate, but they speak of it with great pride. 'I am neither educated, nor do I have much knowledge,' confesses Shams-ud Din, a Mohmand elder in the film, 'but I have heard our leaders saying that the Pushtuns come from Arabia. There was a companion of the Holy Prophet, peace be upon him,

One of the important features of Pushtun tribal life is their rigid devotion to Islam.

who used to speak Pashto. He was a prominent person and a valiant warrior. We are his descendants and we have inherited his characteristics. We have the same sword, the same hand and the same technique of war.' Their reputation for aggression has come to be enshrined in a particular code of behaviour called *pukhtunwali* (literally 'the way of the Pushtun'), whereby a man is duty-bound to defend his honour, if necessary, to the death. That honour means protecting his women, providing hospitality, and defending and observing the rules of Islam. 'When there is a question of honour,' Shams-ud Din claims, 'a Pushtun sacrifices everything, including his money and his head, to defend it. If we have a friend, guest or relative, we must not allow anyone to disgrace him. That is *pukhtunwali*.'

The mechanism that makes the code work and prevents Pushtun tribes from being constantly at war with one another is complex. One of its main features is a kind of democratic court known as the *jirga*, relying on an individual's power of speech to stir society into concerted action.

The men in each Pushtun community gather regularly to discuss and resolve local problems. If they are village matters, only men from that village take part; if the problems are more serious, relating to the whole region or tribe, representatives from the entire area attend. *Jirgas* in Afghanistan would formerly be held even at a national level, with delegates from tribes across the country. But, whether the conference is large or small, the mechanism operates in the same way.

The particular incident in our film concerned a young Mohmand of Kado village, Haji Gul, accused by his father of not respecting his seniority and of not giving him enough support. The older men of the village sit down in a semicircle on the ground and discuss the case informally until the plaintiff Selim, a stooped and elderly man, arrives. Holding out their hands in a position of supplication, they first call out in unison: 'May God give us strength to be just.' Passing their hands down over their faces and beards, they then request Selim to sit before them so that he can put his case. Shams-ud Din begins by questioning the plaintiff as to why he spends so much time arguing with his son. Selim replies that it is a matter of honour for a son to support his ageing father and that, since his own son is known to be wealthy as a result of his labour abroad, it is only just that he should give him as much as 2,000 rupees. Selim claims he needs the money from his father to live in what he considers to be decent comfort.

It is clear from the expressions on the elders' faces that they have little sympathy for Selim and do not regard him as a man who has been much wronged. The reason, it transpires, is that Selim has a deserved reputation as the most cantankerous pest in the village. So they dismiss him and summon his son, Haji Gul. He seems to have come to the *jirga* reluctantly, wearing an air of belligerence. Nevertheless he listens politely as Shams-ud Din again opens the questioning. 'Why,' he asks, 'are you refusing to give your father 2,000 rupees?' 'I have no bad conscience about this,' is Haji Gul's reply. 'I discharge my duty. But my father is a greedy man and has always been a nuisance. He continually demands more money from me and I keep on giving it to him.'

The elders eventually go into private session, fiercely arguing the case to and fro. Several support Selim, wishing the respect due to fathers to be openly recognised. Others have more sympathy for the son, considering the old man's demands unreasonable. They resolve the matter by fining the son and insisting on a public reconciliation with his father. Both are summoned again before the elders. 'The tribe has called a *jirga* to settle your dispute,' they are told. 'The *jirga's* decision is a just one and follows Islamic principles. So, Haji Gul, you will pay your father 1,000 rupees; and you, Selim, will accept the 1,000 rupees and not demand more. The *jirga* will not listen to another demand and will impose a fine of 10,000 rupees if either of you refuses to accept these findings. You must now embrace and accept our decision. And you, Haji Gul, must kiss your father on his beard.' A local religious dignitary, Mian Zarif, then places one large hand on Selim's shoulder and the other on Haji Gul's, and propels the two men together. Everyone bursts out laughing as an obviously reluctant son clasps his father and stoops to kiss his

beard. Following this stage-managed reconciliation, a brief prayer is said and the *jirga* ends.

This incident was not a matter of life and death, but it demonstrated how the system works. In an earlier and more serious case, the same group of elders had discussed whether to punish a woman accused by her husband of infidelity. Had there been supporting evidence, the elders would have had the authority to sentence the woman to death by stoning. Such a decision requires all the members of a village to participate in the execution so that death cannot be attributed to any individual and revenge cannot be taken by a relative of the dead person. In this instance the evidence was weak and the *jirga* recommended divorce instead.

These decisions are respected, though the village has no police force, and to defy the collective wisdom of the elders is to become an outcast. All such decisions are taken after public debate, whether it is a question of supporting an aged parent or of declaring war against the Russians.

The most common disputes in Pushtun territory are over land, women and money. Tribal passion to retain their homeland contributes greatly to the bitterness of what is happening in Afghanistan today. An often-told Pushtun fable puts it well. An elder who owned many fertile acres of land lay dying. As the old man's last breath

A gun with which to defend his honour is the most important possession for any self-respecting Pushtun male (far above). The Pushtun tribes are remarkably democratic.

147

drew near, the Angel of Death appeared, carrying a book in which were listed the names of all those entitled to enter Paradise. 'Tell me your name,' commanded the Angel, 'and I will consult my book.' 'I have been expecting you,' responded the elder: 'Tell me, Holy One, is there any good land I can buy in Paradise?' The Angel repeated his question. 'Of course,' the old Mohmand continued, 'if there is no good land in Paradise I could always buy some poor land and improve it.' Again the Angel asked him for his name. 'Or I would be happy to rent some good land,' suggested the elder. 'Your name!' demanded the irritated Angel. 'I could even reconcile myself to renting some bad land.' *'Your name!'* Finally, with his dying breath, the old Mohmand begged: 'Oh Holy One, if you have nothing else, you must surely have a little land I could sharecrop!'

The Shilluk

The Shilluk of the southern Sudan appear much less openly democratic than either the Mursi or the Pushtuns. Indeed, on first acquaintance they seem to possess all the trappings expected of a 'chief's' society. But the manner in which tribal chiefs achieve and maintain their authority is often far more complex than early notions and observations suggested. So it is with the Shilluk. They have a king, with armed retainers. He has divine powers and apparently unassailable authority. But in reality the 'divine' monarchy of the Shilluk tribe is as constrained and ceremonial as that of present-day Britain.

The 150,000 Shilluk are cattle herders who supplement this activity by cultivating maize and sorghum, irrigating their land with water from the River Nile along whose banks they live. They have been extensively studied by anthropologists because they are accessible. In *The Golden*

The raised village of Pacodo is the residence for the Shilluk king in the Southern Sudan (below).

Before the king or *Reth* is installed, the spirit of the founding king of the tribe is taken in the form of ostrich feathers from village to village throughout Shilluk land (right).

148

Bough, which was first published in 1890, Sir James Frazer used the Shilluk as an example of a society whose existence depended on the well-being of its divine rulers. Thereafter, intrigued by the tales of kings who were ritually killed when their health failed, came scholars intent on research. Among them was Sir Edward Evans-Pritchard, whose studies of the Nuer were even then changing the way anthropologists looked at tribal politics.

In 1975 the Shilluk king, known as the *Reth*, had died, and a new monarch, the thirty-third in succession from the founder of the tribe, was about to be installed. Assisted in the Sudan by Walter Kunijwok, a Shilluk studying his own people, and in England by Paul Howell, an ex-district officer and anthropologist who had published widely on the Shilluk, we tried to unravel the complexities of Shilluk kingship.

Shilluk warriors parade in front of their new king.

Not everyone conducts royal business with the precision and urgency of a Western coronation. Any expectation that the installation ceremony would be as meticulously planned and organised as that of Queen Elizabeth II proved wildly misconceived. After selecting a date, the Shilluk changed their minds and waited for a more auspicious occasion. When the ceremonial process did eventually begin, we certainly got our unique opportunity to witness the making of a king; but he was a monarch that our nineteenth-century colonial forebears or H. Rider Haggard would probably have found unrecognisable.

It was soon apparent that Ayang Anei Kur, the rotund young man about to ascend the throne as the thirty-third *Reth*, would not wield genuine authority over his subjects. Real power was deemed to vest in the spiritual presence of the original founder king, Nyikang. When a Shilluk *Reth* dies, the spirit of Nyikang is believed to flee to the River Nile. It will only reappear when its effigy, made from bamboo and ostrich feathers, is constructed. This, together with an effigy of Nyikang's son, Dak, is then paraded the length of Shilluk land, from village to

village, following the same journey that Nyikang himself is thought to have made in the sixteenth century when he founded the tribe.

As the effigies pass, people flock to pay homage to the founders of their nation, and in every village a shrine is prepared to receive them. Nyikang's effigy rests within the shrine, while Dak's dances outside. The journey takes ten days and eventually reaches the royal capital at the village of Pacodo. Only then can the ceremony of transferring the spirit of Nyikang into the king-elect take place. The period of interregnum is a time of particular tension and danger, for until the spirit of the tribe's founder enters the chosen king at the end of the lengthy sequence of ceremonies, the Shilluk say that 'the world is lost'.

Paul Howell explains: 'Each event in this procedure is a further step towards the transference of the soul of Nyikang from the dead king to his successor, which has always been an essential feature of the Shilluk monarchy. Each stage in the burial and installation ceremonies is another crisis passed, for until the substitution has been made, the Shilluk people are in a condition of extreme spiritual danger as

151

Although it is a long time since the Shilluk fought a war with spears and shields, they demonstrate their fierceness at ritual occasions.

well as of actual political danger; at any time civil war may break out over the choice of the new king.'

During the last two days of the royal installation ceremony in Pacodo, clues to the source of the king's power become clearer. The penultimate day is marked by a ritual battle, a pageant involving people from every region. The northern Shilluk form an army, which is led by the effigies of Nyikang and Dak; the southern Shilluk form an opposing one, led by the king-elect. The two sides, armed with maize stalks instead of spears, attack each other. The battle has a predetermined outcome, for the effigy of Nyikang always captures the king-elect; the office of king is more powerful than the person who occupies it. The spirit of Nyikang now passes into the new king and Nyikang's effigy disappears into the shrine of the royal village.

At this point, the general tension subsides. To complete the ceremonies, the Shilluk chiefs from each village take turns to give short speeches of advice as to how the new ruler should behave. It is their last opportunity for such frankness; from there on they have no power to depose him. He now possesses the divine authority of Nyikang and to oppose him would be to oppose their founder.

One venerable chief urges Ayang Anei Kur to follow the example of his great

The installation of a new king is accompanied by different ritual dances and celebrations.

The finale of the installation of the Shilluk *Reth* is when the village chiefs take turns to advise their new king how he should behave in the future.

153

grandfather, Nyidhok, 'a man of peace, upright and honourable'. A second speaker advises the king to cooperate with the tribal representatives. 'When they pull you, go with them,' he recommends. 'And then – when you pull, they will follow.' A third points out that the young *Reth* will need support from all sides. 'You have ascended the throne in your youth; you are not well known in the south nor in other parts. No person is loved by everybody. One must find friends from all over the land. Take one from here. Take another from there. Spread your net wide. Then no one will question you.'

Finally, the *Reth* himself addresses his subjects; 'My people . . . I have understood all that you said. It was inspiring . . . My dear countrymen, everyone can see what's happening. You without education – your interests come first . . . You're not responsible for the country's unrest. But those others are trouble-makers and I will get them . . . To me they're expendable like the devils whom God casts into eternal fire. Those are my words.'

Ayang Anei is alluding to those Shilluk ministers and high officials in the Sudanese government who, in line with national policy, promise the country more development, education and democracy. In his speech he threatens to stamp out the purveyors of modern ideas which challenge his traditional authority; he is fully aware that modernisation must inevitably lead to the decline of his own power and prestige.

The *Reth* is, in fact, in a difficult situation. He has been imbued with the spirit of Nyikang, thus sanctifying his position, which he retains until his death. In effect, however, his practical power is limited. Shilluk chiefs control the villages that they have inherited from their fathers. Other Shilluk can gain political authority only by working for the central government. The king's power lies mainly in his role as a judicial intermediary in cases of dispute.

He also represents his tribe to the outside world. In the past he would have gained respect and prestige by leading his tribe in war against other tribes; today the Sudanese government has formalised his position in Sudanese society by appointing him a second-class magistrate. He has exchanged limited political power for a more symbolic role as a focus of tribal identity. In the face of the rapid changes that the Sudanese government is trying to impose on its tribal citizens, that role may yet prove invaluable to the Shilluk in maintaining themselves as a tribal entity.

The Kirghiz

The Kirghiz of Central Asia are one of the most isolated societies visited by *Disappearing World*. In 1975, 3,000 of them were living on a high plateau in northwestern Afghanistan. They were under the leadership of one man: their Khan, Rahman Qul. But rather than being a purely symbolic leader, he is a cross between patriarch, high court judge and managing director. His role is akin to that

of his ancestors going back to the first century AD, when the earliest of many Turkic and Mongol tribes swept across the steppes of Asia, to be followed later by Genghis Khan and Timur Lang (Tamberlane). The Kirghiz are one of the tribes defeated by the Mongols who then intermarried with them. The Khan of the Kirghiz was not traditionally a guaranteed hereditary position, nor was he invested with any spiritual force. As Nazif Sharani, the anthropologist who accompanied the *Disappearing World* team, explains: 'The qualities necessary for the candidate of the office of Khan entail bravery, military prowess, honesty, abilities in public persuasion and oratory, sound judgement, being a good Muslim, and success as a herdsman with a large flock and wealth in other tangible goods.'

It took the film crew ten days on horses and yaks to reach the home of the Kirghiz in a bizarre corridor of land created at the end of the nineteenth century as a buffer between the empires of Russia to the north and British India to the south. It looks like

Trapped between the borders of China, the USSR and Pakistan, up to 1979 a group of Kirghiz herders still lived in felt tents like their ancestors.

The chief or Khan of the Afghan Kirghiz is Rahman Qul (above).

Although the Kirghiz are Muslims, they do not require their womenfolk to be veiled or live in seclusion.

months that the summer lasted, and then, before winter closed in, bring them back down again to the warmer valleys of Russia and China. But as the grip of the revolution tightened in those valleys, a group of Kirghiz was forced to flee their settlement in search of their old independence in the mountains of Afghanistan. They soon discovered that they could move only a few miles back and forth across the width of their valley, and were powerless to escape the nine-month winter. With temperatures below freezing for months on end, and up to 70 or 80 degrees of frost on bad nights, milk would dry up and the people would have to melt snow for water. Although they were no longer nomads in the true sense, they retained most of their traditions and followed a pattern of life similar to that of their forebears. They continued to live in circular felt *yurts* and survived off their yaks, sheep, horses and goats; other essential food they had to import from traders who journeyed to the camps from the Afghan lowlands.

In 1975 Rahman Qul wielded almost total judicial, political and economic power over his people. He had not been

a sore thumb, and so it has proved. The Kirghiz living there in 1975 had been trapped in this spot by the rigid boundary policies imposed by the Soviet Union and subsequently by China.

Until the revolutions in those two countries in 1917 and 1949, some two million Kirghiz had roamed the steppes, living off their flocks and trading in grain. A few of them – about thirty households – used to drive their animals up into the high mountains of Afghanistan for the two or three elected by them, nor had he usurped the position of chief. Like previous Khans, he had simply emerged as the obvious candidate. He saw himself as a father figure, doing his best to preserve Muslim traditions; a man who had helped save his people from the fundamental changes Communism was bringing to the two million Kirghiz still living across the borders a few miles away. 'We are imprisoned here,' he explains in the film. 'In winter, it's hard to get in or out of here.

Up until forty years ago, we could cross into Russia. Up to twenty-six years ago, we could cross into China. Before the borders closed, traders travelled between China and Afghanistan, and we could get almost anything. Now no one comes over to this side.'

Much of his power was based on his custom of 'lending' animals to Kirghiz families to breed, thus providing them with milk, wool and fuel. He explains how by shrewd economics and wise investment

Apart from the milk and meat that their animals supplied, all basic foods had to be imported many miles through the high mountains.

The harsh climate and lack of medical facilities meant that the Kirghiz had a very high rate of infant mortality. Surviving children were therefore a particular blessing.

to look after. For the past twenty to thirty years I have owned many animals.' In fact, Rahman Qul's lending system produced herds totalling some 25,000 animals, upon which a large proportion of the Kirghiz survived. Apart from the authority this gave him, it also brought him a considerable annual income.

Although there was little scope for democracy high up in the Pamirs of Afghanistan, most of his followers regarded him as a leader working for their interests. 'I think the Khan's power is good,' comments one shepherd. 'We think first of God and second of the Khan. God has given us the Khan's livestock. If we need any help the Khan helps us. He wants us to be well and to stay well. He tells us to try hard to look after the sheep and yaks and to collect fuel. He tells us not to be lazy, not to sleep too much.' Other herdsmen were less flattering. 'If one man has many and the others have none – is that good? I don't think so. If you are poor, then you are seen as bad; as a thief, corrupt and lazy. If you're poor, you have to be patient and just keep living.'

The Khan expressed fears in 1975 that the Russians would push him out of his homeland. In 1979 things did change dramatically for Rahman Qul and the Kirghiz. After a few skirmishes with the Russians when they sent forces into Afghanistan, the Kirghiz fled and became refugees. The Khan was able to conduct his people to safety in Pakistan and keep them together only because of the economic and political controls he had over them. From his Pakistani refuge he told us: 'The Russians are our enemies, but our case was hopeless. They would have crushed us very soon had we stayed. So now we have to learn to adapt.' The Khan lost his animals when fleeing to Pakistan and so the basis for his authority was weakened. But he was seen as his people's representative and began negotiating on their behalf to try to find a new and permanent home for them. After rejecting the possibility of moving to Alaska, Rahman Qul was finally successful. In 1982 the Kirghiz moved once again, to a new life in eastern Turkey. According to recent reports, he is still investing shrewdly and fast regaining the influence he exerted in the Pamirs.

he had built up his wealth and authority: 'When I started off, I had very few animals. My father owned about 2,000 animals but most of them died in the snow and blizzards. He gave me about 200 and I increased them. In 1941 the Russians raided here and took away all my animals. Once again I started from scratch with only about twenty animals. I looked after them well for many years, until little by little my herd increased. When I had enough, I gave some to one or two families

Rahman Qul's authority over the Kirghiz is based on his character and also his ownership of many of the animals.

6

GAINING CONTROL
KAWELKA, DERVISHES, KWEGU, MASAI

Whatever the political structure of a society – tribal democracy, divine kingship or feudal autocracy – it is clear from the examples of the Mursi, the Shilluk, the Kirghiz and the Pushtun (discussed in Chapter 5), that the maintenance of order is complex. It may or may not involve force, whether explicit or implied.

A. R. Radcliffe-Brown, one of the founding fathers of British social anthropology, recognised this when he described the political organisation of a society as 'that aspect of the total organisation which is concerned with the control and regulation of the use of physical force'. But it has proved difficult to divide the many societies observed by *Disappearing World*, according to whether they sanction the use of force or not. In only one of the instances described below, that of the Kwegu, is the question clearly answerable. Other societies involve a measure of coercion, along with alternative means. The 'big-man' of the Kawelka in Papua

New Guinea battles for power by distributing wealth; the leader of the Kurdish dervishes inherits his power, but only keeps it by exploiting his religious status; and among the Kenyan Masai, power is gained only by individuals progressing through a series of age-grades. In the case of the Kwegu, the power lies elsewhere; it depends upon the patronage of their more powerful neighbours, the Mursi, who are in a position to employ force, or at least threaten to so do, in order to perpetuate the relationship.

The Kawelka

The Kawelka, in the highlands of Papua New Guinea, have no appointed leader. The individual who comes closest to being a chief or leader is the 'big-man' who can influence others through his speech-making. He is, according to the anthropologist Andrew Strathern, 'exuberant yet dignified, boastful yet cautious, bold but canny, innovative and conservative at the same time'. One way for a Kawelka to become a 'big-man' is to hold a lavish gift-giving or party – a *moka*.

A party in the West is an occasion when guests can have a good time. The host can also derive social and economic benefits from it – he can be 'noticed' and make useful contacts among the guests. He can also show off his wealth. The more lavish the celebration, the more people feel obligated to the host. So it is with a 'big-man' of the Kawelka, but in comparison with such occasions in the West, the Kawelka *moka* is of far greater significance for the host.

In the course of following the events leading up to a particularly important *moka* in 1974, we were introduced to one of the most endearing characters in *Disappearing World* – Ongka. *The Kawelka: Ongka's Big Moka* followed his attempts to prepare for the great event and demonstrated its overwhelming importance in the Kawelka community as a source of authority and influence.

We were not seeing Ongka's first *moka*. 'On ceremonial ground after ceremonial ground I have done this,' he explains to Andrew Strathern. 'On these occasions I wore special decorations – the big plaque of multicoloured feathers set on a backing, and the pale blue crest feathers

of the King of Saxony bird. I made these *moka* gifts along with the men of my own clan, the Mandembo, at different times in different years. Sometimes we did the dance in which we bend our knees and make our long aprons sway out in front of us; sometimes we did the stamping dance in which we move round the ceremonial ground in a procession. We did all this many times, until it was all completed, and I was tired of it.' Ongka was by then already a 'big-man'; but the *moka* he was preparing for was to be the biggest and unquestionably the most important of his life.

He had two main motives for it. First, one of his fellow clansmen, Parua, a

The Kawelka have no leaders, but 'big men' can influence others through speech-making.

161

An important ingredient in a Kawelka *moka* is the gift of several hundred pigs.

member of the National House of Assembly, was a man of influence outside Ongka's region. By giving a particularly lavish and generous *moka* for Parua, Ongka knew that he would gain prestige and that Parua would be publicly obligated to him. Secondly, he was aware that changes sweeping across New Guinea and his own region, following the arrival of the Europeans in 1933, were eroding many Kawelka customs and traditions. He wanted a *moka* that would be remembered long after his people no longer held them. As he explains: 'The times had changed and I thought to myself that I would take off my bark belt . . . and my apron, and I would follow the new ways. It seemed to me that we no longer had men of the old style who could do the hard work of rearing pigs or the women to make the strong net-bags for harvesting the sweet potatoes, or to make the ropes for the pigs . . . So I decided, "Well, if the old ways must go, let's at least do something as our last big show."' Ongka summoned men

from three clans and lamented the fact that their fathers had all been true 'big-men', while they, their sons, were wearing long trousers and drinking beer and were now 'rubbish men', as he called them; and that although their mothers were strong women, their daughters had now gone light-headed. 'The old ways,' he told them, 'will be shaken off as we shake clods of earth from a stump of a tree, and we will take on new ways. Everything's crazy now, so let us just do this one thing before it all happens.'

To hold his *moka*, Ongka and his Kawelka group wanted to collect 500-600 pigs, some rare cassowaries, money, a truck and a motorbike: an enormous undertaking requiring several years of preparation. Ongka owned no personal wealth and had to rely on the help of kinsmen and members of his tribe. He counted on their cooperation because he had formerly 'invested' pigs with many of them and could now claim them back with 'interest'. The *moka* would gain him prestige among the Kawelka, and this would reflect on them all; furthermore, Parua would be so indebted to them that eventually they would get their 'gifts' back. 'If Parua does make returns to us, item for item, that will be good,' comments Ongka, 'but it will take drive on his part . . . If he fails to pay us back, I would say to him, "All right, give them to my sister's son". In private, Ongka confided that if Parua did not one day return the *moka*, he would take him behind a bush and slit his throat. But even if Ongka lost his 'investment' he knew he could never lose the glory of having made it: it might be an economic loss but the gain in prestige would make him far more acceptable as a potential political leader.

So he went from house to house urging his relatives and friends to stop drinking beer and wasting time with women and to get on with the important task of preparing pigs for his *moka*. By then there was pressure on him to get everything ready in time. Four of his wives were deputed to look after the pigs, because they are undoubtedly the most important item in the Kawelka economy. 'Pigs are our strong thing,' he explains. 'You need pigs for everything. You must have pigs for a *moka*, to pay for troubles, to get wives. If you don't have pigs you are rubbish – you're nobody.'

In the tense run-up to the *moka*, Ongka, often dressed in ritual feathers and adornments, persuaded and bullied his friends

Pigs are essential currency for the Kawelka, not only for distribution during a *moka*, but also for buying wives.

and neighbours to give him the pigs he needed in the form of a mini-*moka*. Once, he acknowledges a particular contribution with these distinctive words: 'The men's house had fallen down, the young girl's breasts had fallen, the young man's beard grew long. But now that you've given me these pigs, I shall marry the young girl, find a wife for the young man, and build the men's house again.'

Even the best laid plans can be upset. After most of the wealth had been collected, the unexpected death of a 'big-man' in a rival tribe led to an outbreak of fighting that almost ruined all Ongka's preparations. When an individual, especially a 'big-man', dies, sorcery is always

suspected, and men angrily attack the enemy held responsible. Having assembled the items for his *moka*, Ongka learned that his group were being accused of the sorcery that had killed his neighbour. Immediately he despatched a pig to the funeral, with a message disclaiming responsibility. He also sent a special branch used in the ceremony of oath-taking to emphasise the truth of his denial. Ongka's pig was accepted and cooked with others at a distribution of pork to mark the end of the first period of mourning; but although the offering defused the accusation, it did not dispel the suspicion. Everything got held up. For three weeks, until the mourning was over, the Kawelka were uneasy, fearing they might still be attacked, and no *mokas* were held in case they further antagonised the dead man's tribe.

Eventually, Ongka felt safe enough to resume his preparations and, after further delays caused by jealous rivals, finally gave the big *moka* for Parua. The guest of honour received 600 pigs, 10,000 dollars, eight cows, twelve cassowaries, a truck and a motorbike. Ongka was delighted and reported how a 'big-man' from another tribe had complimented him: 'We thought we'd catch up with you and do as you do. You bought cars, and then so did we, but you won over us by obtaining a gun. Se we thought we'd try to get guns too, but then you made your big *moka* and pushed ahead of us again. We thought you might be equalled in that, but then you went and purchased a new car. After that we thought perhaps we too would get more cars, but now you have put more pigs together and cooked them here. It is clear we have no chance of catching up with you; you are a strong man and have your own power.'

Ongka's big *moka* establishes his status as a really strong and important man.

The Qaderi Dervishes of Kurdistan

It took Ongka many years to reach his position as an acknowledged leader among the Kawelka. The driving force was his generosity in holding such a successful *moka*, but he was also recognised as a brave warrior, an eloquent speaker and a shrewd negotiator. In its context, his seemingly strange act of

Kurdish children in Baiveh learn the rituals of the dervishes at an early age.

giving away so much wealth becomes comprehensible. Harder to accept and to understand are the extraordinary rituals of the Qaderi dervishes of Kurdistan. But they, too, can be viewed in a political context. What initially appear to be violent religious practices can be seen to be part of a process by which the leader of the dervishes attains and keeps control over his followers.

The Qaderi dervishes live principally in Iraq, Turkey and Iran, with smaller groups in Syria and the Soviet Union. They are a breakaway religious sect of Islam. Many of them live in villages as integrated communities so they cannot be regarded as a disappearing society or as a 'preliterate', 'tribal' or 'primitive' group. They drive cars and buses, listen to the radio, read books, send their children to school and handle modern rifles very efficiently. On the other hand, they frequently perform rituals of a frightening and bizarre nature. These include piercing their cheeks with skewers, eating glass, playing with poisonous snakes, sending strong electric currents through their bodies and pushing swords deep into the skin of their midriffs.

The Kurds belong to the Sunni branch of Islam. This means that, in common with most of the Arab world, they accept a

165

line of authority passed down from the Prophet Mohammed in the seventh century to the Caliphate. Iran, on the other hand, follows the Shi'ite branch of Islam, so in that country the Kurds have always been in a precarious situation, compounded by the fact that they have ambitions to found an independent Kurdish state. Con-sequently, they have a history of conflict, not only with Iran, but also with all the other nation states within whose borders they live. They are fierce warriors, and frequently remind outsiders of their famous ancestor Saleh-ud-Din, better known as Saladin, the leader of the Arabs against the Third Crusade. It is partly as a result of this turbulent political situation that various breakaway religious sects have taken root among the Kurds; the dervishes are one of the largest.

The dervish sects developed in the twelfth century out of the desire of some individuals for a personalised faith. In Christianity and Judaism, individuals are able to reach God through individual prayer. Buddhists and some Hindus see a personal search for and communion with God as a fundamental part of their faith. Islam, however, relies mainly upon the teachings of the prophet Mohammed and a rigid system of repetitive prayers and devotion. But after Mohammed's death, certain individuals sought 'oneness' with God in different ways and founded the various mystic orders. The Qaderi dervishes of Iran follow the teachings of a twelfth-century leader, Sheikh Abd al-Qadir Gilani, and his descendants. Today, adherents of this order are to be found as far apart as India and Ethiopia.

A young shepherd boy, Ali, explained that he would take out his heart if so ordered by the Sheikh.

Disappearing World went to the village of Baiveh on the frontier between Iran and Iraq, home of the leader of the Qaderi dervishes. In 1973 he was Sheikh Kaka Mohammed, who claimed to be a direct descendant of the founder. But since he was by then aged and ailing, most of the dervish activities in the village were being directed by his twenty-seven-year-old son and heir, Sheikh Hossein.

The dervishes believe that with the Sheikh's permission they will receive the protection of God and of the prophet Mohammed. All things then become possible and they can suffer no pain or injury from their actions. It is proof of God's love for them that they can chew glass or toy with venomous snakes without ill-effect, and also push skewers and swords through sensitive parts of the body and not be injured.

The dramatic ceremonies at which such practices occur are known as *zikrs*. Sheikh Hossein explains why they take place: 'The best Muslim is the one who performs the most *zikrs*. The dervish must have total faith in God – if he sets himself alight he will not be burned, if he cuts himself into pieces he will not die. Yes, if he is cut into pieces it is possible to put him together again; it all depends on a man having total faith. These practices remind us of the Prophet and are wonderful. Man must do it to satisfy God; it is pointless if it isn't for God's sake. In *our* order we show our spirituality openly. The Qaderi way with sword, skewer and fire rituals is unique to us. There are some things even greater than those practices. Some people, for example, can put a skewer through the top of their head until it appears from under their chin. It doesn't matter if it goes through their brain or their face. They will keep their normal sensations.'

His followers accept such statements. One farmer, Izat, zealously explains: 'Sheikh Hossein can give a man permission to electrocute himself. If he tells a dervish to do it, he can without harm. Without permission, a dervish would be killed.' Similarly, Hassan, an odd-job man who frequently swallowed glass and used the sword, says: 'During a *zikr* I call out loud "Zayyid Kaka Mohammed". After calling I pierce my stomach and when I pull out the sword the wound is healed because Sheikh Kaka Mohammed gets

A dervish girl shows off her finery. Very shortly she will go into purdah (seclusion) and will not be allowed to be seen by any men other than her family or husband (left).

During the *zikr* or dervish celebrations, boys and men show their devotion to their Sheikh and their faith in God by licking red-hot spoons or pushing skewers through their cheeks.

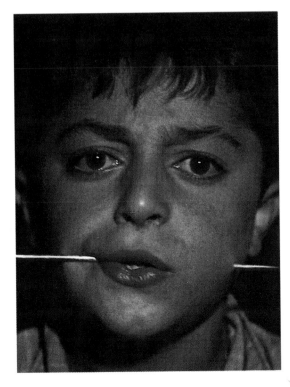

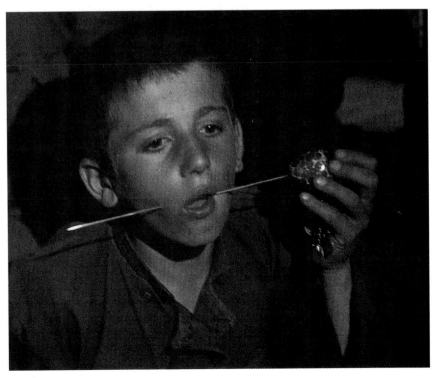

A dervish with poisonous snake wound round his body during the *zikr* ceremony.

Izat, a Kurdish farmer, weeps in ecstasy during a *zikr*.

God to help me. It is God's will and no one else's. In the dervish *zikr* we don't expect anything from anyone except from God.'

The *zikrs* we witnessed in Baiveh were dramatic and spectacular. Young boys licked red-hot metal spoons and pushed skewers through their cheeks. Men ate glass and long nails and drove swords through the skin around their stomachs. Two hundred volts of electricity were applied to one dervish, lighting up a bulb he was holding in his hand, and poisonous snakes wound themselves round arms and necks during the ceremonies. The effect was one of ecstasy rather than pain, although some tears and agonised faces were visible amid the chaos. The religious basis of these incredible performances was self-evident; but in the course of our stay in Baiveh it gradually became clear that the relationship of the Sheikh to his followers had considerable political and economic overtones.

The performers at the *zikrs* were the poorer members of the community. Their devotion to the Sheikh was deep and sincere. One young shepherd boy, Ali, explains why he performs: 'Sheikh Hossein asked me if I wanted to follow the dervish

path. I answered "Yes, I'll follow it". So he initiated me. Now I do everything he tells me – rituals with sword, fire, hot spoons. I shout out loud and I call out to God so that God will take away the pain of the skewer. Otherwise I'd die. Sheikh Hossein gives me permission and he stops me feeling the pain. I'll do anything he wants. Even if Sheikh Hossein's small son told me to do these things I would – I'd cut open my stomach, I'd take my heart out.'

Wealthier members of the community saw no need to perform. 'We order others to perform,' declares one landowner.

The Sheikh and his family have become wealthy farmers, supported by the free labour given by their followers. For them, a practical way to serve God is to serve Sheikh Hossein. That is why Izat the farmer collected rocks for a mosque which the Sheikh was building next to his house overlooking the village. He received no pay for this work, even though he was a poor man. Whenever he could spare time, he sacrificed a day for the Sheikh. 'Because I know that the Sheikh works for God, I work for the Sheikh,' he explains. In this community the poor see no other way of gaining social status in the eyes of the richer members of the society.

Many of the dervishes are the poorer workmen or farmers like Hasan (left).

171

Darchu the Kwegu is an expert hunter, but his people are dominated by the more powerful and numerous Mursi.

treated as second-class citizens by them. The relationship between the two groups is certainly one of domination by the Mursi, but although their supremacy is ultimately upheld by the threat of force, the actual processes through which the two peoples interrelate are ambiguous.

The Kwegu are expert hunters and fishermen who live along the River Omo. They are insistent on their identity as a settled river people, unlike the Mursi, who are nomadic cattle herders who have migrated to the lower Omo area. 'We've always been here,' maintains a Kwegu named Darchu, 'always – and nowhere else. We've stayed here at the river – always. People died, but we stayed on. Our ancestors lived on honey and hunted animals, chasing them in the mud during the rains. They ran in thick mud and speared them. That was the Kwegu way.'

The Kwegu

Among people like the Mursi (see Chapters Three and Five) or the Nuer of the southern Sudan, there are no recognised leaders. No one person within the community controls the lives of others except inside the immediate family where a father determines his children's behaviour, or a husband that of his wife. Among the Mursi, public debating is the essential mechanism which orders the society. But in their relationship with a minority people, the Kwegu, the Mursi show another means of social control.

The 500 or so Kwegu live alongside the Mursi, physically indistinguishable from them but outnumbered two to one and

Darchu builds a trap for a small antelope. His hunting skills are valued by his Mursi patron (left).

The Kwegu are expert canoeists on the dangerous river Omo. Their skill in ferrying their Mursi patrons past man-eating crocodiles to harvest their crops is vital when the river is in flood (below).

173

A new Kwegu canoe is dug out from a tree, burning and chopping the interior in careful stages.

A new Kwegu canoe is dug out from a tree, burning and chopping the interior in careful stages.

The Kwegu perform a vital service for the Mursi. As expert canoeists, they ferry them regularly across the crocodile-infested Omo, so that they can tend their crops. But the Kwegu are regarded by the Mursi as inferiors for one crucial reason: they own no cattle. This simple fact has made them subservient. They have come to accept the Mursi practice whereby a man cannot marry without handing over livestock to his bride's father, and so they depend on Mursi patronage not only for cattle but for the continuation of life itself. By providing cattle or goats for his Kwegu client, a Mursi patron secures control over the man and his descendants.

Sitting with 'his' Kwegu, Kumuli, a Mursi named Bioitongia vividly describes the consequences of the Mursi monopoly of cattle: 'This man is my man, he has no cattle. So when he wants to marry – he sees a girl and wants to marry her – he comes to see me. He says: "I want to marry her". I pick a cow from my herd and go and talk to the girl's father. I take hold of the woman and give her to my man. He now has three wives. I married each one for him, all with my cattle. So he's really my Kwegu. That's how it is.'

The Kwegu consider a Mursi patron essential for everyday protection too. Darchu has an alarming vision of how his life might be without strong support from his patron: 'Imagine I had no Mursi, and I was clearing here at the Omo while the Mursi were still with their cattle. One of them might come and say, "This land you have cleared is mine. Why did you clear it?" "It's mine." "It's not yours. Get off into the bush." I would say to myself, "If I

After weeks of preparation, the new Kwegu canoe is hauled to the river Omo for launching by a team of enthusiastic Mursi.

argue with him, he'll beat me up. What can I do?" So I would go back home and sit down, and people would ask me, "Why aren't you clearing?" "My land has been taken by a Mursi." But if I had a strong Mursi, he would come and find out what was wrong.'

At one level, the relationship between Mursi and Kwegu can be seen as an exchange of services. As David Turton observes: 'Through his possession of a Kwegu client, a Mursi has access to additional resources like hunting and honey gathering, as well as ferrying services. For the Kwegu, the relationship offers access to Mursi cattle and protection.'

The Kwegu say they have always lived at the Omo, while the Mursi arrived more recently.

But since the protection is against other Mursi, and the Kwegu say that in the past they married without handing over livestock, it is apparent that the threat of force underpins the relationship. The Kwegu Kumuli, for instance, is in no doubt about the reality of his situation: 'If we did something bad, the Mursi would toss us in the Omo.'

It might seem surprising that the Kwegu appear content to accept this lower status and do not resent it. David Turton feels that the Kwegu do not recognise that they are getting less out of the relationship than their Mursi patrons. He points out: 'If one asks the Kwegu, "What would you do without the Mursi?" they say, "We wouldn't be able to marry, we wouldn't be able to reproduce, we wouldn't be able to have any children." They see the Mursi as essential to their continued existence. So, despite the very

The Rendille
Wambile is an elder member of a Kenyan nomadic tribe, the Rendille. He is under increasing pressure from a government which fears nomadism. In recent years the government's campaign to settle the nomads has been helped by persistent drought. Many of the camels upon which the Rendille depend have died, and city life in Nairobi has seduced young people away. Many such as Wambile struggle to maintain the traditions and customs that enable the Rendille to remain a successful pastoral community. When he was asked what constituted a good life, Wambile answered: 'When a man ends his service as a warrior, he marries. He increases his herd and God gives him children. If he has many camels he can marry a second wife. The girl he marries is exchanged with camels and she brings him camels. If he has two wives, his children and his herds, that makes a good life.'

important services they provide for the Mursi, they see themselves gaining most from the relationship.' In Turton's view, this is a pattern which might help to explain why other societies accept comparable inequalities.

The Kwegu appear to be in decline as a separate people. In spite of conventional disapproval, occasional intermarriage between Mursi and Kwegu is occurring, although it does not give a Kwegu or his children equal status. Generally the Kwegu find it difficult to get wives outside their society, and because of their own low rate of reproduction, both peoples seem convinced that the smaller tribe will eventually be absorbed by the larger. A Mursi called Ulilibai explains: 'There aren't many Kwegu now. The problem is their wives don't give birth – and when they do they only have one or two children. In the past they would have six or seven. Now they don't. Now they're marrying Mursi, and we're sleeping with Kwegu, their customs are gone.' Darchu agrees: 'Yes, we'll become Mursi. There'll be no Kwegu.'

The Masai

South from the Mursi country, across the border into Kenya, lies the territory of the Masai, a people beloved of novelists and *Tarzan*-type film producers. The Loita Masai, the particular group filmed by *Disappearing World*, live along the Rift Valley of the Western Highlands on the Kenya-Tanzania border. They are exclusively cattle herders, contemptuous both of hunting and of crop cultivation. The status of a Masai man is conditioned by his wealth, his prowess as a warrior and his charisma. But his society is also rigidly divided into age-grades which determine precisely when a boy or a man can compete for higher status. Power is monopolised by the elders, the so-called *ilterekeyani*, who sit in council under the guidance of a respected peer known as the *olaiguenani*. Only the elders can marry and assume responsibility for the women, the children and the family herds; and only they are allowed to take decisions affecting the whole community.

At the beginning of this century, when the British wanted to impose peace upon the warring Masai tribes, they looked for a man they could call a chief. Recognising the communal authority of the elders, they eventually selected one of their number, a man named Ole Nana who appeared to be especially influential. Unfortunately he was a prophet who was consulted on religion and matters of ritual but who had no traditional political authority whatsoever.

The consequence of the Masai's social system is that a young man can achieve status within his age-grade, but can never gain authority or power over other Masai

Masai society is firstly divided into age grades which determines what status a man can achieve.

unless and until he has risen to the grade of elder – a passage marked by a dramatic ceremony called *eunoto*. Having previously led a carefree life as a warrior or *moran*, following this ceremony he now becomes an elder, and is permitted to marry and assume certain political and social responsibilities. 'The end of *moran*hood is good,' explains one elder, 'because you become an elder. People will depend on you. You will look after your herds and try to find a wife. People rely on elders if they're hungry.'

Active *moran*hood begins as soon as a boy is circumcised in his late teens and lasts about seven years. When the next group of boys is old enough to be circumcised, all the existing *moran* are simultaneously promoted to the next age-grade. For a boy to become a *moran* is exciting, far more significant than becoming a teenager in Western society, for it signals a change of status as important as that separating *moran* and elder. 'Is it good to be a *moran*?' one warrior is asked. 'Very good. When you are a child you don't know much. But as a *moran* you become more clever. You visit new places far away. You get to know how to defend yourself. You mature. It's a time for learning. It's like when townspeople send a child to school. A *moran* . . . learns to defend himself and to travel by night. He can brave hardship and he can face hunger. A man who hasn't served as a *moran* is not very clever. He's like a child in Europe who has not been sent to school. The men of his age-grade do not respect him.'

The *morans* learn new things in the course of leaving the family home to travel or live in small encampments hidden away in the forest. They are forced outside the pale of Masai society and into one another's company by a number of rules relating to food and women. They may eat no meat which has been seen by an adult woman, so they have to lead their cattle away into the forest to slaughter them. They are forbidden to drink milk – the Masai staple food – unless another *moran* is present, so they must always be accompanied in their travels around Loita and other parts of Kenya by other *morans*. They cannot marry and are not permitted to sleep with adult women; their only legitimate companions, therefore, are immature or unmarried girls.

The Masai think of this system of restrictions as 'rules of respect', which

The *moran* cannot marry. Their only legitimate companions are *moran* and young unmarried girls (below).

serve to create a mobile body of restless young men with no domestic ties, but held together by bonds of unquestioning loyalty. Formerly, in the days of tribal warfare, they formed the core of the Masai army. The friendships forged within the age group at this period continue as the *moran* progress together through the later stages of life – as junior elders and senior elders and finally as retired elders.

Once a *moran* becomes an elder he is allowed to sleep with adult women and to compete for a wife. In fact, the rule prohibiting a *moran* from going with older women is consistently broken. Husbands are understandably outraged and wives are beaten for the offence, but the breaking of the rule seems to be as much part of the system as the observance of it. The romance of secretly courting the wife of a man in authority typifies the privileges of the elders. When the *moran* becomes an elder in his turn, with the privileges entailed, he knows that the next generation of *moran* will try to seduce his own wife or wives.

The transition from *moran* to elder often proves disruptive to a family. The

young man is now ready to replace his father by taking charge of his mother and his mother's herds. It is not easy for a woman to adjust to the idea of living under the authority and control of her own son.

The promotion from one age-grade to another is the most important factor determining Masai behaviour. It determines a man's relationship with his cattle which, together with the pasture, are gifts from God or Ngai. For as the Masai say: 'Because God gave us both cattle and grass, we will not separate the things God has given us.'

At the elaborate *eunoto* ceremony which marks the transition, the young *moran* shaves his long hair which has been a source of pride and exchanges his elegant clothes for a plain blanket. These rituals symbolise his giving up of an unruly adventurous life for one that is more sombre and responsible.

During the first two days of the *eunoto* filmed by *Disappearing World*, the *moran* paraded about in their typical red ochre, showing themselves off to one another.

Then they visited a river deep in the forest where they decorated their bodies with chalky designs. When they returned they performed a dramatic war dance which went on until late afternoon, by which time they were exhausted. In the evening all forty-nine of the young men were simultaneously shaved.

On the following day nineteen elders, accompanied by the shaven *moran*, went into the forest to sacrifice a cow to God. This represents the most sacred and powerful part of the ceremony. The initiates drink the blood of the animal before the arrival of the other *moran*, who eat the flesh in a rite of communion. During *moran*hood the young men will already have learned the complexities of religious observance and have begun to understand the abstractions of Masai philosophy. The mystical power of the entire *eunoto* ceremony focuses on the hide of the sacrificial animal. The names of Earth and Sky – the twin manifestations of God – are invoked as honey-beer is tossed in the hide. It is then cut into strips and made into rings,

An elaborate ceremony marks the transition of the *moran* from his carefree adventurous life.

which are subsequently worn by the participants and are never removed.

For a few of the graduating *moran*, the big moment of the day is still to come. They are the small minority who have genuinely respected the rule concerning adult women. Each of these innocents now grabs hold of as many female relatives as he can find, and drags them around a ritual house in the centre of a circle, as witnesses to his purity.

Finally, towards the end of the *eunoto* ceremony, a senior elder harangues all the young men as they embark on their new life. 'From now on,' he urges, 'forget the rough ways of *moran*hood. Don't be rude to junior elders or to any woman. Take with you the good influence of this ceremony. Are you listening? Age-mates! The blessing is finished. But we have something to say to you. Go home – respect your people. Respect is the most important thing on earth. We are your moral guardians. And we take our duties very seriously. And you owe us something. The ritual is incomplete without the payment of calves and blankets. You threw away all respect long ago, when you were boys. Then when you became *moran* you thought you were as good as elders, because you tasted tobacco and women. Disperse to your homes and discuss this because we've done our best to organise the ceremony properly for you. Go now and found villages as we did in our time. I shan't tell you again about your faults as *moran* because that's all over now. I shan't remind you again about your stealing and your seduction of the wives of junior elders. Just remember to respect the men who may become your fathers-in-law. You have now entered elderhood.'

The *eunoto* was over. The participants and spectators dispersed. The *moran*, having been admitted to the ranks of junior elders, were now ready to enjoy their new status and to shoulder the burden of new responsibilities.

CHRISTIANS AND PAGANS
AZANDE, UMBANDA, EMBERA

Towards the end of the nineteenth century, travellers, explorers and scholars not only rejected the notion that 'primitive tribes' could have any ordered political system, but also refused to accept that such people had any genuine religious beliefs. The worship of idols, the practice of witchcraft and the use of spells and magic were not seen to represent true expressions of faith on a par with those of the world's recognised great religions. Rather, they were the trappings of ignorant superstition or mumbo-jumbo performed by people arrested at an earlier stage of evolution. The subtleties and complexities of the religion of a people such as the Shilluk, for example, were dismissed as non-existent by the famous explorer Sir Samuel Baker. 'Nor is the darkness of their minds enlightened by even a ray of superstition,' he informed the Ethnological Society of London in 1866.

Thanks to the work of such anthropologists as Sir James Frazer, Sir Edward Tyler and Emile Durkheim, attitudes in the early part of the twentieth century gradually changed. Yet for many people it is still difficult to accept that a man with a bone through his nose and a rattle in his hand, chanting to the beat of a drum, observes a religion just as legitimate and effective as that followed by someone who kneels in front of a cross, praying to the accompaniment of an organ. When a detailed knowledge of how such belief systems work in other societies is lacking, their religions are even harder to accept.

Disappearing World has turned its attention to matters of faith and belief among

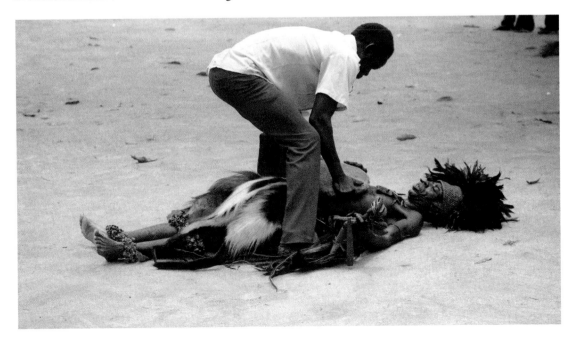

The Azande of Central Africa believe that witchdoctors can help free them from evil influences which bring misfortune.

many different societies, recording religious activities as varied as the shaman performances of the Hmong of Laos *(The Meo)* to the alarming ritual torments at the Sri Lankan festival of Kataragama.

The Azande

Of all the people we have filmed, none has seemed more remote or exotic than the Azande of central Africa. Once, they ruled a great empire that extended from the tropical rain forests of the Congo to the grasslands of the southern Sudan. But they were decimated by the slave trade and broken as a military and political force by the end of the nineteenth century. Gradually the Azande sank into obscurity.

In the 1920s Sir Edward Evans-Pritchard put the Azande firmly on the anthropological map by investigating their system of witchcraft, magic and oracles. One of his students, Mary Douglas, claimed recently: 'Before Evans-Pritchard started the field of African studies of religion, anchoring all the religious beliefs in the social life of the people, there wasn't any study of African religions. There was mythology and there were odd beliefs, and there was fetishism and magic and such like, but nobody had ever thought that you could take the metaphysical ideas of African people which were not written down and treat them with the same seriousness and the same philosophical questioning as you might the ideas of one of the world religions. This was revolutionary.'

The Azande proved ideal for Evans-Pritchard's studies, because witchcraft permeated every part of their lives. 'I had no difficulty in discovering what Azande think about witchcraft, nor in discovering what they do to combat it,' he wrote. 'These ideas and actions are on the surface of their life and are accessible to anyone who lives for a few weeks in their homesteads. Every Zande is an authority on witchcraft. *Mangu* (witchcraft) was one of the first words I heard in Zandeland and I heard it uttered day by day through the months. It was soon clear that if I could gain a full understanding of the meaning of this word, I should have the key to Zande philosophy.'

Fifty years later, we were able to follow in his footsteps. The first thing we found was that witchcraft still plays as important a role as it had a half-century earlier. It seems to provide a means for the people to understand, interpret and combat all misfortune. Incidents and experiences in everyday life for which they have no explanation can be handled by referring to a witchdoctor or a diviner.

The Azande believe that witchcraft can be inherited. If a man or member of his family suffers illness or misfortune, witchcraft may be blamed. Since they have no concept of bad luck, there can be no such

184

thing as a pure accident; something must have made it happen and the commonest cause is witchcraft. To find out who or what is responsible, the Azande resort to one of various oracles which, when consulted, will reveal the truth; other forms of magic can then be used as an antidote. If an individual can discover who is bewitching him, he can then persuade the witch to stop.

The accused person may be quite unaware of the harm he or she is alleged to be doing, and may thus be a witch without knowing it. Evans-Pritchard explained that 'a witch performs no rite, utters no spells and possesses no medicines. An act of witchcraft is a psychic act. Azande believe that witchcraft is a substance in the bodies of witches. It has been described to me as an oval blackish swelling or bag attached to the edge of the liver. They say when people cut open the belly they have only to pierce it and witchcraft substance bursts through with a pop.'

The Azande have a repertoire of oracles for such situations. There is a rubbing board oracle where questions are put to a diviner who rubs together two pieces of lubricated wood and receives his answer when they adhere to each other. The termite oracle works by placing two sticks in a termite mound; the answer depends on which stick the termites eat. The most important of all is *benge*, the poison oracle. A strychnine-based poison is fed to small chickens, and the innocence of the person accused of causing witchcraft depends on whether the birds survive or die. There are parallels here with the ducking-stool trials of witches in medieval Europe. Chief Soro explained how the Azande used the poison in the days of his grandfather, King Gbudwe: 'In the past *benge* was used in the court to prove if a man had used witchcraft to kill. Where today we use *benge* on chickens, King Gbudwe used the same method on human beings. The accused would sit on the floor. The feathers of chickens killed by poison would be stuck in a row in the ground. The man would then have to drink a cup of poison. Then he had to stand and pick up a feather. He had to repeat this five times with five cups of *benge*. Then he had to sit down and someone would frighten him by making a loud noise. If, after that, he was feeling all right, it would show he was innocent and the matter would be ended!'

Oracles are most frequently used to divine whether witchcraft is causing sickness or other misfortunes. They provide the Azande with a method of coping with hardship. 'We take our witchcraft beliefs very seriously,' explains the witchdoctor Marco. 'Our ancestors believed in them before us. They didn't just happen suddenly.'

The system has proved effective for the Azande and they use it to examine the puzzles of everyday life. During our stay in the equatorial forest, an Azande called

In times of trouble, the Azande first consult a diviner who will use various oracles to find out who has caused the problem.

Diviners have several oracles to consult; the strongest is 'benge', a poison given to chicks. Whether the chick lives or dies gives the diviner the answer to his questions.

Witchdoctors see no inconsistency in being a Christian and a witchdoctor at the same time. Witchcraft provides them with practical solutions to misfortune.

each other should the poison kill the chicken. If Gume had no carnal knowledge of Bukuyo, then let the chicken live.' In this case the chicken died.

Several days later, Chief Soro heard that the poison oracle had delivered a verdict and reconvened the court. The accused pair were brought forward to hear the results of the consultation from the sub-chief. To ensure fairness, a second sub-chief, representing Gume, had asked the oracle on *her* behalf whether the first chicken was correct. The answer confirmed the couple's guilt. The chief was now in a position to give a judicial verdict: *Soro*: 'Bukuyo, you did have sex with Gingiti's wife!' *Bukuyo:* 'It must refer to a time several years ago.' *Soro*: 'But you two had sex?' *Bukuyo*: 'Yes.' *Soro*: 'Is that true, Gume?' *Gume*: 'A long time ago.' *Soro*: 'Just answer yes!' *Gume*: 'Yes.' *Soro*: 'And you, Bukuyo?' *Bukuyo*: 'Yes.' *Soro*: 'What a waste of time. You're both found guilty! You should have admitted adultery the other day. Now *benge* has confirmed your guilt.' Even though the adultery had taken place a long time ago, the system of oracles was seen to have worked.

Even if the accused couple had not committed adultery in the past, the fact that *benge* had found them guilty would not have weakened their faith in the system. There are always excuses when the system appears to have gone wrong, such as blaming those concerned for not carrying out the rituals properly. If a Christian prays to God for help without success, the believer does not automatically reject Christianity. The same is true of witchcraft. Success reinforces faith in the system; failure can be explained away.

However, witchcraft is not the universal panacea. The most radical change in Zandeland since the time of Evans-Pritchard's study has been the spread of Christianity. Most Azande nowadays attend one or other of the churches established by the various missionary groups in the region, whether in the bush or in the local town. For people who live in small scattered homesteads in the equatorial forests, deliberately isolated to avoid the consequences of one another's witchcraft, the church provides a useful once-a-week opportunity to get together. But

Gingiti accused his wife Gume of having committed adultery with a neighbour, Bukuyo. The accused couple denied the charges and the case was taken before Chief Soro. Since they had not been caught *in flagrante*, there was no real evidence to prove or disprove the allegation. So the chief resorted to the *benge* oracle, sending a sub-chief with the poison to a diviner to discover the truth. The poison was fed to a chicken while the diviner posed the question: 'Oracle, oracle, here is a man called Bukuyo. He is accused of having sex with Gume. If that is true and they have been lying, *benge* should kill this chicken. This chicken has drunk poison for Gume and Bukuyo. The poison shouldn't work unless they met for sex. Only if they undressed and lay with

There are many churches throughout Zandeland. In times of civil war the church images are often removed for safekeeping.

Without the witchdoctor, Azande have no means of combating the malignant forces that cause them misfortune.

although churches are full and Christianity seems to be flourishing, there is no appreciable decline in witchcraft. The two systems appear to operate alongside each other. Father Jerome, a Catholic priest in Nandi, close to where our filming took place, admitted that he still faces a long struggle before his preachings overcome his congregation's deeply rooted faith in magic, witchcraft and divination. Father Jerome, unlike his fellow priests, is himself an Azande, the only member of the tribe we met who claimed not to believe in the rational power of witchcraft. Magic rituals provide practical answers to everyday problems in a way the church cannot. Failure in the hunt, inexplicable illness, disputed evidence in adultery cases – these are situations for which Father Jerome's church can offer no ready solutions. He claimed to be making progress in his struggle against witchcraft, but believed the Azande use of their traditional system would only disappear when the rural Azande were given access to the better education so far available only to the town-dwellers. 'When I was a child there were no Christians,' said Father Jerome. 'Now, they are practically all Christians. Although they attend services, other things are more difficult for them. For instance, they are still mostly polygamists and most of them still believe in witchcraft. They believe that any illness is caused by the evil-eye which is in turn caused by something invisible inside someone.'

The vast majority of Azande retain their beliefs in witchcraft and magic because these possess an internal logic and are seen to work. Evans-Pritchard gave one explanation: 'In this web of belief every strand depends upon every other strand and one Azande cannot get out of its meshes because it is the only world he knows.' Offered the Christian alternative, the Azande have embraced only those aspects which do not conflict with their traditional beliefs and practices. They welcome the Sunday services and various church celebrations as social occasions, bringing isolated families together. When questioned, they claim to believe in the Holy Trinity, the Crucifixion, the Resurrection and other central features of Catholicism, but are unclear as to what

these things mean and how they relate to daily life. Christianity may offer the Azande some acceptable explanations of the supernatural, but witchcraft and magic continue to provide them with the practical means of coping with it.

Umbanda

In many parts of the world, when Christianity has been introduced to a 'closed' society, its absorption has created a new syncretic religion, an amalgam of the old and the new. *Disappearing World* filmed an example of this in Brazil, where a religious movement called Umbanda has developed from a combination of spiritualism and Christianity. The followers of Umbanda, instead of keeping separate the different belief systems that have arrived in Brazil over the centuries, have managed to combine them. Various African elements have been added to a pot-pourri of Catholicism, local spiritualism and native voodoo practices to produce what is virtually a new faith.

The mixture of African gods and spirits was brought to Brazil by the slaves. The

Umbanda religion has developed from a mixing of African religions, voodoo and Catholicism (above).

This image of Christ shows Yoruba influences from West Africa as well as Christian influences.

189

Offerings to request a favour, North-east Brazil.

Followers of Umbanda contact the spirits through a medium.

saints of the Catholic church arrived with the missionaries, and the spirits were adopted from the beliefs of the South American Indians. Umbandistas maintain that spirits evolve and that they are organised like an army, in lines and phalanxes. The leaders of each line are the most highly evolved. Great spirits can be both saints of the Catholic church and also African gods or *orixás*. Oxala, the highest spirit of all, is closely identified with Christ but also with Yoruba gods from West Africa. St George is also called Ogum, the God of War. Iemanjá is one of the best-loved *orixás*; seen as a manifestation of the Virgin Mary, she is adored as Goddess of the Sea.

Followers of Umbanda use their belief structure, as do the Azande of central Africa, to combat difficulty and misfortune. They make contact with their spirits and gods by consulting and paying a medium for a seance. The spirit enters into the medium while the latter is in a trance, and then, speaking through the medium, advises the client how to act. Sometimes the medium is possessed by a

Iemanjá is worshipped as a blend of the Virgin Mary and Yoruba goddess of the sea.

191

god, but more usually by a lesser spirit who was formerly a man or a woman. The spirits known as 'the old blacks', for example, were once slaves who worked the sugar plantations. They are gentle and wise and good at healing. The *Caboclos* are spirits of Brazilian Indians, who sometimes look more like the indigenous Indians of North America, familiar to most Brazilians from the cinema. The *Caboclos* are brave and noisy, and wear feathered head-dresses.

A follower of Umbanda, who later became a medium, tells the anthropologist Peter Fry in *Disappearing World*'s film: 'I began fourteen years ago. You see I was ill. I didn't believe in Umbanda. I was ill for forty days. I couldn't get up. Then my husband went to see Mother Lourdes. She worked on me and I was able to get up. She said I should put on white clothes. So I did. She said something had been done against me and I was filled with the spirit Eshu. After three days I was cured.' Eshu, a malignant spirit of darkness, is ofen blamed for causing illness and trouble.

The Umbanda religion thrives particularly in the urban regions of Brazil, in large cities such as Sao Paulo and in smaller towns like Campinas. Although it draws adherents from every walk of life and every ethnic background, its principal appeal is to the poor. In the humid town of Belem, 1,500 miles north of Sao Paulo, at the mouth of the Amazon, with its mixed population, Umbanda offers almost the only spark of relief to people whose lives are harsh and monotonous. Here poverty, sickness and unemployment are endemic. Umbanda lends them the strength to endure their problems. One survey into the apparent success of the religion revealed that over sixty per cent of new members were suffering from some kind of illness and were turning to Umbanda for relief or cure.

Umbanda is similar to other new religious movements that stem from Christianity. Dona Lourdes, a famous medium in Sao Paulo, explains: 'Umbanda grows because we believe "Give and it shall be given to you". Here, people come from far and wide. We don't charge for our services. We welcome all with equal affection. We don't know where they come from. We make no class distinctions. The spirit of light embraces all brethren. This creates confidence in the religion and gives people greater faith in the spirits.' In modern Brazil, Umbanda has received increasing social recognition in recent years, attracting a wealthier following, and is recognised as a growing force on the political scene.

The Embera

One influential element in the Umbanda religion has been the spirit world of the South American Indian. Many Indian tribes are convinced that their shamans, like the Umbanda mediums, can, when possessed by spirits, help cure sickness and relieve misfortune. The word 'shaman' is Russian and originally referred to Siberians who were able to converse with the spirit world and so bring help to humans. Similar shaman practices are to be found throughout the world; across Asia, in the Arctic, in the South Pacific and in South America.

The Embera Indians live west of the Andes in the low equatorial strip that borders the Pacific Ocean, in an area of dense rainforest, one of the wettest regions in the world, referred to as the 'graveyard of Colombia' because of the

The spirits of the old slaves are seen as gentle, wise and healing.

The Embera who live in a dense Colombian rainforest are faced with a cultural crisis.

The Embera survived the massacres of the Spanish *conquistadores*; today their cultural identity faces a challenge from Catholic missionaries.

widespread incidence of malaria and yaws. The sixteenth-century Spanish explorers described the people of this region as 'evil and warlike', but it is a reputation they have long since lost.

The Embera are hunter-gatherers who use blowpipes and bows and arrows to kill wild pigs, deer, iguanas, monkeys and birds. They grow some maize, manioc and seed potatoes. They managed to survive extinction when many Indians were massacred by the Spanish *conquistadores* who were looking for labour to mine gold or work in the fields. The Spaniards eventually found it more profitable to import West African slaves to replace the Indians as labourers in the mines and sugar plantations.

Today the Embera again face a crisis, for they are threatened with cultural extinction, as the Colombian government seeks to introduce its own version of civilisation. The greatest influence on the lives of the Indians has been, until recently, the Roman Catholic Church. For the past eighty years the Church has exercised

complete religious and civil authority over the so-called Mission Territories, and today it effectively controls two- thirds of the country. For the Embera, justice and education, as well as religion, have all been dispensed by the Mission and its priests, who travel up river to take young children away to school and who preach tirelessly to reinforce the principles of the Catholic faith among their parents and grandparents.

The anthropologist Ariane Deluz, who spent two years living with the Embera, was especially interested in their traditional religion and wished to assess its chances of surviving the impact of Christianity. 'When you live in such an Indian family for some months,' she says, 'you really have the impression of living in a very polite, upper-class European family. Few words are exchanged, things are always discussed in common between parents. You have the impression of being in Europe much more than when you are in a *libre* (Colombian black) family, where the relationships have not this touch of

Some Embera children are taken away for education in Catholic schools by missionaries.

Priests come up-river to visit the Embera, but the traditional beliefs of the Indians have little in common with Christianity (left).

Embera girls are faced
with two conflicting belief
systems: Christianity and
Shamanism.

lovingness and companionship. The natural
interests of children are always encouraged. Parents are very affectionate to their
children, grandparents to their grand-
children – but not in a very demonstrative
manner.'

She found the links between the
Embera and the Catholic Missions of particular interest: 'When I first arrived, the
Mission was a flourishing enterprise.
Younger priests tried more or less to help
the Indians keep their customs. When I
came back some months later, the young
priests had gone, an older priest had
returned, and there seemed to be an air of
decadence over the Mission, which was
collapsing. Among the Embera the Catholic faith didn't seem to be very strong.'

The traditional beliefs of the Embera,
having little in common with Christianity
or any other world religion, centre on a
supernatural world peopled by spirits –
evil animal spirits and benevolent spirits
of ancestors. The grotesque spirits and
demons in their cosmology cause illness
and death, and need to be countered by
the friendlier, beneficent spirits. In times
of trouble it is the shaman who acts as the
intermediary to appease the evil spirits
and appeal for help from the ancestral
spirits. He is able to communicate directly
with the spirits and has various medicines
and therapeutic techniques, such as
hallucinogens, to bolster his skills.

'You become a shaman,' explains
Ariane Deluz, 'after having yourself

endured crazes, when you see spirits or are possessed by spirits. In order to be cured, you have to accept this spirit coming into you and you then become a shaman.' But she also emphasises the harsh realities of life in the rain forests: 'The Embera are born, live and die with little medical help. Shamanism is one of the best health devices they have because at least all the psychosomatic diseases are cured by the shaman. They are a help; but they can't cure everything.'

Floresmilo is an Embera shaman who used his talents to cure his sick wife and ailing grandson. The rituals included purifying the house with sweet-smelling leaves. Floresmilo called on carved figures, representing his ancestors, to journey from the spirit world to his house and to remove the sickness.

After Floresmilo had performed the necessary rituals to attract the spirits, he left gourds of fermented cane juice to stand overnight. In the morning, the level of the juice had dropped. It was evident to the patients that the spirits had come during the night to drink and that they could hope for a cure.

Body painting is one of the traditions of the Embera.

198

CELEBRATION
CARNAVAL, KATARAGAMA, QUECHUA

All over the world, people come together at regular times of the year to celebrate in mass rituals. In Europe, the major occasion is Christmas; in the United States, Thanksgiving is considered by many to be more important. Some of these events are religious in origin – Christmas was both a Christian and a pagan festival – but over time the religious element has generally become less important than the secular. Christmas is celebrated by millions who are not Christians, and the high level of commercialism and entertainment, which has all but swamped the original religious significance of the festival, is, for believers, a regular seasonal lament.

In some cases we know why these recurring rituals take place – to encourage a harvest, to worship a god, to mark a change in status, to mourn an ancestral death, or perhaps to recall an auspicious event, but often their purpose is unclear.

Carnaval

Of the many cyclic rituals witnessed and recorded by *Disappearing World*, only one appears to happen for the sake of pure enjoyment. This is the *Carnaval* (the Brazilian spelling of 'Carnival') in Bahia, a city in northern Brazil; anthropologists call it a ritual of reversal. During the few days of *Carnaval* everything is turned upside down. People act completely out of character, displaying behaviour that would normally be unthinkable. Sexual practices are relaxed, men and women exchange clothing or wear it back-to-front, relatives hurl ritual insults at one

During the Bahia *Carnaval*, conventions are overturned and anything goes.

another, and people who usually have no voice in society can suddenly make themselves heard. Such rituals were once common in parts of Africa, India and North America, and some of the roots can be traced back to the bacchanalian celebrations and masquerades which were a feature of the Roman empire.

Carnaval in Bahia began as a Portuguese Lent tradition of playing practical jokes – squirting water and throwing flour at passers-by. Today the city's mixture of races and religions has transformed it into something far more complex and popular.

For a few days each year, the *Carnaval* in Bahia allows the city's transvestites to flaunt themselves.

The Rio *Carnaval* attracts tourists from all over the world.

For five days and nights during the week before Lent, the people of Bahia, rich and poor, abandon their everyday roles and enter a world of make-believe. It is a chance to dress up and act out fantasies, to forget daily problems and to let off steam. Normally repressed anti-social behaviour is flaunted. People turn out as thieves, prostitutes, clowns and jesters. Many women dress (or undress) in sexy clothing and dance in a lewd style they would not dream of adopting at other times.

The licence extends to visiting places which normally elicit stern disapproval. Elsa's restaurant, for example, is well off the tourist track. The owner, Elsa, is in fact a man, and his establishment is popular with Bahia's male prostitutes, some of whom are transvestites. At *Carnaval* time they all join enthusiastically in the festivities.

The city streets are suddenly converted into a gigantic stage, and the people appear joyously and unselfconsciously as actors in a spectacular, unscripted play. Costumes are borrowed from every

'The Sons of Gandhi' are one of the Bahia *Carnaval*'s many clubs, many of whch are also inspired by African themes.

201

Lavish and ostentatious decorations typify the *Carnaval*.

culture. Red Indian braves dance alongside New Guinea tribesmen and Ghanaian kings cavort with Portuguese peasants. Milton da Silva, a driver working for the local council, who for the occasion turned himself into Momos, an ancient Greek God of Mockery, confesses to *Disappearing World*: 'It's great to be king – a real nobleman – and enjoy the good things of life. *Carnaval* is everything for us. We can forget daily life for five days of madness – we can forget the other 360 days. We can give free rein to our fantasies. Men dress as women, women dress as men. We sleep in the streets, we make love, we let ourselves go.'

Bahia's colonial history began in the sixteenth century when Europeans first discovered the Bay of All Saints. There is a local legend that the city was founded by a native Indian woman, Katarina Paraguacu. One day, a Portuguese sailor was shipwrecked near her village in the bay. He was rescued and Paraguacu became his wife. When the Portuguese settlers arrived in 1549 to lay the foundations of Bahia, they found part-European descendants of Paraguacu with whom they in turn intermarried. They planted sugar and herded Indians into the canefields to work, many of whom died, while some escaped into the forests. As in Colombia, the Indian workers were replaced by black slaves from Africa.

The two or three million blacks who arrived in Brazil eventually outnumbered the whites of Portuguese origin. Palatial homes sprang up among the canefields. Sugar and slavery proved to be a profitable combination, and for two centuries Bahia remained the country's capital. The central square became known as Pelourinho, Portuguese for 'pillory', the punishment post where slaves were flogged. Catholic churches prospered, lavishly decorated with money from the canefields, and became so numerous that Bahia now claims to have a church for each day of the year. The Catholic priests, as eager to capture souls as the traders had been to capture bodies, baptised the blacks compulsorily, though they were never fully won over.

The Africans brought their own gods with them. Today, their religion, called *Candomblé*, is openly practised and its

temples far outnumber the Catholic churches. At one time, slaves had to worship their gods under the guise of Catholic saints. Today, the whites have taken up *Candomblé*, and in Bahia images from both religions mingle harmoniously. The powerful priestesses who rule the *Candomblé* cult are particularly busy at *Carnaval* time, when many of the faithful visit them to ensure their pleasure during the celebrations.

Bahia is no longer Brazil's capital. Other enterprises have replaced sugar as the main source of wealth in a mushrooming city of two million people. With a large black population, the African influence is exceptionally strong.

Carnaval gives the poor of Bahia the chance to forget the harsh realities of life for five days.

203

Each year hundreds of clubs are formed to organise *Carnaval* activities. One of the most popular clubs, catering both for social activities and hobbies, is called Olodum, meaning 'God of Gods'. Its members are young, black and poor; and African themes are much in evidence. For the 1983 *Carnaval* the club chose to enact the crowning of the King of Oyo in Nigeria. As usual, the director, Ze Carlos, and his friends spent much of their meagre salaries and devoted a great deal of time to organising the *Carnaval* festivities. One way of encouraging a successful outcome to the months of effort is to obtain the blessing of a *Candomblé* priestess. So Ze Carlos went at nightfall to Dona Diva, one of Bahia's most famous practitioners. She sacrificed two chickens in a secret ceremony aimed at protecting the Olodum club against any malign forces. After making her offering to female spirits, Dona Diva explains to us: 'When a club like Olodum gets ready to come out in *Carnaval*, we need to protect them from trouble and violence. Sometimes clubs are jealous of each other. Doing this can fend off someone else's evil wishes.'

Another 'African'-based club carries the name 'Sons of Gandhi'. It was started by poor dockers in 1949 and its members are older than those of Olodum. One of them explained its origins: 'Many British ships came to Bahia in those days. The crews were from India. It was a time of struggle. The Indians were suffering. For us too things were difficult. We couldn't afford an expensive *Carnaval* costume, so we remembered how Gandhi was humble and founded the "Sons of Gandhi".'

In the pre-*Carnaval* months members of the club assemble each Sunday. The meeting begins with a ceremony to cast off evil. The music has distinctive religious associations, with drums and guitars beating out traditional African rhythms. The gods are addressed in Yoruba, a Nigerian language that has otherwise faded from local memory.

Carnaval in Bahia is not reserved for the social outcasts and the poor. Wealthy clubs also join the *Carnaval* processions, competing with one another to show off the most elaborate costumes. And for the many people not affiliated to any club, it is also an opportunity to display individual character. *Carnaval* brings chaos to the city, but the disruption is accepted and welcomed by everyone, politicians included. Bahia's governor is very pragmatic about the personal and communal value of the festival: 'The role of the politician is to please the people. When *Carnaval* is well organised, when the government gives the people the chance to have fun, especially in the street, the people are pleased with the government. Everyone forgets daily problems. Everyone takes to the streets, rich and poor alike. If the *Carnaval* is good, then it's good for me politically.'

After the lengthy preparations, the five days and nights of celebration pass in an orgy of song, dance, drink and procession. Half a million people throng the city centre. The decorated buses and floats of the clubs, which blast out their popular songs at maximum volume wind their set route through the main streets and squares. At every point, onlookers wave and yell from windows and balconies and then spill out on to the streets, singing and gyrating, drunk with the heady brew of beer and *Carnaval*. The atmosphere is irresistible. '*Carnaval* gives our people a chance to display their joy,' says Bahia's mayor. 'Everyone feels equal with no social distinction.'

Kataragama

In southern Sri Lanka, a ritual takes place each year which generates as much colour and excitement as the Bahia *Carnaval*. There are crowds, costumes, pageantry, entertainment and revelry. But *Kataragama* is a strongly religious occasion, attracting people from different backgrounds and different faiths who are seeking some kind of explanation or help.

'I am still a Christian,' confesses one Sri Lankan. 'I still go to church. But when I am in a jam I find it is more effective to go to *Kataragama* and I make a vow and my burden is lifted.' A Hindu engineer had a different reason for attending the festival: 'I came to *Kataragama* to fulfil a vow which I made last year that if I pass my examination I will come this year during the season and do the *Kavadi* dancing for the God.'

The Sri Lankan festival of *Kataragama* attracts followers from many faiths.

Devotees of Kataragama often abase themselves, piercing their skin with hooks or walking on fire to demonstrate their faith and gratitude in the god.

Many poor Sri Lankans, attracted by Kataragama's reputation for helping his devotees, turn to him in time of need.

Many worshippers of the god, despite the harshness of their ritual ordeals, say they feel no pain.

Kataragama is the name of a festival, a place and a deity. Every year, people from all walks of life, Buddhists, Hindus, Muslims and Christians, come here to pay homage to God. In mythology, Kataragama fought and defeated the Titans. He is a living, passionate, almost human deity – worldly, masculine, beautiful and erotic. He does not preach, nor does he make moral judgements; and he will help anyone so long as their devotion is sufficiently strong.

Some who attend the Kataragama festival have recognisably religious motives. Hindu priests come to gain fresh inspiration and power from the god, walking on burning coals to prove their success. Buddhists often come simply to worship. For them the sensuality of the God is most important and the illicit love life he is reputed to have enjoyed is cause for celebration. Penitents may pierce their skin with hooks and humiliate themselves in other painful ways.

Penitence and the search for personal salvation are powerful incentives for many worshippers. Mr Careem, a Hindu teashop owner in downtown Colombo, provides a vivid example of extreme devotion. Ten years earlier he had been an army corporal, involved in an unsuccessful coup against the government. While awaiting trial in his prison cell, he asked Kataragama to save his life, vowing that if the God answered his prayer he would come to the festival for seventeen consecutive years and hang himself from hooks through his back. At his court martial he was acquitted. After humiliating himself before Kataragama for four years, Mr Careem, like many penitents before him, began to feel himself possessed by the God. He became regarded as a kind of holy man, and people started coming to communicate with Kataragama through him.

Many ordinary people, attracted by the God's reputation of omnipotence, turn to him confidently for help in time of need. *Disappearing World* followed the story of the Douglas family and discovered how strongly this belief has taken hold and why so many resort to this form of divine supplication.

Ratnyaka, the Douglas's eleven-year-old son, had visited his grandmother in her village 100 miles away from his home, quarrelled with her and vanished. The distraught parents were convinced that their son's disappearance was symbolic. At some time in the past, a member of the family must have done something which had now caused Ratnyaka to vanish. They decided to resort to astrology. An astrologer cannot look back into the past but he can see and chart the pattern of future events – an individual's destiny or *karma*. Three of the astrologers consulted all said that the boy was still alive but predicted that he would never again return home. A fourth did not ask why the parents had come to see him, but merely based his calculations on their time of arrival. 'Someone has left a place of residence,' he announced. 'There is no other way of getting that person back except by way of Kataragama; not by magic or sorcery. You must go to Lord Kataragama and implore him and give "a life for a life" and whatever else you can afford.'

The parents duly visited their small local temple, paid the priest five rupees and told him to ask the God to get their son back. The priest wrote the boy's name on betel-nut leaves and eventually informed them that Kataragama would bring the boy back within twenty-one days. If not, they should burn the leaves and this would send Ratnyaka into so deep a trance that somehow he would be induced to return. They then made a vow by tying a coin in a cloth and attaching it to the God's lance. The vow stated that if, within twenty-one days, Kataragama brought back their son unharmed, they would plant a young coconut sapling (a symbol of their own lives) for the God, outside the temple. The ritual over, they went home to wait out the three weeks.

Before the time was up, Kataragama had granted their request. Quite suddenly,

In Sri Lanka, religion is very much a part of daily life.

Ratnyaka turned up, with a long story of having been in the capital working in a rice mill, and having being sent home because he was too young. As far as the family was concerned, the God had come to their rescue.

In Sri Lanka religion is not separated from the routine activities of life. Douglas was not a religious man. Although there was a lamp for the Buddha in a corner of his house, it had not been lit for a long time. He went to the God simply because it was a practical thing to do. Thousands of pilgrims come to Kataragama in search of help. Indeed, most people present their problems to the God as naturally as we might take ours to the local welfare or social security department.

Disappearing World found that it wasn't only local people who had reason to be grateful to Kataragama. Ex-sailor Walter Gamage has served on HMS *Drake* in England in 1958. Asked why he returned to *Kataragama* every year to have pins stuck into his body or hooks dug into his back, he explained that he originally came to expiate sins committed while in the Royal Navy. 'In 1963 I thought of coming to *Kataragama* to take part in the fire walking. I got burned badly and was hospitalised for twenty-one days. Before I was moved to hospital I made a vow in order to heal my wounds, to safeguard me and to allow me to go to work.' Now he atones and fulfils his vow every year by having 108 pins stuck in his body. 'I feel that when I do these things I satisfy the God, and I get his full protection. Being a human being I don't think I can live without his protection.'

During the same *Kataragama* ceremony, we witnessed more than 250 people walking over burning coals. The next day, in the emergency hospital, there were twenty-seven cases of burning. These patients were more troubled by the thought that they had been deemed unworthy and had not won the God's protection, than by their burns.

Apart from staging complex, agonising rituals that come from religious observance, *Kataragama*, like *Carnaval*, has other functions, as noted by the anthropologist Gananath Obeyesekere: 'This annual event is also a social gathering for these people; they gossip, renew their friendships (or break them) and generally enjoy themselves by dancing the *Kavadi*, the joyous, exuberant dance in honour of the God. It is also here that mystics talk about their experiences, discuss spiritual matters, invent myths. *Kataragama* is a catalyst of social change.'

The Quechua

On the other side of the world, in the high valleys and plateaux of the Andes, the notion that divine aid and blessing need to be sought every year in an extensive and elaborate ritual is equally powerful. For several million descendants of the great Inca empire, annual ceremonies are a familiar occurrence, featuring dramatic costumes, penitential suffering, music and dance.

Each June, as many as 15,000 Quechua celebrate at the shrine of Senor de Qoyllur

Rit'i. As with *Kataragama*, the festival has deep religious associations and combines Spanish Catholicism with remnants of the ancient religion of the Incas. Today the Quechua religion combines Catholic saints with Inca and pre-Inca spirits. The anthropologist Michael Sallnow believes that the Quechua associate the Virgin Mary with the earth spirit Pachamama, who causes crops to grow and flourish: 'The name of Pachamama is constantly on people's lips, for whenever a person partakes of alcohol he spills a few drops on the ground and calls upon Pachamama to drink with him.'

The village of Kamawara, in southern Peru, is a very isolated Quechua community, where there are no roads, no communications, not even a village street. The few dozen houses are scattered over the hillsides and separated by rocks, fields and animal trails. Anything that comes here comes up the steep mountain footpaths to the village which stands about two and a quarter miles above sea level. Anyone who is not acclimatised struggles to breathe in the thin mountain air. The

Festivals dedicated to Christ and the saints are regularly celebrated.

Quechua girl.

community numbers about a hundred families, living and farming much as they would have done since the Spanish conquest. They are experts in farming potatoes. Apart from a little barley and beans, nothing else grows at these altitudes. Kamawara is sealed off from the rest of the world as effectively as if it were in the heart of the jungle.

For the villagers of Kamawara, the annual pilgrimage to Qoyllur Rit'i is an important event; and for people such as Toribio, the occasion is a time for re-affirming the unity of the family and of the community. The family, father and sons, survives by cultivating potatoes. The potato crop is under the protection of the *apus*, or spirits, who dwell in the natural features of the Andean landscape, in mountains, rocks, streams and lakes, and in the earth itself. The higher the mountain, the more powerful its *apu*. Christianity exists in this area, but the *apus* remain.

Each year more than 10,000 pilgrims make the punishing climb to Qoyllur Rit'i, within sight of Ausangate, the highest mountain in southern Peru. The shrine, like others at which the Quechua worship, is a place where a vision of Christ has appeared. 'He was seen here by two boys,' says one of the Kamawara villagers. 'Having been seen by man, he hid himself away with the little boys. So the three of them stayed together. He gave the boys bread which they lived on for three weeks.

211

Quechua man with knitted
headgear.

212

Then, as the boys watched, Christ died, but miraculously he lives on.'

In Kamawara, there is a great deal of argument over the position of 'patron' of the pilgrimage. It is an expensive honour, since the patron must provide food, drink and firewood for everyone on the journey; he pays for musicians and is expected to slaughter a pig or a sheep, a rare luxury, for feasting after the pilgrimage. His generous gift brings him prestige but no authority. Another official, the 'maestro', is chosen to lead the contingent to the shrine, and two young women are appointed as cross-bearers. The villagers fortify themselves for the gruelling pilgrimage to the shrine with a strong home-made brew called *trago*, firewater made from sugar cane. In Kamawara, possibly because the houses are cut off from one another and the rest of the world, there seem to be barriers of aloofness and mistrust which can only be broken down by alcohol.

The principal focus of the pilgrimage is a small painting of Christ, a kind of ikon known as the *lamina*. Wrapped for safe-keeping, it is the most revered object in Kamawara. The main purpose of crossing the mountains annually to Qoyllur Rit'i is to recharge the *lamina* with the sacred properties that have drained away during the year. It is thought, too, to contain all

Kamawara's sins accumulated since the last visit, which will vanish after the rigorous journey to the shrine.

The first day's walk takes the villagers to a meeting ground at the foot of a trail leading to the shrine. Here the thousands of pilgrims form an enormous camp, waiting in readiness for the final part of

Fertility rites are held annually for the various domesticated species – llamas, alpacas, cows and sheep. The animals are sprinkled with liquor, and the spirits of the earth and of the surrounding hills are invoked to protect them and make them multiply.

Ritual dancing is a feature of many highland Quechua festivals and pilgrimages. The masked dancer is an *ukuku*, and represents a bear. The other dances are *wayri ch'unchos*; with their headdresses of macaw feathers they represent the tribal peoples of the lowland jungle to the north (left).

213

Mongolia

The great celebrations in Mongolia are the *Nadam*, public festivals of games, horse-racing, wrestling and other sports. Since the 1930s, when Professor Owen Lattimore first saw a *Nadam*, they have become celebrations of the anniversary of the Communist Revolution in 1917. Lattimore describes the traditional elements that have been maintained: 'Wrestlers are presented as winners by heralds who still use the traditional forms of chanting. There is a particular kind of singing which is supposed to encourage and strengthen the spirit of the horse before the child-riders go out and start

the race. The classic distance for an important horse-race is eighteen to twenty miles.'

During the Qoyllur Rit'i fiesta, *ukuku* dancers climb the treacherous glacier which overhangs the shrine to recover a cross that has previously been planted there.

the journey, an exhausting five-mile climb up a single narrow footpath to the sanctuary. The shrine lies some 15,000 feet above sea level, high enough even for the local people to gasp for air. The piles of rocks that mark the approach to the sanctuary are treated with as much reverence as the cross placed on top.

To escort the *lamina* along the final stretch, the villagers of Kamawara, like all the other pilgrims, change into their dancing costumes, which are stylised caricatures of Indians and other South American people. There is no special explanation for these costumes. It may be that by dressing as pagan outsiders the pilgrims are trying to protect themselves as they bear the *lamina* along the last few yards to the source of sacred power.

Inside the sanctuary, above the altar, is a figure of Christ painted on a rock. At the altar the Kamawarans hand their *lamina* to a lay brother, one of the festival organisers. The dancers kneel in prayer and the *lamina* is left overnight in the presence of the Senor to be recharged with grace. Above the shrine is a grotto dedicated to the Virgin Mary, where the pilgrims can

Ukuku dancers kneel on the glacier above the Qoyllur Rit'i sanctuary, candles planted in the snow, and pray to the spirits of the mountains (above.)

The cross marking the entrance to the sacred precincts of the Qoyllur Rit'i shrine.

The shrine of Qoyllur Rit'i consists of an image of the crucified Christ on a rock, around which a sanctuary has been built. The image dates from an alleged miraculous appearance of Christ at the spot in 1783. Its popularity has waxed and waned over the years, and is currently enjoying a surge of popular devotion.

ask personal favours or beg for good harvests, abundant livestock and health.

The villagers dig in for the night, well apart from the other groups, huddling together in the bitter cold for warmth and protection. Next morning they dance once more up to the shrine to retrieve their *lamina*, which can now be taken back to the village in triumph. Home at last, they bear it in procession so that the rest of the villagers can see it and receive its blessing.

Like Kataragama, Qoyllur Rit'i is a focal point for enjoyment. In a society almost devoid of relief from the harsh everyday struggle for survival, the annual celebration for their patron saint is of tremendous importance. The Quechua do not let themselves go like the Bahian revellers at *Carnaval* time, overturning all accepted everyday values; but the festivities perform the essential function of revitalising the community.

MEN AND WOMEN
ASANTE, MOROCCANS, MASAI, MEHINAKU

An anthropologist who worked among the Sherpas of Nepal, Sherry Ortner, once wrote that 'everywhere, in every known culture, women are considered, in some degree, inferior to men'. In the West, many preconceptions about the roles of men and women have, in recent years, been overturned. Today we are witnessing the beginnings of a revolution in which women are successfully competing with men for equal or superior status, confounding traditional beliefs that sexual roles are pre-ordained by biological, social or cutlural imperatives. In *Men and Women Among the Azande* (1974), Sir Edward Evans-Pritchard wrote of male chauvinism: 'If we may be inclined to pass judgement on the Zande male for his attitude to his womenfolk, should we not remember that the battle for women's rights in Britain is only just over, if indeed it is?'

Anthropologists, with an array of examples for comparison, have been aware longer than most how varied the roles of the sexes can be. Although no evidence supports the myth of an Amazonian people dominated by powerful female warriors, there are many societies where, in certain spheres, women exert considerable influence and even a measure of economic control. Everywhere, however, sex roles are divided, and men rarely accept that their position is in any way inferior to that of women. On the contrary, men view female domination of certain areas of life as reinforcing their own superiority, since women's work is generally regarded as inferior and demeaning.

This chapter looks at the different roles played by men and women in four very different societies, the Asante in Ghana, the Moroccans in Marrakech, the Masai in Kenya and the Mehinaku in Brazil. We should bear in mind what Margaret Mead wrote about the ways the sexes behaved and were expected to behave. 'Every single culture that has ever existed has valued the male activities more than the female. It did not make any difference what these activities were – even dressing dolls – if the men did them, they were valuable.' Despite the often considerable influence wielded by the women in the four examples shown here, Margaret Mead's comment still applies.

The Asante

The Asante or Ashanti, who number over one million, live across the southern half of Ghana. They formed their own nation state in the eighteenth century and were among the fiercest and most successful opponents of the British through the nineteenth century until, after six wars, they were finally defeated in 1901. During those troubled times the Asante were ruled by a king, who controlled his people and territory by appointing powerful regional chiefs. Although the chiefs and leaders of Asante society were invariably men, senior women were always chosen to advise and to supervise the moral welfare of females. And in the Asante economy women also played a more central role.

Each day up to 70,000 people throng Kumasi's market, which handles every kind of merchandise from tomatoes to

Kumasi market in Ghana, one of the largest in Africa, is run entirely by women.

talcum powder. Decisions about what is sold, who sells it and at what price, are made by women. The only men in the market nowadays are employed as labourers and secretaries by the women, who have organised themselves into tightly run produce associations, each with its own elected leader known as a Queen Mother. She, together with a committee of elders, takes all the important decisions. Oba, the Queen Mother of the plantain section of the market, explains: 'I have been an "elder" or "leader" for a long time. At times I go to the Regional Minister because of the women I represent. I go to the union office, I go to the

Palace, I go to funerals. When the plantain comes in the women often quarrel and fight. I settle the disputes. It's not an easy task, I swear by your mother. Even in a disunited home there must be a leader and with 500 people, if they have no leader, there will be chaos.'

The Queen Mothers have power to punish offenders by fining them or banishing them from the market, and also to exercise control over the quantity and quality of the produce sold. This would appear to give some women considerable wealth and influence; but as Oba explains, such local influence only partially compensates for the disadvantage Asante women experience in other walks of life: 'If you look around you will see only women buying and selling plantains. No men sell plantains. Our work is difficult, we have to work very hard so that one day, if your husband is not there, you can look after the children, since they don't inherit from the father.'

Oba was referring to the fact that Asante society is matrilineal, meaning that sons do not inherit from their fathers or their fathers' relatives, but from their mothers' relatives. A man's wealth passes, not to his own son, but to his sister's son. Although in theory this should give women more influence and status, in practice it often entails great hardship for a woman, since on the death of her husband his property goes not to her and her children, but to his sister's children. She is therefore left to support her children alone until they can inherit from her brother.

During his lifetime, a father has strong ties and moral responsibilities for his own sons and daughters but no legal authority over them. Nevertheless, it is recognised that he cannot be expected to love his sister's children as much as his own. The anthropologist Meyer Fortes believed that the Asante matrilineal kinship structure resulted in greater equality between the sexes than in many other societies, because even though men exercise far more political power, this power is inherited through women. A son's property and a chief's authority are similarly derived from the mother's family.

It is in marriage and the system of polygamy, whereby the men can have, and prefer to have, more than one wife, that Asante women perceive themselves to be at a disadvantage. One man observes: 'Having two wives is useful for us. Any time things are not going right – for example, if a woman is menstruating she cannot cook for you, it is not allowed – if you have only one wife and she is menstruating, how will you and your family eat? Therefore if you have two wives and one is menstruating, the other will cook for you.'

Women are therefore at a grave disadvantage because their husband, without legal responsibilities for their children, can easily abandon them for a new wife. This is what happened to Oba, who is bitter about marriage. She is her husband's second wife, and when asked whether she felt that having more than one wife is a good thing, her response is vehement: 'It's really wrong, but how can we complain? Your husband does not even come from your own family; it's like a clash of two trains. How can you force your laws on him? You can't if he does not obey. All you

Although Asante women run the market and children inherit through their mothers, many women feel that they are still disadvantaged in Ghanaian society.

can do is just keep quiet. Once you speak out, you are finished. Marriage! It's really like a long story. No matter how much time you devote to it, there is still a lot to talk about. You can talk about it walking all the way from here to Europe. Men in Asante are really, really bad. Sooner or later they will desert you, so you have to work hard to support yourself. All that marriage brings you is trouble.' Because of these tensions, an Asante woman's most important relationship is with her children and her mother. Links between mothers and daughters are so strong that even after marriage some wives live apart from their husbands.

One of Oba's friends in the Kumasi market is Ama Sewa, the Yam Queen Mother. Like Oba, she has sought economic security in order to protect her children from a system where the father's responsibilities are minimal. Her story also demonstrates how differently the sexes regard marriage: 'When I grew up I married a man; we had eight children, one

died but the rest are all alive, and they are all from one mother and one father. During that time I learned to trade – to sell yams. Through this yam selling I managed to look after my children and send them to school. But in those days, if your husband wanted to take another wife, all he need do was compensate you. Usually the compensation was about thirteen shillings but if he loved you it could be as high as four pounds. My husband gave me four pounds' compensation and so I gave him permission to marry the other woman. We arranged things on a weekly basis. When my husband said he was going to sleep with his other wife, I would know that he was making love to her.'

The men may understand why many women feel bitterness towards the system, but for them it provides convenience and comfort without responsibility. Kwame Ajuman, from Ama's village, accepts that taking a second wife brought problems, but he insists that in the long run it is an asset for the first wife as well as for him. 'No woman likes to have competition. This is because a woman may be with you for a long time and help you along, and the moment you get prosperous you take another wife. This makes her bitter because she will have to share whatever you give to her. But if you arrange things properly, she will thank you because you have brought someone in who will help her.' His explanations for fixing a rigid sexual rota are equally pragmatic. 'This is because I get many visitors and the women get jealous of each other, so if I am not sleeping with one of them now, then she won't cook for my visitors . . . Everyone stays in their own house and I make a timetable for them; one stays for two weeks; after that the other sleeps at my house for the next two weeks. She leaves when her time is up and she takes away the bed sheets and bedding to wash. The one who comes also brings her own bedding and when she goes away she'll take them away.'

The position and role of the Asante market women is a reflection of other sections of society, including the royal family. King Opuko Ware II was elected in 1970, mainly because of the support he received from the Asante Queen Mother, the most powerful woman in the kingdom. All members of the royal family are related to her. When a king dies it is she who nominates his successor to the committee of elders, who makes the final decision. But this measure of apparent power has to be viewed in a wider context. By and large, women wield only limited influence in Asante society.

'It is an accepted fact with Asante,' explains one man, 'that God did not make us to worship women. Women must worship men. God did not make us to cook. God said that we should live by the sweat of our brow. So we work to earn what we give to our wives to cook for us. A man would only get near a fire if he does not have a wife or has led a useless life. It is very good to have a resourceful wife and much better if there are two. They do some petty trading. They can provide for the housekeeping. They can cook for you. So it helps me a lot! The different wives also compete and it gives pleasure in the marriage.'

The Moroccans of Marrakech

The independence that some Asante women have acquired through trading and the formation of tightly controlled associations would be unimaginable in the Islamic society of Marrakech in Morocco. The divine messages received by the Prophet Mohammed in the seventh century, which were later to form the Koran, were to have a revolutionary impact on the treatment of women in Islamic society by their menfolk over the next thirteen centuries.

The Prophet was influenced by the traditions and customs that prevailed in contemporary Arabia, and many of the

In the city of Marrakech, ancient Islamic customs about women are strictly observed.

Only in the seclusion of their family houses may women remove their veils and relax (right).

Hajiba, a dancer, is regarded as a woman without honour in Marrakech society because she allows men outside her family to see her unveiled (below).

behavioural rules and restrictions practised today by Muslims originated at that period. Laws such as the one which limited each man to four wives were established in the Koran. Following the customs of his own tribe, the Quraysh, Mohammed required a woman to act and dress with modesty. 'Say to the believing women that they cast down their looks and guard their privy parts and display not their ornaments except those of them that are external; and let them pull their veils over the opening of their chemises at their bosoms and not display their ornaments save to their husbands or their fathers.' (Koran 33) The literal interpretation of that statement in the Koran has led to women in many parts of the Muslim world being unable to venture outside their homes without being veiled; and although Mohammed made no mention of it, in later years a system of purdah was adopted, whereby women were kept behind the walls of their home so as not to be seen by any men other than those in their direct family.

In the city of Marrakech the rules of the Koran are strictly observed. The public places belong exclusively to the men; in the streets, the business houses, the mosques and the cafés, they mingle with friends and strangers. They are expected to be sensitive to slights upon their honour, and in public they cultivate an

image of aggressive virility. Women, on the other hand, must not be gazed at by strange men, and are kept in the seclusion of private courtyards, behind the high walls of the houses. They are wholly subordinate to their husbands and brothers.

Every Moroccan family is jealous of its honour, which is determined by the behaviour of the men in the public world and by the chastity of the women. Men consider women to be sexually irresponsible by nature. The merest whisper of gossip which casts doubt upon a woman's virtue threatens the family honour; so she must demonstrate her innocence visibly to the outside world. She is prohibited from

223

meeting or having any contact with men from other families; and since her reputation depends on her seclusion from strangers, when she emerges from the house she is expected to hide her face. A married woman goes out only at the discretion of her husband, and to do so without his consent can lead to suspicions of adultery. Most of the women who venture out into the streets of Marrakech still wear a veil and the cloak known as the *jellaba*. This costume is a tacit statement that a woman does not really belong in the public world of men, suggesting that she is not actually outdoors.

The Moroccans, too, are strictly patrilineal; inheritance passes from father to son. The father is responsible for the economic welfare of his children, and indeed the system of secluding women makes it virtually impossible for them to support themselves or their children should the marriage break down. For a Moroccan woman to attempt to earn and live independently would place her outside the acceptable bounds of society.

It is difficult for Muslim women to complain of their lot, particularly in front of non-Muslim foreigners. In their film *Some Women of Marrakech*, anthropologist Elizabeth Fernea and director Melissa Llewelyn-Davies were able to overcome this reticence by working with an all-female film team and relying on Fernea's intimate knowledge of Islamic society. One young Marrakech woman, Hajiba, explained to them how few choices are left to a woman if the protection of her immediate male relatives is removed. Her father was dead and she was separated from her husband. so she became a dancer. 'It's something I had to do,' she explains. 'I had no choice, I did it partly because of my little brothers and sisters. I wanted them to stay together in our village. I didn't want them to start running around after my father died. If we leave our land, it's like there's no trace of us left. My dancing helps the family stay together. The day my father died my elder brother said in front of everyone at dinner that I must leave! He threw my belongings into the street . . . I left the village and came here to Marrakech. Some months later he came after me, with a knife. He threatened me and said I was ruining his reputation.'

A woman such as Hajiba is regarded as without honour in Moroccan society and as a person who has brought disgrace to the whole family. Yet she enjoys a freedom undreamed of by other women. She sings and dances at social events in villages and towns and is much in demand for important festivities. At the same time, because Hajiba and women like her perform in front of strange men, they are thought to be women of easy virtue. Their freedom from the usual restrictions is looked on with awe by more traditional women; for the dancers of *shaikhaat* have the power to harm people who offend them by performing a special spell-casting dance.

Islam permits polygamy, and a wealthy Moroccan man is supposed to treat his wives equally, with his attention and wealth divided impartially among them. But a discussion with the elder wife of one polygamous marriage suggested that women in Morocco have problems that would be well understood by their Asante counterparts. 'He has four wives altogether,' confides this wife, 'and we each have our turn, one night at a time. Recently he took a new wife. We brought him children and did everything for him. He brought this new one and bought her a house near the city gates. He went off with her and left us living on our own, to make out as well as we can. That's the way the world is. We eat well, we live well, praise God. I suppose we must be thankful for all the things you see here surrounding us.'

But Morocco is changing, and the role of women is no longer maintained as strictly as traditionalists would like. One wealthy lady recounts how things had been in the past. 'We only went out once a fortnight,' she recalls. 'We'd put on our veils and our slippers and go to the steam-bath and stay there from the midday prayer until sunset. Then we'd come home and cook food for our husbands, praise the Prophet. But now all that's over. We've got our freedom. Since Morocco got independence we began to go out. Now, praise be to God, we move with the times. Like our children and everybody, we're in the grip of change.'

For the poor, change has come about from economic need. Not all families can afford to keep their women at home occupied only by domestic chores, or to

The main complaint of many women is the lack of attention they get when their husbands take additional younger wives.

225

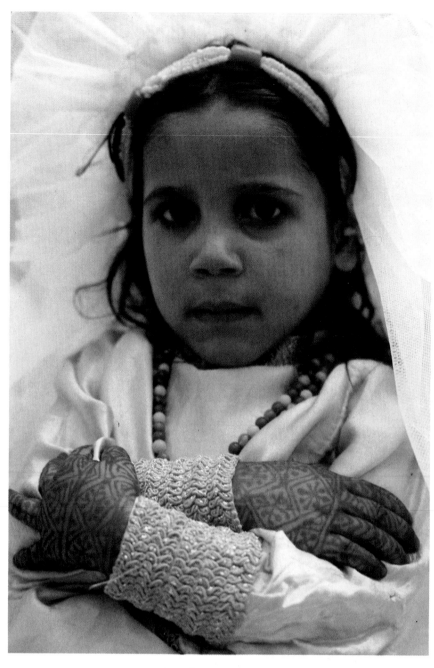

customs. She shouldn't go out uncovered. She shouldn't gossip or try to set evil on other people. That is how a woman should live whether she lives in Marrakech or in the countryside.' But a woman who wishes to stand by such ideals needs the support of her menfolk.

The ties between a woman and her father's family remain strong until marriage. When a girl marries, she enters her husband's family. This important transition is marked by a great ritual – the central point of which is the defloration of the bride. Her virginity, respresenting the honour of her father's family, is celebrated by the exhibition of her blood-stained clothing, which is borne off through the streets to her mother's house.

Women have to accept their role in Moroccan society. In a religious school girls learn to recite: 'In the name of God, the Compassionate, the Merciful. Men have authority over women because God has made the one superior to the other and because they spend their wealth to maintain them. Good women are obedient. In the name of God, the Compassionate, the Merciful.'

The Masai

In both Asante and Moroccan society, women are often indignant about their menfolk taking more than one wife; but they have little opportunity to object. So the reaction of a young Masai woman in Kenya who was asked by Melissa Llewelyn-Davies if she minded that her husband had acquired another wife is surprising.

'No,' was the reply. 'We're not jealous like you Europeans. If he brings even twenty more wives, that's fine. If we're jealous we're beaten and sent back home. To us, a co-wife is something very good because there is much work to do. When it rains, the village gets mucky. And it's you who clears it out. It's you who looks after the cows. You do the milking and your husband may have very many cows. That's a lot of work. You have to milk and smear the roof and see to the calves . . . So when you give birth and it rains, who will smear the roof if you have no co-wife? No one. Who will clear the muck from the village? No one. So Masai aren't jealous because of this work.'

employ servants to run errands outside the house. Aisha bint Mohammed comes from a family of small farmers who live some thirty miles outside Marrakech. She herself has spent most of her life in the city and is married to an unskilled labourer. She shares a small courtyard with six other families whose rented rooms open on to it.

In Marrakech jobs are hard to come by and it is sometimes easier for a woman than a poorly educated man to find work. Aisha has worked as a maid, in a laundry and in a bakery, icing pastries. She is a very religious woman and a strong believer in the conventional ideals. 'A woman should pray to God and observe our religion. She should follow our

Among the Masai, a woman is regarded as wealth.

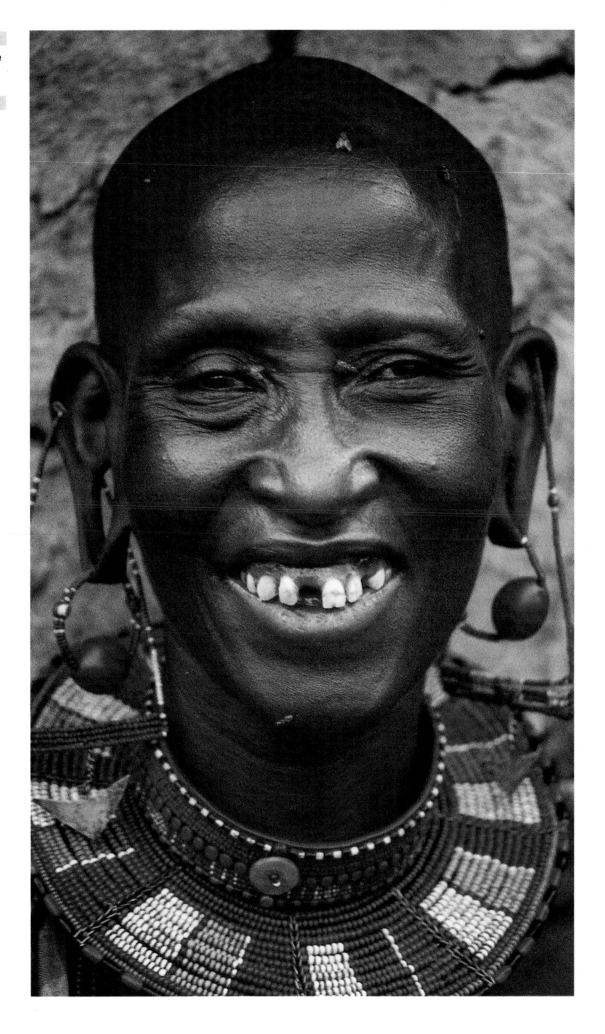

Nolpiyaya is one of twelve wives of a wealthy Masai elder and prophet.

Part of the difference in attitude lies in the Masai conception of wealth. Among these cattle-herding pastoralists along the Kenya-Tanzania border, wealth is measured in terms of cattle, women and children. In other societies wives and children may be regarded as expenses; here they represent wealth. A Masai man's riches may be measured by the size of his village, which includes not only the number of cattle in his herd but also the number of his female dependents. He needs a woman to build a house for him, to milk his cows and to do the household chores. But she needs a man far more. A woman is not permitted to own any animals, and to survive she must attach herself to a man – be he father, husband or son – with cattle. The essential thing for a Masai woman is to marry and bear sons, for it is they who will care for her.

This is especially important because of the age difference between husbands and wives. Women marry young. Men do not marry until they have been through warriorhood – from the age-grade of *moran* to that of junior elder (see Chapter Six). A junior warrior is aged between twenty-five and thirty, and even so it is not easy for him to acquire sufficient wealth to afford a bride. Girls of marriageable age therefore find that their husbands are wealthy senior elders.

In the film, Melissa Llewelyn-Davies asks Nolpiyaya, one of the twelve wives of an affluent Masai elder and prophet, whether a girl was happy to get married. 'Yes,' replies Nolpiyaya, 'because at home brothers mistreat you. You don't have your own cows to milk. But when you're married you build your own house and sit on your own bed.'

'And your husband?' asks Melissa.

'He's happy to have a wife to bear him children and to create a village.'

'Does a woman mind if her husband is old?'

'Sometimes she minds; she won't go near him. So she is tied up and beaten. And her family say: "You must marry that man." So you come to love him.'

For a woman, preparing for marriage is a lengthy and painful process. As a young girl she has led a fairly carefree life. She doesn't have much work to do, is flattered by the attentions of handsome warriors and has a secure home in her father's village. A girl's only anxiety, as she gets older, is not to get pregnant until she has been formally initiated into maturity. However, as she nears marriageable age, she gets ready to be circumcised.

The female circumcision ceremony begins as a private family affair. For the girl it is her farewell to childhood and also to her father's village, because she will marry soon afterwards. From a giggly adolescent she will now be transformed into a mature and thoughtful woman. Her head is shaved, she relinquishes her childhood name and she gives away her jewels to a younger sister. It marks the total shedding of her previous identity.

After circumcision, a woman is considered fertile and entitled to become pregnant. Nolpiyaya explains why this is so important: 'A girl wants to hurry up and be circumcised. It's a very good thing so long as she is not pregnant. When a girl grows up she no longer wants to get near men because she doesn't want to get pregnant. She just goes and plays around with warriors and then goes to sleep in her mother's house.'

All marriages are arranged by men, and the bride knows neither her husband nor his village. The marriage itself is also the focus for an important ritual. On her arrival in her new husband's village the bride is surrounded by the village women,

A married Masai woman has milking rights over her husband's cows, but she does not own them.

All Masai marriages are arranged by men, and the bride is a stranger to her husband and to his village.

including her new co-wives, who proceed to hurl insults at her. 'Look, there's a thief coming!' screeches Maliyani. The others join in: 'She'll bring shame on us. She must be a thief. Leave her alone, she cried all night. She didn't eat yesterday. What have you come here for? Hyenas will crunch your bones tonight. Look at her teeth!'

All Masai women have to endure this humiliation. They are compelled to leave their mothers and to settle among strangers. The ritual of public insult dramatises the isolation of the young bride, exposing her anxieties to the women who are already established in the village – the very women on whom she will rely for friendship and support.

Maliyani's behaviour appears curiously ambivalent. Although she hurls some of the worst threats at the new wife, she seems anxious to protect her: 'Go on, cry! There's no one to help you. Your husband's only got one cow and that's got rabies. Hurry up because we're ready to brand you. Your husband's got no cows, only pumpkins. Stop crying now.'

A married Masai woman is given milking rights over some of her husband's cows; but not one of them really belongs to her and if her husband decides to sell or slaughter any, she can do nothing about it. As Nolpiyaya puts it: 'No Masai woman can ever say, "I shall sell a cow; I have a purpose in mind." She is only holding them in trust for her sons.' Marriage is more concerned with organising rights over animals than with friendship or affection. If a woman cannot choose her husband, she can choose a lover, often from the ranks of the young *moran*. Husbands will beat their wives if they find out; but there is no dishonour attached to adultery as there is in western society.

Masai and Moroccan women both have to accept that they do not control their own lives. While Muslim women refer to the Koran, Masai wives explain their position by means of a myth: 'Elephants used to carry things for women long ago. Buffal-

Marriage among the Masai is chiefly about the apportionment of rights over livestock.

The Mehinaku of Brazil believe that in the past men took care of children and domestic duties while women hunted and worked in the fields.

oes were our cows. Gazelles were our goats. Warthogs were our sheep. Zebras were our donkeys. Those were our animals. One day the women got up early to slaughter an animal and every woman said: "My son won't go herding today. He'll stay to eat kidney." So the animals went off into the forest. They all became wild . . . That is why we women no longer own animals. Men own all the cows. We became men's servants, because our cows went off on their own. So we own nothing. All we have now is our gourds to milk into. That's the way it is.'

The Mehinaku

On a tributary of the Xingu River in central Brazil live the Mehinaku, a tribe of hunters, gatherers, fishermen and slash-and-burn farmers. Like the Cuiva (see Chapter Two), the Mehinaku never stop long in one place. After three or four years, when they have exhausted the soil in a particular area, they move on and clear another, preparing to plant the manioc which is essential to their diet.

The Mehinaku, like the Masai, have a myth to explain why men and women differ and why they perform separate

233

Mehinaku girls understand their role at an early age.

The Mehinaku have many rituals to ensure the success of their crops.

functions. Originally, according to the myth, men took care of children, breast-fed babies, prepared flour from the manioc and wove hammocks, while women fished, hunted and cleared the fields. In that mythical age women had a special house, which was sacred and used for ceremonies: 'A man who dared enter the woman's house during their ceremonies would be gang-raped by all the women of the village.' The women protected the sacred flute used in their rituals. But, continues the myth, the men learned from their chief to frighten the women and captured the flutes: 'We grabbed the flutes and took over the houses. Today if a woman comes in here and sees our flutes, we rape her. Today the women nurse babies, process manioc flour and weave hammocks, while we hunt, fish and farm.' The flutes represent the dangerous spirit Koiuku; and as the Mehinaku chief Ayuruwa explains: 'A woman doesn't go into the men's house. If a woman saw the flute spirit inside, she would die in a month.'

The roles of women in Mehinaku society are determined at a very early age. Children are everywhere brought up to understand and play the role that is socially acceptable for their sex. This is reflected in their games, many of which are detailed imitations of adult behaviour. During one of their popular games, the boys and girls, aged from five to twelve,

The *pequi* spirits are fed to guarantee a good harvest.

acted out Mehinaku marriage rituals; 'husbands' pretended to hunt and fish, returning with leaves in place of animals, while 'wives' prepared manioc. Then, like their elders, the children paired-off and made for a hidden area to imitate sexual intercourse. 'The Mehinaku are sexually free,' explains the anthropologist Thomas Gregor, 'and most children have had some degree of experience by the time they are adolescent.'

After adolescence, the games become serious. One of the most demanding of female domestic roles is the preparation of manioc. On poor forest soils, manioc provides the Mehinaku with a reliable diet. The women extract the edible portions of the tuber by scraping and grinding them to a pulp so that the unwanted parts are washed away. The women shape the manioc flour into loaves and leave them to dry in the sun. Another important domestic task is the making of hammocks. A man often refers affectionately to his wife as 'my little hammock', reflecting her household skills.

236

Most children have sexual experience by the time they are adolescent.

A Mehinaku man in ritual clothing waiting for his turn to participate in the ceremonies.

The different roles of men and women are not confined to domestic matters. They each have their separate assembly places in the village. The men's hut is exclusively male territory, upon penalty of gang-rape. When they are not hunting, fishing or working, that is where they should be. On the other hand, the house and its immediate surroundings are feminine areas; the men are not encouraged to spend too much time there. Those who do are referred to, behind their backs, as 'rubbish-yard men' or simply 'women'.

The sexual divide in the everyday life of the Mehinaku is most clearly expressed in their ritual activities. One of the most important ceremonies, held in the autumn, is for the spirits of the *pequi* fruit. Each year, after the fruit is harvested, the Mehinaku set about ensuring that next year's crop will be a good one. They have a long-standing relationship with the spirits that in return for food and entertainment an abundant crop will be guaranteed. Yumuy, the son of the Mehinaku chief, explains: 'We have rituals for the *pequi* spirits, to let them have their own food. Otherwise they're sad. They eat fish and *pequi* nuts and drink porridge. If we didn't

feed the spirits there would not be any *pequi*. We bring the spirits into the village to feed them. That is a really beautiful ceremony.'

The sexual associations of the *pequi* fruit are revealed in the story of its origins. In ancient times, two sisters went down to the river to bathe. Yakajukuma, a great alligator, came out of the water and the women began to run away. But the skin of the alligator peeled open and out stepped a handsome young man. He became the lover of the girls and every day returned to have sex with them. They would duly call out from the river bank, 'Great alligator spirit, let us have sex.' When the men of the village discovered what was happening, they ambushed the alligator spirit and killed it. The grieving girls buried the body, and from its sexual parts grew the first *pequi* tree.

The *pequi* rituals last a month, some of them spaced out over several days. The final elaborate *mapulawaja* ceremony goes on for four days. Each owner of a *pequi* orchard sponsors two men to bring in a *pequi* spirit. The men return to the village, bearing *pequi* leaves, and assume the identity of the spirits. They are stopped by

239

the women, who give them food, and then approach the men's house, where they are asked about the prospects for the coming year. They are joined by other male spirits, and this heralds the arrival of a different spirit known as Aripi, in the guise of a grotesque old woman. When all the spirits are assembled, they get the food and share it with the people present. The climax of the *mapulawaja* ritual comes when the men playing the part of Aripi take up painted gourds, which represent vaginas, and taunt the village women. Inside one of the huts, the men dance in a circle around the centre pole while the women form a straight line facing them. The men wave their gourds and continue

to provoke the women until, in mock anger, they attack their tormentors.

Even though Mehinaku rituals tend to emphasise and confirm the separate roles of men and women, the distinction between the sexes is, in certain respects, less rigid than in many other parts of the world. Thomas Gregor pointed out how the village tolerated deviant sexual practices; although such inclinations were not encouraged, no attempt was made to interfere with male or female homosexual encounters when they became known. Even when a man assumed the duties of a woman, adopting feminine clothes and paint, and taking male lovers, he was still an accepted part of the community.

Films in the series DISAPPEARING WORLD up to 1988

Title	Group	Producer/Director	Research
A Clearing in the Jungle	PANARE, Venezuela	Charlie Nairn	
The Last of the Cuiva	CUIVA, Colombia	Brian Moser	
Embera – the End of the Road	EMBERA, Colombia	Brian Moser	
War of the Gods	MAKU, BARASANA, Colombia	Brian Moser	
The Tuareg	TUAREG, Algeria	Charlie Nairn	
The Meo	HMONG, Laos	Brian Moser	Chris Curling
Dervishes of Kurdistan	KURDS, Iran	Brian Moser	André Singer
Kataragama – A God for all Seasons	SINGHALESE, Sri Lanka	Charlie Nairn	Angela Burr
The Mursi	MURSI, Ethiopia	Leslie Woodhead	André Singer
The Mehinacu	MEHINAKU, Brazil	Carlos Pasini	
Masai Women	MASAI, Kenya	Chris Curling	Melissa Llewelyn-Davies
The Kawelka: Ongka's Big Moka	KAWELKA, Papua New Guinea	Charlie Nairn	Pattie Winter
The Quechua	QUECHUA, Peru	Carlos Pasini	David Ash
The Sakuddei	SAKUDDEI, Indonesia	John Sheppard	
Masai Manhood	MASAI, Kenya	Chris Curling	Melissa Llewelyn-Davies
The Kirghiz of Afghanistan	KIRGHIZ, Afghanistan	Charlie Nairn	André Singer
Mongolia: On the Edge of the Gobi*	KHALKHA, Mongolia	Brian Moser	
Mongolia: The City on the Steppes*	KHALKHA, Mongolia	Brian Moser	
The Shilluk	SHILLUK, Sudan	Chris Curling	André Singer
The Eskimos of Pond Inlet	IGULINGMUIT, Canada	Michael Grigsby	Pattie Winter
Some Women of Marrakech	MOROCCANS, Morocco	Melissa Llewelyn-Davies	
Saints and Spirits*	MOROCCANS, Morocco	Melissa Llewelyn-Davies	
The Rendille	RENDILLE, Kenya	Chris Curling	
The Sherpas	SHERPAS, Nepal	Leslie Woodhead	Pattie Winter
The Umbanda	UMBANDISTAS, Brazil	Stephen Cross	
Khyber*	PATHANS AND BRITISH, North-West Frontier	André Singer	Andy Harries
Afghan Exodus*	PATHANS, KIRGHIZ, HAZARA, Pakistan	André Singer	David Ash
The Pathans	PATHANS, Pakistan	André Singer	Andy Harries
The Kwegu	KWEGU, Ethiopia	Leslie Woodhead	Andy Harries
The Azande	AZANDE, Sudan	André Singer	David Jenkins
Asante Market Women	ASANTE, Ghana	Claudia Milne	Jane Gabriel
Inside China: Living with the Revolution*	RURAL HAN, South East China	Leslie Woodhead	Claire Lasko
Inside China: The Newest Revolution*	RURAL HAN, South East China	Leslie Woodhead	Claire Lasko
Inside China: The Kazakhs*	Kazakhs, China	André Singer	David Jenkins
In Search of Cool Ground – The Mursi Trilogy: The Mursi (reversion of 1974 film) The Kwegu (reversion of 1982 film) The Migrants (new film)	MURSI, Ethiopia KWEGU, Ethiopia MURSI, Ethiopia	Leslie Woodhead Leslie Woodhead Leslie Woodhead	André Singer Andy Harries David Wason
An Invisible Enemy*	SAMI, Norway	Peter Carr	Liz Andrew
The Basques of Santazi	BASQUES, France	Leslie Woodhead	David Wason
The Kayapo	KAYAPO, Brazil	Michael Beckham	Peter Connors
The Lau	LAU, Solomon Islands	Leslie Woodhead	David Wason
Lamalera	LAMAHOLOT, Indonesia	John Blake	David Wason
Gypsies	VLACH GYPSIES, Hungary	John Blake	Fiona Moffitt
The Wodaabe	WODAABE, Niger	Leslie Woodhead	David Wason

Series and executive producers: BRIAN MOSER, JEREMY WALLINGTON, ANDRE SINGER, STEVE MORRISON, ROD CAIRD *Produced by

Camera	Sound Recordist	Editor	Anthropologist	First British Transmission	
Bob Bolt	Neil Kingsbury	Gerry Dow	Jean-Paul Dumont	May 1970	CLEARING
Ernest Vincze	Bruce White	Dai Vaughan	Bernard Arcand	April 1971	CUIVA
Michael Whittaker	Colin Richards	Kelvin Hendrie	Ariane Deluz	May 1971	EMBERA
Ernest Vincze	Bruce White	Martin Smith	Peter Silverwood-Cope, Stephen and Christine Hugh-Jones	June 1971	WAR OF GODS
Michael Dodds	Eoin McCann	Dai Vaughan	Jeremy Keenan	April 1972	TUAREG
Michael Davis	Eoin McCann	Dai Vaughan	Jacques Lemoine	July 1972	MEO
Michael Dodds	Christian Wangler	Dai Vaughan	Ali Bulookbashi and André Singer	November 1973	DERVISHES
Ernest Vincze	Bruce White	David Naden	Gananath Obeyesekere	November 1973	KATARAGAMA
Michael Dodds	Christian Wangler	Kelvin Hendrie	David Turton	November 1974	MURSI
Stephen Goldblatt	Bruce White	Gene Ellis	Thomas Gregor	November 1974	MEHINACU
Charles Stewart	Ian Bruce	Dai Vaughan	Melissa Llewelyn-Davies	November 1974	MASAI (1)
Ernest Vincze	Bruce White	Shelagh Brady	Andrew Strathern	December 1974	ONGKA
Stephen Goldblatt	Mike MacDuffy	Gene Ellis	Michael Sallnow	December 1974	QUECHUA
Dick Pope	Bob Alcock	Andrew Page	Reimar Schefold	December 1974	SAKUDDEI
Charles Stewart	Neil Kingsbury	Dai Vaughan	Melissa Llewelyn-Davies	April 1975	MASAI (2)
John Davey	Eoin McCann	Francesca Ross	Nazif Shahrani	December 1975	KIRGHIZ
Ivan Strasburg	Eoin McCann	Jane Wood	Owen Lattimore	December 1975	EDGE OF GOBI
Ivan Strasburg	Eoin McCann	Dai Vaughan	Owen Lattimore	December 1975	CITY ON STEPPES
Ernest Vincze and Ivan Strasburg	Bruce White	Ted Roberts	Walter Kunijwok and Paul Howell	January 1976	SHILLUK
Ivan Strasburg	Mike McDuffy	David Gladwell	Hugh Brody	January 1977	ESKIMO
Diane Tammes	Marilyn Grant	Dai Vaughan	Elizabeth Fernea	January 1977	MARRAKECH
Diane Tammes	Marilyn Grant	Terry Twigg	Elizabeth Fernea	(spin-off: not UK)	SAINTS + SPIRITS
Charles Stewart	Bruce White	Terry Twigg	Anders Grum	February 1977	RENDILLE
Michael Dodds	Christian Wangler	Kelvin Hendrie	Sherry Ortner	April 1977	SHERPAS
Michael Thomson	Phil Taylor	Jeff Harvey	Peter Fry	November 1977	UMBANDA
Michael Thomson	Alan Bale	Jack Dardis	Akbar Ahmed and Louis Dupree	June 1979	KHYBER
Michael Thomson	Ray French	Alan Ringland	Akbar Ahmed and Rémy Dor	August 1980	AFGHAN EXODUS
Michael Thomson	Alan Bale	Andrew Sumner	Akbar Ahmed	November 1980	PATHANS
Michael Blakeley	Phil Smith	Oral Norrie Ottey	David Turton	March 1982	KWEGU
Michael Thomson	Ray French	Jack Dardis	John Ryle	March 1982	AZANDE
Diane Tammes	Diana Ruston	Andy Sumner	Charlotte Boaitey	March 1982	ASANTE
Michael Thomson	Ray French	Oral Norrie Ottey	Barbara Hazard	April 1983	CHINA 1
Michael Thomson	Ray French	Oral Norrie Ottey	Barbara Hazard	May 1983	CHINA 2
Michael Blakeley	Phil Taylor	Oral Norrie Ottey	Shirin Akiner	May 1983	CHINA 3 (KAZAKHS)
					MURSI I, II, III
Michael Dodds	Christian Wangler	Kelvin Hendrie	David Turton	October 1985	
Michael Blakeley	Phil Smith	Oral Norrie Ottey	David Turton	October 1985	
Michael Blakeley	David Woods	Oral Norrie Ottey	David Turton	October 1985	
Mike Rainer and Nicholas Plowright	Phil Smith		Georg Henriksen	February 1987	SAMI
Michael Blakeley	David Woods	Oral Norrie Ottey	Sandra Ott	June 1987	BASQUES
Michael Blakeley	David Woods	Paul Griffiths-Davies	Terence Turner	June 1987	KAYAPO
Jon Woods	Ray French	Oral Norrie Ottey	Pierre Maranda	June 1987	LAU
Lawrence Jones	John Curtis	Paul Griffiths-Davies	Robert Barnes	In Production	LAMALERA
			Michael Stewart	In Production	GYPSIES
			Mette Bovin	In Production	WODAABE

the DISAPPEARING WORLD team, but not transmitted under series title.

The Anthropologists

The brief notes below relate to the anthropologists who contributed to *Disappearing World*.

AKBAR AHMED is an anthropologist with twenty years' experience as a government servant in the North-West Frontier Province of Pakistan. He is currently Commissioner, Sibi Division, Baluchistan. From 1987-8 he was Iqbal Fellow at the University of Cambridge. He has written extensively on Pathan society, including *Pukhtun Economy and Society: Traditional Structure and Economic Development in a Tribal Society*.

SHIRIN AKINER is Lecturer in Central Asian Studies at the School of Oriental and African Studies, London. She has travelled widely in Central Asia and speaks a number of local languages. She is the editor of the *Central Asian File* and her publications include *The Islamic Peoples of the Soviet Union*.

BERNARD ARCAND is Professor titulaire in anthropology at the University of Laval and an executive member of the Canadian Association of Sociologists and Anthropologists. He has published extensively on his field work among the Cuiva Indians of Brazil, including *The Urgent Situation of the Cuiva Indians of Colombia*, 1972.

ROBERT BARNES is Lecturer in Social Anthropology at the University of Oxford. He has conducted research with the Lamalera at Kédang in Eastern Indonesia since 1969 and has written extensively about them, including *Kédang: a Study of the Collective Thought of an Eastern Indonesian People*.

CHARLOTTE BOAITEY has been practising as a barrister since 1982. After obtaining a Diploma in Social Anthropology from Oxford University in 1985 she acted as consultant anthropologist to *Disappearing World*. She has lectured on African family law and the role of women in African societies.

HUGH BRODY is an Honorary Associate of the Scott Polar Research Institute, Cambridge. He has continued to write about and film in the Canadian North since he collaborated with *Disappearing World* in 1975. His books include *The People's Land, Maps and Dreams* and *Living Arctic*. His films include *Treaty 8 Country, People of the Islands* and *On Indian Land*.

ALI BULOOKBASHI did field work in Azerbaijan and Kurdestan towards his doctorate at Oxford University before returning to Iran to work for the Ministry of Culture on folklore and anthropology.

ARIANE DELUZ holds a senior research position at the Laboratoire d'Anthropologie Sociale du Collège de France de l'Ecole des Hautes Etudes en Sciences Sociales in Paris. She has written extensively on African societies, particularly the Guro of the Ivory Coast. During 1968-71 she conducted field work among the Embera of Colombia.

REMY DOR is a Researcher for the French National Centre for Scientific Research and Professor at the School for Oriental Languages at the Sorbonne, Paris. He has specialised in the Turkic peoples and the languages of Afghanistan and Central Asia. He has written or edited seven books on the Kirghiz, the Uzbek and their oral literature.

JEAN-PAUL DUMONT is currently Professor at the Department of Anthropology of the University of Washington. His areas of specialisation are France, the Philippine lowlands and the South American lowlands. His publications include *Under the Rainbow: Nature and supernature among the Panare Indians*.

LOUIS DUPREE is Adjunct Professor of Anthropology at Pennsylvania State University. He has been conducting ethnographic and archaeological research in Afghanistan and Pakistan for nearly forty years. He has held numerous academic positions and written very extensively about Afghanistan, including a classic work *Afghanistan*, first published in 1973.

ELIZABETH FERNEA is Senior Lecturer in Middle Eastern Studies and English at the University of Texas at Austin. In 1982 she was involved in the production of three half-hour films about social change in the Arab world from the woman's perspective. Her publications include *Middle Eastern Muslim Women Speak*.

PETER FRY first taught anthropology at University College, London following field work on cults in Zimbabwe. He founded the anthropology department in the University of Campinas in Brazil from 1973 and left in 1984 to become Director of the Ford Foundation in Rio de Janeiro. His best known book is *Spirits of Protest*, 1976.

THOMAS GREGOR is Professor of Anthropology at Vanderbilt University, Nashville, Tennessee. His major interests are the study of gender and sexuality and of conflict and war among the Indians of South America. His publications include *Mehinaku: The Drama of Daily Life in a Brazilian Village*.

BARBARA HAZARD did extensive research into Chinese communes and was Visiting Lecturer in Sociology in the Nankai University in Tianjin in 1981-2. She was Associate Professor of the Sociology of Modern China at the Free University of Berlin until 1984 when she became Director of the Chinese Language Department in the Polytechnic of Central London. In 1986 she returned to the US to study law. Her publications include *Peasant Organisation and Peasant Individualism*.

GEORG HENRIKSEN is Senior Lecturer in the Department of Social Anthropology at the University of Bergen. He has conducted field work among the caribou-hunting Naskapi Indians of Labrador, the Turkana nomads of Kenya and the Saami (Lapps) of Norway (1982-3).

PAUL HOWELL is a Fellow of Wolfson College, Oxford and Director of Development Studies Courses at the University of Cambridge. As a District Commissioner he spent many years among Nilotic tribes in the Southern Sudan and was an anthropological observer at the burial and installation of three Shilluk kings. His publications include *Nuer Law*.

CHRISTINE and STEPHEN HUGH-JONES have both conducted field work in Colombian Amazonia. Stephen Hugh-Jones is Lecturer in Social Anthropology at the University of Cambridge and a Fellow of King's College. His publications include *The Palm and the Pleiades: Initiation and Cosmology in Northwest Amazonia*. Christine Hugh-Jones's main publication is *From the Milk River: Spatial and Temporal Processes in Northwest Amazonia*.

JEREMY KEENAN is a Professor of Social Anthropology at the University of Witwatersrand, Johannesburg. He has worked extensively in both the Sahara and Southern Africa and has written at length about both regions. His publications include *The Tuareg: The People of Ahaggar*.

WALTER KUNIJWOK studied folklore at Khartoum University before completing a doctorate at Oxford University in race relations. He was Minister for Labour and Social Security in the Sudanese Government until 1987.

OWEN LATTIMORE was Professor of Chinese Studies at Leeds University until 1970, when he retired after a distinguished career in several fields. His early childhood was spent in China. He first visited in Mongolia in 1926 and has been returning regularly ever since. His publications include a number of classic works.

JACQUES LEMOINE is Director of the Centre for the Anthropological Study of South China and the Indochinese Peninsula, Paris. He is in charge of several research projects on the Southern Han Chinese, the Mia Yao and the Tai peoples. His publications include *L'Initiation du Mort chez les Hmong*.

MELISSA LLEWELYN-DAVIES conducted two years' field work among Masai women towards research at Harvard University before joining Granada Television as a researcher and later producer/director of *Disappearing World*. In 1984 she completed a five-part film *Diary of a Masai Village*, which was transmitted by the BBC.

PIERRE MARANDA is Professor of Anthropology at Laval University. He first visited the Lau of Malaita in the South Pacific in 1966, and his research on them continues. His publications include *Folklore and Culture Change: Lau Riddles of Modernisation*.

GANANATH OBEYESEKERE is Professor and Chairman of the Department of Anthropology, Princeton University. He has written extensively about the ethnography and sociology of Sri Lanka. His publications include *The Cult of the Goddess Pattini* and, with Richard Gombrich, *Buddhism Transformed: Religion and Social Change in Modern Sri Lanka*.

SHERRY ORTNER is Professor of Anthropology at the University of Michigan. She has been conducting research into Sherpa society since 1966. Her publications include *Sherpas Through Their Rituals* and she is preparing a study of the culture and history of the Sherpa monasteries.

SANDRA OTT is Director of the Ithaca College London Centre and Adjunct Professor of Basque Studies, University of Nevada, Reno. She holds a D.Phil in Social Anthropology from the University of Oxford for her work on the French Basque community filmed by *Disappearing World*. This was published as *The Circle of Mountains: A Basque Shepherding Community*.

JOHN RYLE studied English and Social Anthropology at Oxford University. From 1976-9 he was an Assistant Editor of the *Times Literary Supplement*. His publications include *Warriors of the White Nile: The Dinka*.

MICHAEL SALLNOW is Lecturer in Anthropology at the London School of Economics. Since 1972 he has been researching the Cusco region of the Peru-

vian Andes. His publications include *Pilgrims of the Andes: Regional Cults in Cusco*.

REIMAR SCHEFOLD is Associate Professor in Cultural Anthropology at the Free University, Amsterdam. He has done field work in Indonesia and in Africa (Tunisia and Senegal). He has numerous publications in the areas of Symbolic Anthropology and Material Culture.

NAZIF SHAHRANI is Associate Professor of Anthropology at the University of California at Los Angeles. His publications include *The Kirghiz and Wakhi of Afghanistan*, and *Revolutions and Rebellions in Afghanistan: Anthropological Perspectives*, for which he was both a contributor and Senior Editor.

PETER SILVERWOOD-COPE worked on Edmund Leach's Northwest Amazonian project of 1968 to 1972. He returned to Britain in 1971 and wrote his Ph.D at Cambridge University. He is currently Professor of Anthropology at the University of Brasilia, Brazil.

ANDREW STRATHERN is Mellon Distinguished Professor of Anthropology at the University of Pittsburgh. He has carried out extensive field work in the Highlands of Papua New Guinea since 1964. His publications include *One Father, One Blood: Descent and Group Structure among the Melpa People*.

TERRY TURNER is Professor of Anthropology at the University of Chicago. He has been conducting field work among the Kayapo for twenty-five years. His numerous publications include 'Kinship, Household and Community Structure among the Kayapo' in *Dialectical Societies* by David Maybery-Lewis.

DAVID TURTON is Senior Lecturer in Social Anthropology at the University of Manchester. He has conducted field work among the Mursi of Southern Ethiopia since 1968, and has written extensively about them. He is currently preparing a definitive study of the Mursi.

BIBLIOGRAPHY

Introduction

BEATTIE, John, *Other Cultures*, New York: Free Press 1964.

EVANS-PRITCHARD, E.E., *Essays in Social Anthropology*, London: Faber and Faber 1962.

EVANS-PRITCHARD, E.E., *Social Anthropology*, London: Cohen and West 1951.

HENLEY, Paul, 'Recent Developments in Ethnographic Film-making in Britain', *Anthropology Today* 1985.

LEACH, E.R., *Social Anthropology* London: Fontana Masterguides 1982.

LEWIS, I.M., *Social Anthropology in Perspective*, London: Penguin 1976.

LIENHARDT, Godfrey, *Social Anthropology*, Oxford: Oxford University Press 1964.

LOIZOS, Peter, 'Granada Television's Disappearing World Series: An Appraisal', *American Anthropologist* 1980.

MAIR, Lucy, *An Introduction to Social Anthropology*, Oxford: Oxford University Press 1972.

POCOCK, David, *Understanding Social Anthropology*, London: Hodder & Stoughton 1975.

STREET, Brian, *The Savage in Literature*, Routledge & Kegan Paul, 1975

WEAVER, T., Ed., *To See Ourselves: Anthropology and Modern Social Issues*, Illinois: Scott, Foresman, 1973.

WOODBURN, James, Ed., *The Royal Anthropological Institute Film Library Catalogue* 1982, (revised in 1988)

CHAPTER I

THE WINDS OF CHANGE (Tuareg, Eskimos, Basques)

BALIKCI, Asen, *The Netsilik Eskimos*, New York: Museum of Natural History 1970.

BIRKET-SMITH, K., *The Eskimos*, London: Methuen 1959.

BREEDEN, Robert L., Ed., *Nomads of the World*, Washington: National Geographic Society 1971.

DUMOND, Don E., *The Eskimos and Aleuts*, London: Thames & Hudson 1987.

GREENWOOD, Davydd J., *Unrewarding Wealth: The Commercialization and Collapse of Agriculture in a Spanish Basque Town*, Cambridge: Cambridge University Press 1976.

KEENAN, Jeremy, *The Tuareg: People of the Ahaggar*, London: Allen Lane 1977.

MAGEMAU, Martina, *et al.*, *Arctic Life: Challenge to Survive*, Pittsburgh: Carnegie Institute 1983.

MERKUR, Daniel, *Becoming Half Hidden: Shamanism and Initiation among the Inuit*, Stockholm: Almqvist & Wiksell 1985.

MURPHY, Robert F., 'Tuareg Kinship', *American Anthropologist*, 1967.

NICOLAISEN, Johannes, *Ecology and Culture of the Pastoral Tuareg*, Copenhagen: National Museum of Copenhagen 1963.

NORRIS, H.T., *Indigenous Peoples of the Sahara*, Oxford: Pergamon Press 1984.

OTT, Sandra J., *The Circle of Mountains: A Basque Shepherding Community*, Oxford: Clarendon Press 1984.

PITSEOLAK, Peter and Eber, Dorothy H., *People From Our Side: An Eskimo Life Story in Words and Photos*, Bloomington and London: University of Indiana Press 1975.

RICHES, David, *Northern Nomadic Hunter-Gatherers: A Humanistic Approach*, London: Academic Press 1982.

STEPHENS, Merc, *Linguistic Minorities of Western Europe*, Llandysul: Gamer 1978.

TREMBLAY, Marc-Adelard, Ed., *The Pattern of 'Amerindian' Identity*, Quebec: Presses de l'Université Laval 1976.

CHAPTER 2

CLASH OF CULTURES (Cuiva, Kayapo, Sakuddei, Maku and Barasana, Meo)

Arcand, Bernard, *The Urgent Situation of the Cuiva Indians of Columbia*, Copenhagen: International Work Group for Indigenous Affairs 1972.
Arcand, Bernard, 'The Cuiva Band', in G.A. Smith and D.H. Turner, Eds., *Challenging Anthropology*, Toronto: McGraw Hill 1979.
Beauclair, Inez de, *Tribal Cultures of Southwest China*, Taipei: Orient Cultural Service 1970.
Campbell, Margaret, *et al.*, *From the Hands of the Hills*, Hong Kong: Media Transasia 1981.
Cowell, Adrian, *The Heart of the Forest*, London: Gollancz 1960.
Geddes, William R., *Migrants of the Mountains: The Cultural Ecology of the Blue Miao*, Oxford: Clarendon Press 1976.
Hames, Raymond B. and Vickers, William T., Eds., *Adaptive Response of Native Amazonians*, New York: Academic Press 1983.
Kunstadter, Peter *et al.*, Eds., *Farmers in the Forest*, Honolulu: University Press of Hawaii 1978.
Lebar, Frank M., Ed., *Insular Southeast Asia: Ethnographic Studies*, New Haven: Human Relations Area Files 1976–7.
Lemoine, Jacques, *Un village Hmong vert du haut Laos*, Paris: CNRS 1972.
Maybury-Lewis, David, Ed., *Dialectical Societies*, Cambridge, Mass., and London: Harvard University Press 1979.
McKinnon, John and Bhruksasri, Wanat, Eds., *Highlanders of Thailand*, Kuala Lumpur: Oxford University Press 1983.
Schefold, R., 'Religious Involution: Internal Change, and its Consequences, in the Taboo-System of the Mentawaians', *Tropical Man*, 1976.
Turner, Terrence S., 'The Ge And Bororo Societies as Dialectic Systems: A General Model', in David Maybury Lewis, *Dialectical Societies*, Cambridge: Harvard University Press 1979.
Turner, Terrence S., 'Kinship, Household and Community Structure among the Kayapo', in David Maybury-Lewis, *Dialectical Societies*, Cambridge: Harvard University Press 1979.
Villas Boas, Orlando and Villas Boas, Claudio, *Xingu: the Indians, Their Myths*, London: Souvenir Press 1975.
Walker, Anthony R., Ed., *Farmers in the Hills*, Penang: Penerbit Universiti Sains Malaysia 1975.

CHAPTER 3

A MATTER OF CHOICE (Lau, Sherpas, Mursi Migrants)

Axelsen, Hans Guldberg, *The Sherpas in the Solu District*, Copenhagen: Munksgaard 1977.
Bourdillon, Jennifer, *Visit to the Sherpas*, London: Collins 1956.
Douglass, William, *Echalar and Murelaga: Opportunity and Rural Exodus in Two Spanish Basque Villages*, London: Hurst 1975.
Fuerer-Haimendorf, Christoph von, *Himalayan Traders: Life in Highland Nepal*, London: John Murray 1975.
The Sherpas of Nepal: Buddhist Highlanders, London: John Murray 1964.
The Sherpas Transformed: Social Change in a Buddhist Society of Nepal, New Delhi: Sterling 1984.
Ivens, W.G., 'The Island Builders of the Pacific' – Seeley, Service and Co Ltd, London, 1930.
Maranda, E.K. 'Lau, Malaita. "A woman is an alien spirit".' Article in 'Many Sisters', Collier Macmillan 1974.
Maranda, E.K., 'Folklore and Culture Change: Lau riddles of modernisation.' Vancouver, University of British Columbia 1974.
Maranda, P. 'The Popular Subdiscourse' – Current Anthropology 19, 1978.
Ortner, Sherry B., *Sherpas through Their Rituals*, Cambridge: Cambridge University Press 1978.
Turton, David, 'Spontaneous Resettlement after Drought: An Ethiopian Example' in *Disasters* No 8 1984.

CHAPTER 4

BEHIND THE CURTAIN (Mongols, Kazakhs, Han)

Akiner, Shirin, *Islamic Peoples of the Soviet Union*, London: Kegan Paul International 1983.
Bacon, Elizabeth E., *Central Asians Under Russian Rule: A Study in Culture Change*, Ithaca: Cornell University Press 1966.
Crook, David and Crook, Isabel, *The First Years of Yangyi Commune*, London: Routledge & Kegan Paul 1965.
Crook, David, *Revolution in a Chinese Village: Ten Mile Inn*, London: Routledge & Kegan Paul 1959.
Dragadze, Tamara, Ed., *Kinship and Marriage in the Soviet Union*, London: Routledge and Kegan Paul 1984.

HAZARD, Barbara, Ed., *Peasant Organization and Peasant Individualism: Land Reform, Cooperation and the Chinese Communist Party*, Saarbrucken and Fort Lauderdale: Breitenbach 1981.
HINTON, William, *Shenfan: The Continuing Revolution in a Chinese Village*, New York: Random House 1983.
HUMPHREY, Caroline, *Karl Marx Collective: Economy, Society and Religion in a Siberian Collective Farm*, Cambridge: Cambridge University Press 1983.
WEISSLEDER, Wolfgang, Ed., *The Nomadic Alternative*, The Hague and Paris: Mouton 1978.

CHAPTER 5

ORDER, ORDER, ORDER (Mursi, Pushtuns, Shilluk, Kirghiz)

AHMED, Akbar, *Millenium and Charisma among Pathans*, London: Routledge & Kegan Paul 1976.
AHMED, Akbar, *Pukhtun Economy and Society*, London: Routledge & Kegan Paul 1980.
AHMED, Akbar, *Social and Economic Change in the Tribal Areas*, Karachi: Oxford University Press 1977.
ASAD, Talal, 'Market Model, Class Structure and Consent: A Reconsideration of Swat Political Organization', *Man*, 1972.
BACON, Elizabeth E., *Central Asians Under Russian Rule: A Study in Culture Change*, Ithaca: Cornell University Press 1966.
BARTH, Frederik, *Political Leadership Among the Swat Pathans*, London: Athlone 1959.
DOR, R., *Contribution à l'étude des Kirghiz du Pamir Afghan*, Paris: Publications Orientalistes de France 1975.
DUPREE, Louis, 'Tribal Warfare in Afghanistan and Pakistan' in A. Ahmed, and D. Hart, Eds., *Islam in Tribal Societies*, London: Routledge & Kegan Paul 1984.
DUPREE, Louis, *Afghanistan*, Princetown: Princetown University Press 1973.
EVANS-PRITCHARD, E. E., *The Divine Kingship of the Shilluk*, Cambridge: Cambridge University Press 1948.
FISHER, James F., *Himalayan Anthropology: The Indo-Tibetan Interface*, Paris and the Hague: Mouton 1978.
FUKUI, Katsuyoshi and TURTON, David, Eds. *Warfare among East African Herders*, Osaka: National Museum of Ethnology 1979.

HOLY, Ladislav, Ed., *Segmentary Lineage Systems Reconsidered*, Belfast: Queen's University Press 1979.
HOWELL, Paul and THOMSON, W.P.G. 'The Death of a Reth of the Shilluk and the Installation of His Successor', *Sudan Note and Records*, 1946.
LATTIMORE, Owen, *Pivot of Asia*, New York: AMS Press 1975.
LIENHARDT, Godfrey, 'The Shilluk of the Upper Nile', in C.D. Forde, Ed., *African Worlds*, London 1954.
LINDHOLM, Charles, *Generosity and Jealousy: The Swat Pukhtun of Northern Pakistan*, New York: Columbia University Press 1982.
MICHAUD, Roland and MICHAUD, Sabrina, *Afghanistan*, London: Thames & Hudson 1980.
OGOT, Bethwell A., *Kingship and Statelessness among the Nilotes*, Oxford: Oxford University Press 1964.
RIASANOVSKY, Valentin, *Customary Law of the Nomadic Tribes of Siberia*, Bloomington: Indiana University Press/The Hague: Mouton 1965.
SHARANI, N., *The Kirghiz and Wakhi of Afghanistan*, Seattle: University of Washington Press 1979.
SINGER, André, *Guardians of the North West Frontier: The Pathans*, Amsterdam: Time-Life 1982.
SINGER, André, *Lords of the Khyber*, London: Faber and Faber 1984.
SINGER, André, 'Problems of Pastoralism in the Afghan Pamirs', *Asian Affairs*, 1976.
TAPPER, Richard 'Holier than thou: Islam in three tribal societies' A. Ahmed and D. Hart, Eds., *Islam in Tribal Societies*, London: Routledge and Kegan Paul 1984.
TURTON, David, 'The Relationship between Oratory and the Exercise of Influence among the Mursi', in M. Bloch, Ed., *Political Language and Oratory in Traditional Society*, London: Academic Press 1975.
TURTON, David, 'Territorial Organisation and Age among the Mursi', in P.T.W. Baxter and U. Almangor, Eds., *Age, Generation and Time*, London: Hurst 1978.
WIRSING, Robert G., *The Baluchis and Pathans*, London: Minority Rights Group 1981.
WOODHEAD, Leslie., *A Box Full of Spirits: Adventures of a film maker* London: Heinemann 1987.

CHAPTER 6

GAINING CONTROL (Kawelka, Dervishes, Kwegu, Masai)

BERNARDI, Bernardo, *Age Class Systems: Social Institutions and Politics Based on Age*, Cambridge: Cambridge University Press 1985.
BRUINESSEN, M. Van, *Agha, Shaikh and State: On the Social and Political Organization of Kurdistan*, Utrecht 1978.
FUKUI, Katsuyoshi and TURTON, David, Eds. *Warfare among East African Herders*, Osaka: National Museum of Ethnology 1979.
GULLIVER, Philip H, *Social Control in an African Society*, London: Routledge & Kegan Paul 1963.
HOLY, Ladislav, Ed., *Segmentary Lineage Systems Reconsidered*, Belfast: Queen's University Press 1979.
MAIR, Lucy P., *Primitive Government*, London: Scholar/Penguin 1977.
SALZMAN, Philip C., *Contemporary Nomadic and Pastoral Peoples*, Williamsburg: College of William and Mary Press 1982.
SINGER, André, 'Dervishes', in T. Stacey, Ed., *Peoples of the World*, London 1973.
SINGER, André, 'The Dervishes of Kurdistan', *Asian Affairs*, 1974.
STRATHERN, Andrew, *One Father, One Blood: Descent and Group Structure among the Melpa People*, London: Tavistock 1972.
STRATHERN, Andrew, *Ongka: A Self-Account by a New Guinea Big-Man*, London: Duckworth 1979.
STRATHERN, Andrew, *The Rope of Moka*, Cambridge: Cambridge University Press 1971.
RUBEL, Paula G. and ROSMAN, Abraham, *Your Own Pigs You May Not Eat; A Comparative Study of New Guinea Societies*, Chicago and London: University of Chicago Press 1978.
TURTON, David, 'A Problem of domination at the Periphery: the Kwegu and the Mursi' in D. Donham and W. James, Eds., *The Southern Marches of Imperial Ethiopia*, Cambridge: Cambridge University Press 1986.

CHAPTER 7

CHRISTIANS AND PAGANS (Azande, Umbanda, Embera)

BASTIDE, R., *Les Religions Africaines du Bresil*, Paris: Presses Universitaires de Frances 1960.
BAXTER, P.T.W. and BUTT, Audrey, *The Azande and Related Peoples of the Anglo-Egyptian Sudan and Belgian Congo*, London: International African Institute 1953.
BROWN, D., 'Umbanda and Class Relations in Brazil', in M.L. Margolis and W.E. Carter, Eds., *Brazil Anthropological Perspectives*, New York: Columbia University Press 1979.
DAVIES, Douglas James, *Meaning and Salvation in Religious Studies*, Leiden: Brill 1984.
DELUZ, A., 'L'Initiation d'un chamane Embera', *Bulletin de la Société des Americanistes*, 1975.
EVANS-PRITCHARD, E. E., *The Azande: History and Political Institutions*, Oxford: Clarendon Press 1971.
EVANS-PRITCHARD, E. E., *Witchcraft, Oracles and Magic among the Azande*, Oxford: Clarendon Press 1976.
FARON, L.C., 'Marriage, Residence and Domestic Groups among Panamanian Choco', *Ethnology*, 1962.
LEACOCK, Seth and LEACOCK, Ruth, *Spirits of the Deep: A Study of an Afro-Brazilian Cult*, New York: Doubleday 1972.
LEWIS, I.M., *Ecstatic Religion: An Anthropological Study of Spirit Possession and Shamanism*, London: Penguin 1971.
LIENHARDT, Godfrey, 'Modes of Thought', in E.E. Evans-Pritchard, *et al.*, *The Institutions of Primitive Society*, Oxford: Oxford University Press 1954.
PERELBERG, R.J., 'Umbanda and Psycholanalysis as Different Ways of Interpreting Mental Illness', *British Journal of Medical Psychology*, 1980.
PRESSEL, E., 'Umbanda Trance and Possession in Sao Paulo, Brazil', in I. Zaretsky, Ed., *Trance, Healing and Hallucination*, New York: Wiley-Interscience 1974.
SINGER, André and STREET Brian, Eds., *Zande Themes*, Oxford: Basil Blackwell 1972.
WILLEMS, E., 'Religious Mass Movements and Social Change in Brazil', in E.N. Baklanoff, Ed., *New Perspectives on Brazil*, Nashville: Vanderbilt University Press 1966.

CHAPTER 8

CELEBRATION (Carnaval, Kataragama, Quechua)

BASTIEN, Joseph W., *Qollahuaya Rituals*, Ithaca: Cornell University Press 1973.

GIFFORD, Douglas F. and HOGARTH, Pauline H., *Carnival and Coca Leaf*, Edinburgh and London: Scottish Academic Press 1976.

GOMBRICH, Richard, *Precept and Practice: Traditional Buddhism in the Rural Highlands of Ceylon*, Oxford: Clarendon Press 1971.

ISBELL, B.J., *To Defend Ourselves: Ecology and Ritual in an Andean Village*, Austin: University of Texas Press 1978.

LEWIS, I.M., *Ecstatic Religion*, London: Penguin 1971.

OBEYESEKERE, G., *Medusa's Hair: An Essay on Personal Symbols and Religious Experience*, Chicago and London: University of Chicago Press 1981.

OBEYESEKERE, G. 'Social Change and the Deities: Rise of the Kataragama Cult in Modern Sri Lanka', (*Man* 1977.)

O'FLAHERTY, Wendy, *Asceticism and Eroticism in the Mythology of Siva*, London: Oxford University Press 1978.

SALLNOW, Michael, WHITBURN, Richard and CUTLER, Vivienne, *Peru: The Quechua*, Oxford: Basil Blackwell 1978.

SALLNOW, Michael, *Pilgrims of the Andes: Regional Cults in Cusco*, Washington: Smithsonian Institution Press 1987.

STEIN, W.W., *Hualcan: Life in the Highlands of Peru*, Ithaca: Cornell University Press 1961.

URTON, Gary, *At the Crossroads of the Earth and the Sky*, Austin: University of Texas Press 1981.

WIRZ, Paul, *Kataragama: The Holiest Place in Ceylon*, Colombo: Lake House Investments 1966.

CHAPTER 9

MEN AND WOMEN (Asante, Moroccans, Masai, Mehinaku)

BASSO, Ellen B., *The Kalapalo Indians of Central Brazil*, New York: Holt, Rinehart & Winston 1973.

BERNARDI, Bernardo, *Age Class Systems: Social Institutions and Politics Based on Age*, Cambridge: Cambridge University Press 1985.

BROWNE, Angela W., *Craft Industry and Rural Employment in Ghana*, London: Recordak Microfilm Records 1978.

CAPLAN, Ann P. and BUJRA, Janet M., Eds., *Women United, Women Divided: Cross-Cultural Perspectives on Female Solidarity*, London: Tavistock 1978.

EVANS-PRITCHARD, E.E., *Man and Woman Among the Azande*, London: Faber & Faber 1974.

FERNEA, E.W., *A Street in Marrakech*, New York: Anchor/Doubleday 1976.

GOODY, Jack, Ed., *Changing Social Structure in Ghana*, London: International African Institute 1975.

GREGOR, Thomas, *Anxious Pleasures: The Sexual Lives of an Amazon People*, London and Chicago: University of Chicago Press 1985.

GREGOR, Thomas, 'Exposure and Seclusion: A Study of Institutionalized Isolation among the Mehinaku Indians of Brazil', *Ethnology* 1970.

GREGOR, Thomas, *Mehinaku: The Drama of Daily Life in a Brazilian Village*, Chicago and London: University of Chicago Press 1977.

GULLIVER, Philip H., *Social Control in an African Society*, London: Routledge & Kegan Paul 1963.

LLEWELYN-DAVIES, Melissa, 'Two Contexts of Solidarity amongst Pastoral Masai Women', in P., Caplan and J. Bujra, *Women United, Women Divided*, London: Tavistock 1978.

MACLEOD, Malcolm, *The Asante*, London: British Museum Publications 1980.

MAHER, V., *Women and Property in Morocco*, Cambridge: Cambridge University Press 1974.

MAIR, Lucy P., *Primitive Government*, London: Scholar/Penguin 1977.

OPPONG, Christine, Ed., *Female and Male in West Africa*, London: George Allen & Unwin 1983.

REICHEL-DOLMATOFF, Gerrardo, *Amazonian Cosmos*, Chicago: University of Chicago Press 1970.

ROBERTS, John M. and GREGOR, Thomas, 'Privacy: A Cultural View', in J.R. Pennock and J.W. Chapman, Eds., *Privacy* 1971.

SCHNEIDER, David M. and GOUGH, E. Kathleen, Eds., *Matrilineal Kinship*, Berkeley and Los Angeles: University of California Press 1961.

SPENCER, Paul, 'Opposing Streams and the Gerontocratic Ladder', *Journal of the Royal Antropological Institute*, 1976.

VILLAS BOAS, Orlando and VILLAS BOAS, Claudio, *Xingu: The Indians, Their Myths*, London: Souvenir Press 1975.

ADDITIONAL REFERENCES

BARNES, R.H., *Kedang: A Study of the Collective Thought of an Eastern Indonesian People*, Oxford: Clarendon Press 1974.

BARNES, R.H., 'Marriage, Exchange and the Meaning of Corporations in Eastern Indonesia', in L. Comaroff, Ed., *The Meaning of Marriage Payments*, London: Academic Press 1980.

BARNES, R.H., 'Concordance, Structure, and Variation: Considerations of Alliance in Kedang', in James Fox, Ed., *The Flow of Life*, Cambridge, Mass.: Harvard University Press 1980.

HENLEY, Paul, *The Panare: Tradition and Change on the Amazonian Frontier*, New Haven and London: Yale University Press 1982.

JONES, Mervyn, *The Sami of Lapland*, Minority Rights Group Report 55, 1982.

SATO, S., 'Pastoral Movements and the Subsistence Unit of the Rendille of Northern Kenya with Special Reference to Camel Ecology', *Senri Ethnological Studies*, 1980.

SPENCER, Paul, *Nomads in Alliance: Symbiosis and Growth among the Rendille and Samburu of Kenya*, London: Oxford University Press 1973.

INDEX

A

Afghan Exodus   29
Afghanistan   29, 34, 41, 102, 144–7, 155–8
Africa   8, 35, 39, 68, 69, 139, 184, 189, 190, 194, 199, 203–4
Agua Clara   61
Ahaggar   65–6
Ahmed, Akbar   34, 145
Ajuman, Kwama   220
Akiner, Shirin   37
Alaska   158
alcoholism   73, 86
Alexander the Great   144
Ali   170–1
Allan Quatermain   17
Amadror   69
Amandumatkerei   94
Amazon   9, 12, 52, 57, 58, 88, 98, 192, 217
Anaviapik   72–3
Andes   27, 47, 83, 192, 208, 211
Aqsaqal   130
Arabia   145, 221
Arabs   62–4, 165–6
Arcand, Bernard   10–11, 19–20, 84, 86
Arctic   30, 62, 71, 192
Arhex, Father Joseph   80–1
Ari   121
Aripi   240
Asante   37, 217–21, 224, 226
Asmara   123
Ausangate   211
Ayuruwa   234
Azande   34, 37, 42, 45, 57, 184–9, 190, 217
Azande, Men and Women Among the   217

B

Baffin Island   71
Bahia   199–205, 216
Baiveh   168–71
Baker, Sir Samuel   183
Ballantyne R.M.   16

Banks-Smith, Nancy   30, 37
Barasana   21, 97–100
Basques   9, 14, 39, 62, 74–6, 78, 81
Bateson, Gregory   18
Baxter, Paul   33–4
Bay of All Saints   203
Beattie, John   35
Beckham, Mike   39, 52
Belem   192
Berbers   62
Berka   119–23
Berreman, Gerald   29
Bioitongia   174
Boaitey, Charlotte   37
Boas, Franz   15–6, 22–3, 29, 41, 55
Bodi   141–4
Bordeaux   81
Brasilia   91
Brazil   9–11, 27, 39, 45, 56, 57, 88–92, 189, 192, 199–203, 217, 233
British   34, 144–5, 148, 177
Brody, Hugh   30, 71
Buddhism   24, 95, 115, 166, 206, 208
Bukuyo   186
Bulookbashi, Ali   24
Burr, Angela   13

C

Caboclos   192
Caliphate   166
Campinas   192
Canada   71, 73
Candomblé   203–4
Careem, Mr   207
Carlos, Ze   204
Carnaval   199–205, 208, 216
Caspian Sea   124
Catholicism   98, 100, 188–90, 194, 196, 203, 210
Cathy Come Home   21
Ceylon   24
Charlongtonga   142
Chernobyl   78
China   37, 54, 100, 106, 115, 124–5, 130–7, 156
Christ   190, 211–4
Christianity   72, 95–6, 107–13, 166, 183–98, 199, 205, 206, 211, 213–6
Cinaru   85
circumcision   178, 229–30
City on the Steppes, The   31
Clayton, Sylvia   34
Clearing in the Jungle, A   57
collectivisation   106, 125–7, 130–7

Colombia   10, 12, 20, 21, 48, 83–4, 92, 97, 100, 192, 194, 203
Colombo   207
Communism   124, 130–7, 157
Communist Revolution   130, 136, 214
Conan Doyle, Sir Arthur   16
Congo   184
Conquistadores   12, 194
Conrad, Joseph   16
Cooper, Merian C.   8
Cuiva   10, 12, 19–20, 41, 61, 83–6, 88, 92, 233
Cultural Revolution   131, 135–7
Curling, Chris   12–3, 24, 33, 52
Custom   107–13

D

Dak   150–3
Darchu   172, 174, 177
Darjeeling   114
Deluz, Ariane   194, 196
dervishes   24, 161, 164–71
Dervishes of Kurdistan, The   24
Din, Shams-ud   145–6
Ding family   136–8
diseases   12, 72–3, 88, 127, 198
Diva, Dona   204
Douglas family   207–8
Douglas, Mary   184
Dumont, Jean-Paul   57
Dupree, Louis   34
Durkheim, Emile   183

E

Ecuador   32
education   66, 73, 78, 92, 94, 110, 114, 118, 133–5, 194
Egypt   16
Elsa's restaurant   201
Elwafil   69
Embera   21, 192–8
Engels, Friedrich   133
Eritrea   123
Eshu   192
Eskimos   15, 30, 41, 52, 62, 71–4, 107
Eskimos of Pond Inlet, The   29, 30, 52
Ethiopia   24, 37–8, 50, 53, 56, 107, 118–9, 123, 139, 166
eunoto   178, 181–2
Evans-Pritchard, Sir Edward   23–4, 34–5, 41, 45, 149, 184–6, 188, 217
Everest, Mount   113

F

Fernea, Elizabeth 30, 224
Firth, Sir Raymond 24
Flaherty 8
Floresmilo 198
Forman, Denis 9, 19, 24
Fortes, Meyer 24, 219
Foueda 108–13
France 14, 39, 64, 74–5, 80
Frazer, Sir James 18, 149, 183
Fry, Peter 192
Funafou 108–13

G

Gamage, Walter 208
Gandhi 204
Gbudwe, King 185
Ghana 37, 203, 217
Gilani, Sheikh Abd al-Qadir 166
Gingiti 186
Gluckman, Max 24
Gobi Desert 125
Gobi, On the Edge of 31
Goillart family 76–8, 81
Golden Bough, The 18, 148–9
Gombrich, Richard 24
Goosile 108
Gorotire 46, 88–90
Gouzdez, Gabriel 84
Grass 8
Greeks 144, 203
Gregor, Thomas 27, 236, 240
Grigsby, Mike 30
Guayaquil 32
Gul, Haji 146
Gume 186
Guozong, Zhu 135

H

Hajiba 224
Halbertsma, Niels 12
Han 37, 124, 132–3, 135–8
Harratins 68–9
Hassan 169
Hazara 102
Hazard, Barbara 37
Henley, Paul 22
Hillary, Sir Edmund 113
Himalayas 47, 52, 54, 107, 113
Hinduism 166, 205, 206, 207

Hirafok 69
Hlamu, Pasang 117–8
Hmong 21, 42, 100, 184
Hola 135–8
Honiara 110
Hossein, Sheikh 168–71
Howell, Paul 149–50
Hudson Bay Company 71
Hugh-Jones, Stephen and Christine 12, 99–100
Huns 124

I

Iemanjá 190
Iklan 69
Incas 208, 210
India 16, 114, 155, 166, 199, 204
Indian Ocean 47
Indians 10–12, 15, 19–20, 46, 194, 196, 203–4, 214
Indians, Amazonian 19, 139
Indians, Brazilian 192
Indians, Colombian 20–1
Indians, Kwakiutl 15
Indians, North American 192
Indians, Red 203
Indians, South American 190, 192
Indo-China 102
Indonesia 24, 92, 96
Inuit (see Eskimos) 71–4
Inukuluk 73
Invisible Enemy, An 78
Iran 8, 24, 42, 102, 165–6, 168
Iraq 42, 165, 168
Islam 24, 30, 37, 95, 130, 132, 135, 145–6, 155, 157, 165–71, 206, 221, 224
Istanbul 130
Izat 169, 171

J

Japanese 135–6
Jerome, Father 188
Jie 13
Judaism 166
Junet family 78–81

K

Kado 146
Kalabeti 113

Kamawara 210–4
Kami, Ali 115
Kanyonk 90–1
Kataragama 24, 184, 205–8, 210, 216
Kataragama 24
Katmandu 114, 117–8
Kavadi 205, 208
Kawelka 27, 30, 52, 56, 61, 160–4
Kawelka, The: Ongka's Big Moka 161
Kayapo 9–13, 39, 45, 52, 88–92
Kayapo, The 9–13, 29
Kazakhs 54, 124, 130–5
Kazakhs of China, The 37
Kaziza 133, 135
Keenan, Jeremy 65–6, 70
Kenya 27, 52, 118, 161, 176, 177, 179, 217, 229
Khalka 124
Khan 155–8
Khan, Genghis 124, 155
Khyber 34
Kiangsu 124, 135
Kililea 108
King Solomon's Mines 139
Kipling, Rudyard 16
Kirghiz 29, 41, 58, 102, 155–8, 160
Kluckholm, Clyde 139
Koiuku 234
Komorakora 123
Komorokibo 142
Kumasi 37, 217, 220
Kumuli 174, 176
Kunijwok, Walter 149
Kupranpoy 91
Kur, Ayang Anei 29, 150–5
Kurdistan 24, 164–71
Kurds 42, 161, 165–71
Kwakiutl 15
Kwegu 37, 160–1, 172–7

L

Lao, Pathet 102, 105
Lao, Royal 102, 105–6
Laos 12, 21–2, 42, 100–2, 184
Lappland 78
Latin America 9, 12
Lattimore, Owen 31, 124, 126–7, 214
Lau 39, 107–8, 110–3, 114, 118
Lau of Malaita, The 108
Lawrence T.E. 64
Leach, Edmund 12
leaders 92–3, 106, 114, 132, 139–47, 148–55, 155–8, 160–2, 165, 172, 177–8, 218, 221

Lemoine, Jacques 21, 100, 104, 106
Lent 199–201
Libya 62
Ligoleta 79–80
Liping, Chen 135
Live with Herds, To 13
Llaneros 10, 20, 84–6
Llewelyn-Davies, Melissa 13, 27, 30, 224, 226, 229
Loita 177, 179
Loizos, Peter 32
Lourdes, (Mother) Dona 192

M

Maanabeu 110
Maanabisi 110
McDougall, David and Judith 13
Mago 119–23
Mair, Lucy 24
Maku 21, 56, 97–8
Malaita 107, 111
Mali 62
Malinowski, Bronislaw 14, 23
Maliyani 232
Man of Aran 8
Mandembo 161
Mangu 184
Mao, Chairman 136–7
Maranda, Pierre 39, 108, 113
Marcel, Gabriel 41
Marco 185
Marrakech 217, 221–6
marriage 135, 174, 176, 219–21, 222, 224, 226, 229–33, 236
Marx, Karl 133
Masai 13, 27, 161, 177–82, 217, 226–33
Masai, Loita 177–82
Mason, A.E.W. 16
Mead, Margaret 18, 83, 217
Mehinaku 27, 56, 58–61, 217, 233–40
Mekong river 104
Melpa 27
Meo 12, 21–2, 28, 100–6
Meo, The 21–2, 106, 184
Metzger, Ron 97–8
Migrants, The 38
Milne, Claudia 37
missionaries 21, 71–2, 97–100, 108
Mitatu 143
Moana 8
Mohammed, Aisha bint 226
Mohammed, Prophet 166–9, 221–3, 225
Mohammed, Sheikh Kaka 168–9

Mohammed, Sidi 66–70
Mohmands 145–6, 148
Moizoi 142
moka 27, 161–4
Momos 203
Mongolia 30, 31, 32, 124–8, 130, 132, 155, 214
moran 178–82, 229
Morocco 30, 217, 221–6
Moser, Brian 8, 20–4, 28, 31–2, 41, 48–52, 56, 61, 83, 100, 126
Moser, Caroline 9, 32
Mukai 131
Mursi 13, 24, 37–9, 56, 57, 58, 118–23, 139–44, 148, 160, 161, 172–7
Mursi, The 24, 45
Muslims 132, 135, 155, 157, 165–71, 206, 222, 224, 232

N

Nadam 214
Nairn, Charlie 12, 21, 24, 27, 52, 54, 56, 57, 61
Nairobi 176
Nana, Ole 177
Nandi 188
Nangpala pass 115
Nanook of the North 8
Nepal 30, 113–4, 117, 217
Ngai 181
Ngokolu 142
Niger 62, 69
Nigeria 204
Nile river 148, 150
Nolpiyaya 27, 229–32
nomadism 12, 62–70, 83–6, 88, 127, 130, 156, 176
North America 199
Norway 78
Nuer 45, 149, 172
Nyidhok 154
Nyikang 150–4
Nzài, Njuan 105

O

Oba 218–20
Obeyesekere, Gananath 24, 208
Obidullah 102
Ogum 190
Olha 78–9
Olodum 204
Omo river 119, 121, 172, 174, 176

Ongka 27, 30, 52, 161–4
Opuko Ware II, King 221
Orinoco river 83
Ortner, Sherry 114, 217
Ott, Sandra 14, 39, 75–6
Oxala 190
Oyo, King of 204

P

Pachamama 210
Pacific 16, 107, 192
Pacodo 150–3
Pakistan 34, 102, 144–5, 158
Pamirs 158
Panare 57
Papua New Guinea 23, 27, 52, 56, 61, 139, 160–4, 203
Paraguacu,Katarina 203
Parua 161–4
Pasakiat 93
Pashto 146
Pasini, Carlos 27, 56, 58, 61
Pathans, The 34
Peking 124
Pelourinho 203
Peru 27, 210–1
Phou Phai Mai 104
Plowright, David 9–10
Polo, Marco 124
Pond Inlet 71–3
Popolzai 102
Portuguese 12, 199, 203
Pushtun 34, 102, 144–8, 160
Pyrenees 9, 14, 39, 62, 75–6, 81

Q

Qaderi 164–71
Qair, Abdur 130–1, 133, 135
Qoyllur Rit'i, Senor de 208–16
Quechua 27, 208–16
Queen Mothers 218–21
Qul, Rahman 29, 155–8
Quraysh 222

R

Radcliffe-Brown, A.R. 160
Ratu 108
Red Sea 123
religion 57, 72, 81, 94–6, 97–100, 107–13, 115–7, 126, 135, 165–71, 181, 183–98, 199, 203, 205–8, 210–16

Renberg, Tomas 78
Rendille 52, 176
Rendille, The 33
Reth 149–55
Revolution, Living with the 37
Revolution, The Newest 37
Rice Burroughs, Edgar 16
Rider Haggard, H. 16–7, 139, 150
rituals 24, 88, 91–2, 94–5, 98, 111–3,
   128, 150–4, 161–4, 165, 168–72,
   181–2, 184–9, 198, 199–216, 226,
   230–2, 234, 239–40
Roba 110
Ropni 88–91
Rouch, Jean 8
Russia 102, 144, 147, 155–8, 192

S

Sahara 52, 54, 62–4
St George 190
Sainte Engrâce 76
Sakkudei 24, 28, 47, 54, 57, 92–6
Saleh-ud-Din (Saladin) 166
Sallnow, Michael 27, 210
Sami 78
Samoa, Coming of Age in 18
Santazi 75–6, 80–1
Sao Paulo 192
Sarney, President 91
Schoedsack, Milton 8
Scythians 124
Selim 146
Sewa, Ama 220
shamanism 98, 104, 184, 192–8
Shanghai 135
Sharani, Nazif 155
Shefold, Reimar 28
Sheppard, John 24, 28, 47, 54, 57
Sherpas 30, 54, 113–8, 217
Shi'ite 166
Shilluk 30, 52, 148–55, 160, 183
Siberians 192
Siberut Island 24, 28, 47, 92,96
Silk Route 124
Silva, Milton da 203
Silverwood-Cope, Peter 12, 97–8
Singer, André 13, 54
Sirdar 118
slaves 69, 189, 192, 194, 203
Solomon Islands 39, 107, 110–1
Somalia 123
Soro, Chief 185–6
Sousou 110
South America 192, 214

South Pacific 39, 61, 107, 113, 192
Soviet Union 126, 130, 156, 165
Spain 12, 75–6, 81, 194, 210, 211
Sri Lanka 24, 184, 205–8
Strathern, Andrew 27, 30, 161
Street, Brian 18
Sudan 30, 45, 52, 57, 69, 118, 123,
   148–9, 154–5, 172, 184
Sukulu 110–3
Sumatra 47, 92
Sunni 165
Surkhel camp 102
Syria 165

T

Tajik 102
Tamanrasset 70
Tanzania 177, 229
Tawarek 62
Tayler, Donald 12
Tenzing, Dorje 115
Tenzing, Mingma 30, 117–8
Tenzing, Purwa 114–5
Tenzing, Sherpa 113
Thami 113–8
Tibet 114–5
Tien Shan mountains 130
Timur Lang (Tamberlane) 155
Tit, battle of 64
Titans 206
Toata, Hatley 111
Togorro 94
To'ou, Dede 108–10
Toribio 211
tourism 81, 113, 117–8
Trobriand Islands 23
Tsultim, Ang 118
Tuareg 21, 52, 54, 62–70, 71, 74, 107
Tuita 110
Turiba river 57
Turkey 42, 58, 102, 124, 130, 155, 158,
   165
Turner, Terry 39, 88, 91–2
Turton, Andrew 21
Turton, David 24, 37–8, 41, 53, 56,
   123, 139–44, 176–7
Tyler, Sir Edward 183

U

Uganda 13
Ulan Bator 128
Ulikuri 123

Ulilibai 177
Uma 93
Umbanda 57, 189–92
United States of America 15–6, 104
Urumchi 132–3
Utuva 73
Uzbek 102

V

Vaughan, Dai 14
Venezuela 21, 57, 83
Vientiane 104
Vietnam 21, 102, 105–6
Vincze, Ernest 10
Virgin Mary 190, 210, 214

W

Wallington, Jeremy 13, 29
Wambile 176
Wason, David 48
Weaver, Thomas 28
White, Bruce 11
Winter, Pattie 13
Witchcraft Among the Azande 34, 45
*Witchcraft, Oracles and Magic Among the
   Azande* 34
Women of Marrakech, Some 224
women, role of 110, 123, 135, 137–8,
   145, 217–21, 222–6, 229–40
Woodhead, Leslie 14, 24, 37–9, 141
World in Action 21
Wuxi 124, 135–8

X

Xingu 10, 12, 27, 88, 233
Xinjiang 124, 130, 132, 135

Y

Yakajukuma 239
Yao, Chu 104–5
Yeti 117
Yoruba 190, 204
Yumuy 239

Z

Zande 184, 186, 217
Zarif, Mian 146